Advanced praise for Tony McKinley and
From Paper to Web

"Mr. McKinley's expertise has proved invaluable in staying up to date with the latest technology in optical scanning, recognition and retrieval. His ability to clearly and concisely address the interrelated technical, archival and managerial aspects of document digitization makes him a clear leader in this emerging field."

Dr. David Graper, Director, ASC Computer Center
Annenberg School for Communications, University of Pennsylvania

"Tony McKinley really knows document imaging and OCR. His knowledge and understanding of the technology and our application enabled us to make the right imaging product choice at BIOSIS. Tony keeps his eyes and hands on the cutting-edge technology. He is constantly evaluating and comparing the new and improved products against the tested and proven."

Sam Couchara, Data Entry Manager, BIOSIS

"Tony McKinley not only understands the technical aspects of products and technology but knows how to communicate the application and value to all levels within the industry. His years of experience enable him to provide insight and direction to our product plans and programs to ensure we are hitting key user requirements."

Wayne Crandall, VP of Sales and Marketing, Xerox Desktop Document Division

"Tony's diverse industry experience provides an excellent platform for his clear and insightful analyses. From Paper To Web provides an invaluable and refreshing look at imaging products from a business solutions perspective, a refreshing change from the typical editorial reviews that are all too often a shallow focus on features instead of substance."

Jon Karlin, President/CEO, ZyLAB International, Inc.

"Uniquely, Tony combines his extensive practical experience, market knowledge and writing skills to consistently produce accurate, up-to-date publications that contain lots more useful information than the fluff I usually read."

John Solomon, VP and Co-founder, Input Solutions, Inc.

i

From Paper
to Web

How to make information

instantly accessible

by Tony McKinley

Adobe Press

San Jose, California

Library of Congress Catalog No.: 96-78987

ISBN: 1-56830-345-9

10 9 8 7 6 5 4 3 2 First Printing: February 1997

Published by Adobe Press, Adobe Systems Inc., http://www.adobe.com

Printed in the United States of America by GAC Shepard Poorman, Indianapolis, Indiana.

Published simultaneously in Canada.

Editorial and Production: Van Cleve Britton Publishing Ltd. Design: Bradford Foltz

Chapter opener images: ©1996, PhotoDisc, Inc.

Adobe Press books are published and distributed by Macmillan Computer Publishing USA. For individual, educational, corporate, or retail sales accounts, call 1-800-428-5331, or 317-581-3500. For information address Macmillan Computer Publishing USA, 201 West 103rd Street, Indianapolis, IN 46290, or at http://www.mcp.com.

Dedication

I lovingly dedicate this book to my wife, Patty
and my children, Laura, Tony and Hugh.

table of contents

Chapter 6: Decisions in Indexing 117

Part 3: Searching Digital Content

Chapter 7: Acrobat Search 131

Chapter 8: Enhanced PDF Collections on the Web 159

Chapter 9: Advanced Navigation for Superior Information Access 179

Part 4: Using Digital Content

Part 5: Advanced Resource Guide

Acknowledgments

I must thank Patrick Ames, Publisher of Adobe Press for giving me this opportunity to work on this labor of love. My editors, Mike Britton and especially Suzanne Van Cleve provided insight and direction that shaped this book and made this book better than I ever imagined it could be. Bradford Foltz designed the pages and gave the lively feel and openness that a book about the Web should have. Diane Boccadoro fine-tuned the text and any errors remaining are purely my own.

I'm also compelled to acknowledge my colleagues, customers and friends who lived through the history of scanning and recognition with me, always providing comfort and encouragement: John Solomon, Wayne Crandall, Steve Goodfellow, Jon Karlin, Sam Couchara, Dave Abbott, Joanne Tremonte, Peter Atwood, Larry Shiohama, Mike Schofield, Bob Boerner and so many others I'd like to list. It's been a pleasure and a privilege working with Adobe people, Chris Hunt, Alan Williams, Judy Kirkpatrick, Anna Kjos; and the guys from Emerge, John Cook, Andy Young and Glenn Gernert. For making the Internet and the Web feel like my own backyard, I'll always be grateful to Jeff Miller (Sysop) at ONIX (my ISP) and online friends David Orr, Todd Gerbert, Andrew Sutherland, Philip Yip (Technoid, Camel, Egghead & Qwerty) and the rest of the gang. And for giving me the chance to contribute, I thank Bruce Hoard and Andy Moore of Imaging World.

I'd like to thank my Mom for believing all along that my degree in Creative Writing was not for naught. Thanks, Mom.

Finally, for reading everything and providing those critical first line editing services and patient analysis, support, and Common Sense, cutting out the dense jargon and shinola, translating everything to human-readable sentences: my wife, Pat McKinley, read every word of this and aimed to make it understandable by the largest number of people.

Introduction

In this book I've tried to share my excitement and enthusiasm for the great new technology that is providing easy and unprecedented access to information. It might seem like a strange obsession, but I've been dedicated to turning paper into digital form for over 15 years and finally — everything works!

Dating back to the earliest Optical Character Recognition machines, I've worked at finding better ways than typing to get information into computers. Of course, in the early days we mostly wanted to just get information off paper to simply edit it or recompose it and then print it right back out on paper. But, even that was exciting. Look, a machine that reads and types!

By the early '80s, more interesting things were being done with electronic information, and I had the opportunity to work with such online database pioneers as Mead Data Central, Chemical Abstracts and BIOSIS. Now that digital information itself was being consumed over online terminals, OCR seemed to have found a higher calling and I was lucky enough to work for Kurzweil Computer Products.

The information that we wanted to convert to digital form was now in typeset form, unlike the far simpler typewritten documents that early OCR could handle. We could "train" our Kurzweil scanners to recognize magazines for Mead's NEXIS database, and for the giraffe-high stack of Chemical Abstracts published in hard cover. Compared to OCR's earlier limitations of being able to read only about a dozen typestyles, Kurzweil Intelligent Scanning Systems were a real breakthrough.

In those days, there were precious few prospects for our scanners. One limitation may have been the $50,000+ price tag, but the more severe limitation was that there just wasn't much you could do with digital documents. By the late '80s local area networks and personal computers had become more powerful and popular. But still, to equip a PC to run a moderately fast scanner, we had to add special hardware boards that often cost more than the computers they were installed in. By 1990, I took great pride in the fact that we could put together a decent one-seat scanning system for about $25,000.

But every step of the way was still very expensive, and everything had to be beefed up for imaging applications, including storage, networks, displays and printers. The high speed OCR systems still cost $20,000-$30,000 or more. Then, as Moore's law kicked in over a few generations of PCs the computers finally grew into the demanding requirements of imaging and recognition. But still, transmitting images beyond the LAN was demanding and expensive, requiring dedicated communications lines. And CD-ROM readers cost in the thousands, and CD recorders were beyond the reach of all but the hardiest companies boldly investing in electronic publishing.

It was a lot of fun, but document imaging never had the great breakout that we all expected for so long. We were still limited to niche applications, not far removed from the earliest industrial and professional imaging applications. Then, the Web came along and woke up the slumbering giant of the Internet. Suddenly we had something to do with all the digital documents we could create!

The fact that the PCs, CD drives, storage, monitors, modems and every other piece continually got faster and cheaper certainly helped move things along too.

But my personal expectations remained unfulfilled. Optical character recognition was still expensive because it was difficult to reproduce the appearance of paper documents and it was costly to edit and clean up the results of OCR.

Then one day a couple of years ago, I was walking by the Adobe booth at the AIIM show, the biggest annual event in the imaging industry. It was curious that Adobe was even there, but what I was seeing on the big screen monitor was even more curious. They had just scanned a page, done recognition, and were displaying the results. Unlike the results of OCR, which contains tildes for unrecognizable characters in the text, there were small images of the suspect words blended into the document! And the output looked just like the original! To someone who had spent 15 years toiling in the field of OCR, spanning hundreds of installations and millions of dollars worth of systems, this was absolutely incredible.

As soon as it became available, I got my hands on a copy of Adobe Acrobat Capture 1.0 and put it to the test in our Online OCR Lab. I was stunned. I literally sat in front of my computer in wide-eyed astonishment. Now, I don't expect everyone to feel that way, but then not everyone has personally done more than 2,000 OCR demos like I have. If I'd had Capture over the years I could have met the needs of hundreds and hundreds of customers that conventional OCR simply could not satisfy.

I have one more confession to make, and that is that my interest in converting paper to digital documents goes back beyond my years in OCR. My inspiration for this field comes from Buckminster Fuller, in his 1962 book Education Automation. In that typically freewheeling talk Bucky proposed a universally accessible digital library that would enable anyone, anywhere to study, learn and grow. Bucky figured that this intellectual freedom of the masses would bring humanity's best ideas to reality.

Now, that may sound like a lofty goal, but if we're going to get there, the path is clear before us. The theme of this book is that we can now provide superior access to information. It's not just that we can digitally miniaturize books and get them out of the library without leaving home. The key is that we can provide instant access to the information within the documents.

In my study of Acrobat Capture, I explored the efficiencies of Adobe's Portable Document Format, which offers a range of features from cross-platform viewing and printing to a built-in set of management and search capabilities. Not only does Capture do what my 2,000 OCR demo customers ask for, but PDF seems to meet the vaguely defined but clearly required needs of digital documents and digital libraries.

I've tried to address the entire experience of moving from paper to digital documents on the Web. After finding the most efficient way to create the new documents, we move on to the even more important question of how to organize the information within the digital library. Finally, the issues and techniques of Information Retrieval are explored to give both publishers and users some useful tips and tools for finding what they seek on the Web.

While the lessons learned in this book came from many years in business and academic applications of this technology, I still aspire to the ideals espoused by Bucky Fuller. Now that the technology to make the world a better place that he predicted is here, we're on our way.

    — T.M. - 1/20/97

Key Elements

The idea of writing a paper book about global digital libraries could not be more ironic to anyone than it is to me. Focused on this meeting of paper and digital, we have tried to blend this book into the Web in both look and function by employing the following array of easily recognizable elements:

Tip (tip)

Things to look out for, mistakes to avoid, the voice of experience.

Web Links (http://imagebiz.com/PaperWeb)

The Web Links let you explore the Internet right along with the samples and lessons. We picked these links by their projected long life reliability. All of the links are available at our web site above.

Blast from the Past

These Blasts put today's technology into perspective with earlier developments and projections.

Fringe

According to your interests, there are many fine points to explore in this rapidly expanding world of global access.

Tech Details [T]

Things you might bump your head on.

Jargon ◉

Definitions of the more obscure technical terminology.

About the Author

Tony McKinley is a industry analyst, writer and consultant, and is a principal in Intelligent Imaging. Mr. McKinley's dedication to document imaging and recognition began in 1978, and includes five years at Kurzweil Computer Products, and six years as President and Founder of an early imaging systems integration company. Mr. McKinley's Online OCR Lab has performed testing for some of the largest vendors in the field, and recent analysis and writing clients have included Adobe, Xerox, Caere, Fujitsu, Canon, Open Text, Excalibur Technologies and ZyLab. He is a Contributing Editor for *ImagingWorld Magazine*. He lives near Valley Forge, Pennsylvania.

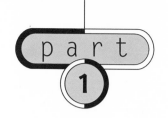

part
1

creating
digital
content

the past:

a paper
legacy

chapter one

The Users And Tools Have Gone Digital, But The Information Is Stranded On Paper

"By 2004, the pile of information on your desk will be 30 percent paper and 70 percent electronic, compared to 90 percent paper today," states Dr. Keith T. Davidson, Executive Director of Xplor International.[1] Dr. Davidson illustrates our business dependency on paper by citing statistics such as: "Executives spend as much as three hours every week looking for missing information, the average document is copied 19 times, 200 million pieces of paper are filed away each day."[2]

For more information, visit the Xplor web site at http://www.xplor.org

This expensive and time-consuming medium of paper is growing: more paper documents are produced now than ever before. This isn't just a problem for legacy information, but an ongoing requirement to handle increasing volumes of paper in today's information-dependent business environment. The Gartner Group estimates that 5.46 billion office documents are produced each year, 59 percent of which are accessed and retrieved manually.[3] Put another way, the Gartner Group estimates that 170 miles of new files are generated every day.

Paper And Microfilm: Imperfect Mediums

Compared to electronic alternatives, paper information is much more expensive to create, reproduce and store. In a study conducted by KPMG/Peat Marwick that analyzed conversion from paper to electronic documents, it was conservatively estimated that Adobe Systems would save $950,000 per year[4] with a full-scale change to the new paradigm.

Due to its physical nature, paper is limited in distribution by the number of copies generated. The fact that virtually every office and even every department has a copier is a testament to this limitation. Add to that manual updates to previously distributed documents, and you multiply the single task of document management by the number of users.

Conventional filing systems provide only one index field for the file, which is the paper file folder tab. To efficiently store and retrieve files in a file cabinet, all users must understand the indexing scheme. More important, files must be returned to the proper position in the cabinet because it may take hours of manual searching to find a misfiled document. It has been estimated that 7.5 percent of paper documents get lost completely.[5] This risk of misfiled and unreturned documents is virtually eliminated in an electronic file system because the documents themselves are never moved.

Paper isn't particularly useful as a groupware tool, either; changes to paper documents need to be republished on paper to spread the news. An electronic document can be annotated by many users, and the latest updated version of the document is always available to all users on the network.

Microfilm was the earliest means of preserving documents mechanically through photography, one of the ancient wonders of the Industrial Revolution. Through the use of high-power optics, entire books could be faithfully captured on a small amount of film. The negative of the film could be easily reproduced, providing a new distribution medium. Microscope-like readers displayed the pages and allowed users to peruse these miniature documents.

This new microfilm system had undeniable benefits and annoying drawbacks. On one hand, it was cheaper and easier to ship a few ounces of microfilm to distant offices than it was to ship a few hundred pounds of paper. At the remote office, a single file drawer could match the storage capacity of an entire file room, and a single administrator could manage an entire library of documents.

Users found microfilm to be fairly clunky. If you work for the FBI, the IRS or any other large user of critical source documents, using microfilm is infinitely better than wading through the comparable wilderness of paper. And microfilm works fine if you always search by a strictly defined field like Purchase Order or Customer Number.

The primary advantage is the simple physical compression of large collections of files. Unfortunately, access to information on microfilm is much more opaque than access to information in books on shelves or cabinets full of files. Access to pages on microfilm is usually strictly serial, and it is best to know exactly which page you are seeking. Without a dedicated computer-assisted retrieval system, there is no way to query or search the content of microfilm. Since the images must be displayed one-by-one on a viewer, the only practical means of access is the index.

Digital vs. Paper Documents

We refer to books, file cabinets and libraries as comparisons to digital information. Specifically, we compare digital documents to conventional books. Books are highly evolved information transmission vehicles that illustrate the benefits of 500 years of human ingenuity and development. Books contain illustrative contents, from the finest typography to the most glorious graphics and photography. Books also contain highly advanced navigation and finding aids, such as table of contents, index, glossary and footnotes.

In their physical form, books are durable and compact vessels of information. We use books as a basis for comparison because simpler documents do not possess the features to compare to the richness of a digital document.

Nominal Definitions Of A Page

A text page = 2,000 characters

An image page = 50,000 characters

These sizes are widely accepted as the rule of thumb for page calculations.

These figures are for discussion purposes only. The actual page sizes should always be measured and used in planning any actual implementation.

Tools For Global Distribution

The earliest online databases were pure text databases, with no graphical content. The early LEXIS & NEXIS databases, provided by Mead Data Central, offered information in the fields of law and news, respectively. LEXIS guaranteed to have Supreme Court findings online within 48 hours of publication in Washington, D.C. In the beginning, all documents were manually rekeyed into the system, and eventually OCR was used to speed up the process. These methods gave Mead Data users rapid access to important information as soon as possible.

Through the world-spanning communication facility of the Internet, digital documents can be made available for global instant access. For example, Adobe Systems distributes software on the Internet, and thousands of programs are downloaded every day.

An evolution in paper documents occurred when laser printers replaced impact printers, and another leap occurred for electronic documents with the development of graphical user interfaces. Just as laser printers provided more flexible fonts and page layouts, GUIs gave developers a much richer palette with which to paint.

Weightless Shipping: Comparing Paper To Digital Documents

Pages On Paper Compared To Same Number Of Pages On CD-ROM

A typical CD stores about 650 MB (1 MB = 1024 x 1024 bytes = 1,048,576 bytes) of information, which equates to 340,000 pages at 2,000 characters per page, or about 170,000 single-spaced, double-sided pages.

If these duplex pages are printed on 20-pound bond paper, the stack of paper required to match the information capacity of a CD would weigh 1,700 pounds.

For reference, 170,000 sheets of 8.5 inch x11 inch 20-pound bond paper weighs 1,700 pounds.

New Languages Are Born For The Web

Another evolution came with presentation languages, and the birth of the World Wide Web is attributed to one such language. HyperText Transport Protocol (HTTP) introduced the fantastic ability of "Click to Go." Remember, the Internet existed long before the birth of the Web; it was just difficult to get around without a solid UNIX background.

Suddenly, with the development of HTTP, hypertext links were embedded within the documents. A user reading a remote document can simply click on a highlighted word or phrase and be instantly connected to another computer. Thus the documents themselves are linked, and the global wiring that accomplishes this miracle becomes invisible to the user.

Vannevar Bush, science advisor to FDR, described the memex as a desktop device to access and contribute to worldwide knowledge. The article "As We May Think" appeared in the Atlantic Monthly in 1945, describing something that sounds a lot like the World Wide Web.

The document language of HTTP is HyperText Markup Language (HTML). HTML can be considered the original word processor of the World Wide Web. The concept of hypertext itself is relatively ancient, going back to the dawn of computer time, as described by Vannevar Bush 50 years ago. But in addition to the crucial functionality of the links in hypertext, HTML was developed as a page composition language, which included a wide range of text attributes and graphical capabilities. In the long run, HTML added much more in terms of document connectivity, rather than in terms of the presentation of Web documents.

Even the most simple paper documents contain elements that have always been troublesome to represent on a computer monitor, and they have been even more troublesome to capture through a scanner. A signature on a letter is a very basic example of this "richness" that has separated paper from electronic documents. In the same way that a signature validates the letter, the lack of the signature on a reproduction may invalidate it.

When we take one small step further in the "richness" scale of common paper documents, we consider the broad universe of page composition and typesetting. Starting with basic reports that include charts and graphs, and moving into the complexity of books, newspapers and magazines, we encounter an entire "language" for the presentation of information. Using this "language," a tremendous amount of information is represented in a very dense, but instantly understood, form.

Adobe Systems introduced Acrobat and the PDF format to bring this richness to electronic documents. The Portable Document Format makes electronic documents much more familiar to users who grew up in a world of paper. PDF files are designed to be the analog to PostScript files in the sense that they can be used on virtually any output device. Whereas the output devices for PostScript are laser printers, the output devices for PDF are graphical user interfaces on virtually any hardware and software platform. PDF also retains all of the PostScript abilities to re-create rich hard copies through printers and faxes.

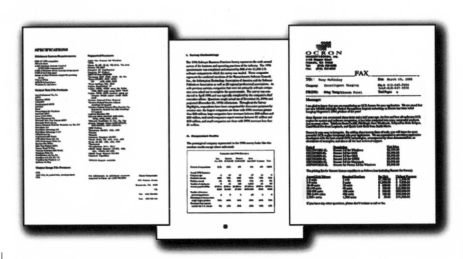

These samples are also available at

Columns, tables, letterhead: All are preserved with PDF format.

http://imagebiz.com/PaperWeb

The goal of PDF is to recapture the rich layout and presentation of information in a form that is equal to the presentation already out there in the vast realm of information residing in paper documents. To keep this evolution in perspective, think of the languages as generations that inherit all the capabilities of the former. ASCII was the first, HTML was the second, and PDF is a third generation language for electronic documents.

Portable Document Format is designed to bring rich composition to electronic documents, and Acrobat Capture offers a direct path from paper to PDF.

Paper is a physical universal format;

PDF is an electronic universal format.

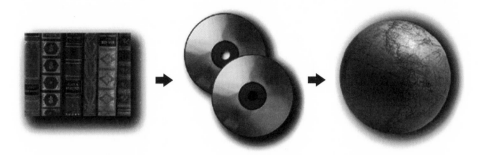

To achieve global reach, a document will be duplicated and copied to multiple sites on the Web.

Mirroring: The same collection of documents resides on many servers on the global Internet. For example, Adobe, Microsoft and many others mirror their software releases on many sites on the Web to accommodate the greatest possible number of users with the best possible performance.

If you would like to get a copy of the Acrobat 3 Reader for Windows 95, simply point your browser to the following URL (Universal Resource Locator):

```
http:www.adobe.com/acrobat/
```

You will begin the download process. When the file READER.EXE is completely received on your computer, use the RUN command to choose this self-installing application. By following the attached instructions, it only takes a few minutes to configure Acrobat 3 Reader with your Web browser, usable as both a stand-alone program and as an integrated online viewer on the Web. When PDF files are downloaded, the Acrobat 3 Reader is immediately invoked to display the files.

For access to all of the software offered by Adobe, browse its Technical Support Library

```
http://www.adobe.com/supportservice/custsupport/tsfilelib.html
```

Benefits Of Electronic Documents

Searching makes electronic documents superior to paper documents. A full text search capability enables the user to search the entire document for words of interest, and can fill in the gap left by indexes. Even the most extensive indexing systems are limited by the goals of the original index scheme.

An Index is (a few descriptive words) about the document;

Full Text is (each word contained within) the document.

Comparing Telecommunications Methods In Pages

To move the same 340,000 pages discussed in the previous section, the time requirements over common telecommunications methods

---

28,800 modem
@ 1.44 pgs/min
63 hours

ISDN modem
@ 5.6 pgs/min
15.75 hours

T1 Line
@ 77.2 pgs/min
70 minutes

The primary attraction of a text database is the ability to search for information by performing a simple word search. At first glance, this appears to be the ideal way to retrieve documents from a database. However, a poorly designed search may retrieve either no documents or far too many documents.

Even the earliest text-searching engines included tools to refine the search and increase the user's productivity. Advanced Text Search techniques are covered in Chapter 12.

The limited life span and gradual decay of paper can be overcome by transforming books into digital form. Some optical media claim 100-year durability, as magnetic tape has claimed for many years. Lacking time machines to verify the claims, archives can still be confidently built based on the digital format in which the data is encoded, whatever the physical media. Once digital, that electronic item can be converted to new media as it develops in the future.

The most dramatic advantage of digital over paper documents is the ever-increasing liveliness of the online medium. Mouse movements trigger sounds, clicked icons initiate videos, and interactive programs allow the user to move in a 3-D virtual reality. Beyond gimmicks, interactivity offers a tremendous breakthrough in technical and educational documents. While books are limited to a few illustrations and step-by-step instructions, a digital document can provide instant access to complete visual, audio and 3-D demonstrations.

Problems On The Digital Road

The road to instanly accessible information has some potential delays and complications.

All of the technology is in place: powerful CPU chips, wireless communication links to the Internet, more efficient batteries, better screens, voice input. The portable Web TV is selling well. But the price is high for the latest equipment, most of which will be considered outdated within six months of purchase.

It's important to carefully assess the costs and benefits of any large scale digitization project before buying equipment on site. In addition, consider the costs of staffing and training when evaluating a solution. Look for a system that's both flexible and compatible on multiple platforms, today and in future years. The long-term accessibility of your information depends on the planning you do now.

Complicated Scanning Names

Regular desktop scanners run at truly prodigious speeds, sucking in images of paper pages and crystallizing them as digitized files. One step up, like the Mustang GT upgrade in a Ford, and the scanners have tons of extra image-gobbling horsepower. It is simply good sense to figure out what you hope to do with that thing before you pump the pedal and stomp on it.

Very basic scanner controller software will follow even the least-informed user's bidding and run that machine at maximum controllable speed. Low-level software will spit out a stream of images, and this pile of images will be perfectly usable by any C Programmer. Such snowblower-like output of naked digital files is not very handy for a normal person to deal with.

If the images are going to be captured through a very low-level interface, the user must be careful and consistent with file names. These file names are often very constrained in length because low-level controllers insist upon room within the file name itself for incremental numbering.

The Office Of Technology Assessment: A Virtual Agency Gone But Not Forgotten

The OTA was established by an Act of Congress to provide an unbiased analysis of technology across all industries and disciplines. About 775 reports were generated in the 23 years that OTA was in operation, and these were all distributed in printed form, courtesy of the Government Printing Office.

To call the products of OTA Research Projects "reports" may be misleading to readers. The published documents often looked more like text books. The average document was 80 to 100 pages and in-cluded photos, illustrations, charts and free-form art.

The Washington Post announced the closing of this taxpayer-owned think tank in the Sept 28, 1995 edition: "The Office of Technology Assessment closes Friday, the first government agency eliminated under the new Republican revolution." Richard Nicholson, Executive Director of the American Association for the Advancement of Science, was quoted as saying, "There used to be a time that knowledge was power. Now it seems like Congress has decided it's a nuisance."

When the closing was announced, the agency was inundated with requests for complete collections of the entire library of OTA Reports. In the end, 85 sets

(t i p)

Incrementally Numbered Page Image File Names

Given Name:	**FILENAME.ext**
File Names:	**FILE0001.ext … to FILE9999.ext**

Document-scanning software often dedicates the last four characters of file names to a four-character numeric field to track page numbers. This allows one document to be up to 9,999 pages long. While this may seem like a good idea to a programmer, a scanner operator is best advised to keep scanned batches to a limit of 50 to several hundred pages.

The reason for processing small batches of images are manifold:

- **Simpler recovery from any failure on one batch**
- **Smaller files to store and read from disk**
- **Smaller documents to handle in workstation memory**
- **Smaller files to move over any network**

One 500-page book may be scanned in 10 batches of 50 pages each. Actually, there are only 25 paper pages in each batch, but because they are printed on both sides, they add up to 50 page images.

of books were scrounged together and sent out to repositories around the world.

This would have been the sad end of a noble endeavor if not for the lifesaving capabilities of a new technology. The OTA will live on as a "virtual agency" on CD-ROM and the World Wide Web. Acrobat Capture technology provided a means to transform paper documents into rich electronic documents at an affordable cost.

"Our major objective is to preserve a legacy of OTA," declares Peter Blair, Assistant Director for the Industry, Commerce and International Security Division of OTA. "These are very long shelf-life documents," Blair explains, "and our goal is to provide a research tool for our traditionally demanding users."

"We started distributing this information, bought and paid for by the taxpayers of this great nation, as raw ASCII on an FTP server in the early days of the Internet," says Blair. "We are now distributing an entire history of the agency on a five-CD-ROM set, including a history of the way OTA worked in our original mission."

In addition to CD distribution, the OTA Studies are now mirrored on a myriad of robust sites on the World Wide Web. A fragile paper collection has attained global digital immortality.

If we are scanning Moby Dick, these batches might be called

Moby0001.tif	**Pages 1-50**
Moby0051.tif	**Pages 51-100**
Moby0101.tif	**Pages 101-150**

Of course, they could just be called Moby1, Moby2, Moby3, etc., but in this example the file name itself lets the user know which page the batch starts on.

At the end of the process, the document might be called MobyDick.pdf.

Note that the 8.3 convention of FILENAME.ext is by far the most widely acceptable file name format on the Web, and for that reason it is often recommended to Mac and UNIX authors.

Since these files are being handled with such minimal information attached, it is important that they be managed through the system as the blind, clumpy files they are. Files can be handled and cleaned out just like temporary files and unique names, so they should be deleted after one or two warnings.

If the documents are going to be captured and archived under a more orderly system, it is important to find the most common denominator of understanding in the basic index fields.

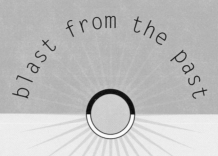

Alan Kay's Original Dynabook

The Dynabook, as described by Kay in 1968, and by some accounts
modeled in cardboard, was about the size of a three-ring binder and could fit into
a bookbag. It had a flat screen display and wireless communications. The screen
was envisioned as a touch-sensitive Liquid Crystal Display that could serve as a
keyboard when necessary.

The vision has been almost realized several times, by Xerox, Apple and other
bold pioneers. Today's most important development, predicted long ago by
Alan Kay, is an Intelligent Agent software, which may open the door between human
and computer information processing. The availability and quantity of information
is already drowning even the most devoted users. It's time to stop surfing and
start sailing on seas of info.

The future Dynabook can go to the beach, or into the bathtub, or out to a
peaceful park bench, and still be connected to the global digital library, and the
global community of connected users who are within instant reach.

Competing With The Comfort Of Paper

Paper documents are so familiar that the intelligence built into them has become transparent, invisible. In the 500 years since the development of movable type in the Gutenberg Press, printing has taken on all of the rich nuances of spoken language. The very appearance of words and paragraphs tells us a great deal about the information embodied therein. Headlines lead us around a number of stories, at once telling us the main point of interest and defining the location and shape of the article. Within the text, punctuation shows us the flow of the facts, and symbols like quote marks sharply define the action and actors.

This is a vast, even infinite, topic, and this book examines the depth of information embedded in the appearance of the document. However, the easiest and first way to archive and disperse a document is to make copies of it.

Of course, to old-fashioned purists, paper books will still have their allure. They can be easily scribbled on and otherwise marked, and they can be read in almost any light or environmental conditions. Books can contain your father's signature, the weight of his hand and the strokes of his handwriting. It will be at least a human generation or two before digital books can carry such physical presence and emotion, if they ever can.

Working With Digital Documents

A key consideration is the large file size of scanned images. The rule of thumb is to estimate 50K per page image. It should be noted that this is based on a simple text page, and the file size of pages including graphics and fine text could be much higher. In addition, the textual contents of the page will make up another 1,000 or more characters in overall file size. Once again, the estimate of 2,000 characters of text would be on single-spaced, typewritten page. A typeset page with small text could contains two to five times more characters, while a simple memo or letter may be only a few hundred characters. In addition, to provide text searching capability, an index is included with the page or document, adding more characters to the size of the file.

Acrobat Portable Document Files are much smaller than the aggregate file described above while still retaining the appearance of the original. Acrobat Capture retains only the image of graphical elements that can not be converted to text. The page layout and the appearance of the text itself are preserved, including type styles and font attributes such as size, bold, italic and underlined. This conversion to text greatly reduces the overall file size.

Another important issue of digital documents is the comparison between content and appearance. Let's review the benefits of image and text.

1. Image files faithfully reproduce the look of the original page and document = Appearance

2. Text files allow word-by-word searching of the data in a document = Content

The ideal solution would provide an accurate depiction of the *appearance* of the document, which can be navigated through, and a complete text version of the document for searching the *content*.

Adobe's Acrobat files are the Internet version of PostScript files. PostScript became a global de facto standard because it formed a common language that could reproduce richly composed documents on a variety of hardware and software platforms.

Software and hardware develop separately, but both develop prodigiously. As the many editing packages blossomed for each operating system, laser printers evolved to outperform earlier generations of very capable dot-matrix printers. Prior to Post-Script, each word processor and page composer required a dedicated printer to produce even the most basic pages. Electronic documents are evolving on the same path to richer presentation that computer-generated paper documents went through in the '80s and early '90s.

> **(t i p)**
>
> **Page composition has been developed over 500 years, always with the goal in mind to present information more densely and in a more orderly way. The logic behind this design trend becomes very simple if you consider paper as very precious. To conserve this highly valuable resource, scrupulous use of page space is critical.**
>
> **Now, we have to constrain ourselves to the much less dense medium of the computer display. With a tiny fraction of the resolution to present complex images, we need to be very crafty and parsimonious in our presentation of information. Considering the patience of our busy readers, we must design our information vehicles to deliver the goods quickly.**

Text Only: Original pages are converted to formatted electronic text

Benefit: Results in the smallest files, fully text searchable

Disadvantage: Discards the image of the original page

Image Only: Original pages stored as full-page bitmap images without converted text

Benefit: Provides exact copies of originals

Disadvantage: Search and retrieval limited to a few index fields

Image + Text: Original pages are stored as full-page bitmap images with links to text

Benefit: Allows text searching and retrieves images of originals

Disadvantage: Results in the largest files

Evaluating Access To Text

Text can be considered the opposite of image as a type of digital document. Whereas the image faithfully reproduces the form of a document, the text makes up the content of a document. Though this is not a perfect comparison, since pictures and graphs are part of the content of many documents, it serves to illustrate the primary difference between image and text.

Until relatively recently, text was the only practical content for online services due to hardware limitations. The capacity of 1200/2400-baud modems was limited, as were the user terminals. Very early LEXIS/NEXIS terminals were dedicated teletype machines, which were completely incapable of reproducing graphic images. Fax was the only answer for remote use of "images" of documents, which, of course, was still a great improvement over the mail.

If the density of the information in a computer file could be weighed, a text file would be an extremely dense file. Information, in this case, being defined as data that can be easily read by a human. In a pure text file, there is nothing but the barest of layout elements, only tabs and carriage returns, to create the presentation or appearance of the information. Almost every single character in a text file is data.

OCR: Optical Character Recognition, software that converts scanned images of documents to text and data; contents of documents can be searched by word and phrase.

The single greatest disappointment of optical character recognition is that the results are not perfect. Forget the fact that many people can not read and write perfectly or type accurately. Users expect OCR to produce perfect results. Why OCR bears this unique burden is a mystery—it probably has to do with every human's sci-fi-propelled desire to beat the computers. And OCR is one of the few things that computers have tried to do that they don't do perfectly. (Stifle the snickering.)

In most applications of OCR, the accuracy rates will be around 95-99 percent. This means that there will be unrecognized text in the output of raw OCR processing. Even when OCR gets 99 out of every 100 characters correct, there will still be 20 errors on the average page that need to be fixed. Since these corrections are done by people, they occur at human rates rather than the super-human rates of OCR. The costs to clean up the OCR process are always the largest component of the overall costs of an OCR project.

Enhancing Access To Text

What makes digital documents better than paper documents is instant access to information within the documents. Most current document enhancement techniques are simply the computerized versions of proven traditional methods. The cut-out thumb tabs of large hardback dictionaries are the original bookmarks, cut on a beveled angle to allow readers of a 5,000-page book to arrive roughly in the right area of the book.

Of course, bookmarks in digital documents can be more precisely accessible, and there can be far more of them, in almost infinitely nested sublevels. Once again, digital documents are more valuable precisely because of instant access, not just the physical advantages of tiny size and easy transmissibility.

If there had to be one single differentiator between paper and digital documents, it's hypertext links. While links are built on conventional footnotes and references, they don't just reference another document, they provide an instantaneous path to the other document. These links automate the paths of reference through information, enabling study at a real-time pace. Users may follow their inspiration to rapidly pursue specific ideas in vast seas of information.

Deciding which tools to use becomes rather obvious with practice. Key fields, such as those inserted using Adobe Acrobat at the time of scanning, may be the fastest route. However, it all depends on the thought process of one very important person: the key word creator. If he or she is familiar with your operation and documents, your key words can accurately reflect your information-searching needs.

Alternatively, if you chose to do a full text search, you'll have to carefully construct your query. If it's too tightly constructed, you won't find anything. If your search terms are too vague, you'll get hundreds of hits and wind up mostly frustrated. If your search is just right, you can successfully use the tool with little work on the inputting side.

Consider the nature of your material and the types of searches you're likely to do before embarking on your scanning project. That preliminary time investment will pay off handsomely in the near future.

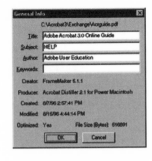 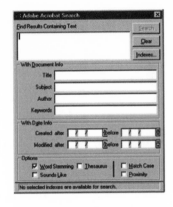 

Acrobat Search

Left

General Info available for every PDF file, some of which is entered by the author and some is derived from the applications used to create the file.

Center

You can customize the performance of the Search Engine under File-Preference-Search in Acrobat 3. Using any combination of criteria, you can refine the search for more useful results.

Right

Search results can be sorted and highlighted to your preference to expedite access to files.

It is an easy mistake to assume that full text searching is obviously better than any index database. After all, we know what we are looking for and can just search on the right terms, right?

In extremely large databases or constantly expanding databases, like various search engines on the Web, it's handy to focus the search function. Here's where investing in intelligent index information to a large collection of files pays off. Like key word insertion, time devoted to categorizing and tagging files adds immeasurably to the value of a collection of documents.

Chemical Abstracts, Biological Abstracts and Current Contents are all designed to provide scientists with a very up-to-date awareness of all scientific papers being published in each particular field. These few, specialized publications keep scientists informed on literally thousands of technical and professional journals.

These tightly focused secondary publishers add value to an otherwise impenetrable avalanche of data. For example, in a typical edition of a scholarly journal, several papers will be published. The value and reliability of the information in each published article has usually been criticized and judged by a jury of peers. Only worthy material gets published.

This material goes through a second round of judges, when the editors of the secondary publishers decide which articles are worth entry into the database. This database is called a Bibliography and contains at least the following fields of data.

Info that is specific to the article

Title	Affiliation	Key Words
Author	Abstract	

Info that is specific to the published journal

Issue	Date	Pages

Even when the finest minds in the world are working on the job, and every present-day topic of interest is being faithfully tagged and preserved, there is more information here than can ever be packaged in any sort of abstract or bibliographic index.

Journal Info — Accession # for database

Amer. J. Bot. 69(9): 1410-1419. 1982.

308196-1

Title

MORPHOLOGICAL STUDIES OF THE NYMPHAEACEAE:12. THE FLORAL BIOLOGY OF CABOMBA-CAROLINIANA

Edward L. Schneider and John M. Jeter

Department of Biology, Southwest Texas State University, San Marcos, Texas 78666

Authors and Affiliations

ABSTRACT

Observations have been made on the pollination ecology of *Cabomba caroliniana* Gray in Texas. Flowers are trimerous with morphologically similar perianth parts. The adaxial corolla spurs are nectariferous and attract small Diptera (e.g. *Notiphila cressoni* and *Hydrellia bilobifera*). Anthesis occurs for 2 consecutive days with flowers opening about 10:00 a.m. and closing around 4 p.m. on each day. First-day flowers have short, indehiscent stamens and longer pollen-receptive stigmata which arch outward over the nectaries. In 2nd-day flowers the stamens have elongated to the level of the stigmata and extrorse dehiscence occurs above the nectaries. Stigmata of 2nd-day flowers are pressed together at the center of the flower and are nonreceptive to pollen. Insects attracted to 2nd-day flowers in search of nectar become dusted with pollen (due to the position and extrorse dehiscence of the anthers) and as insects fly to 1st-day flowers, achieve cross-pollination by virtue of the stigmata position over the nectaries. Seed anatomy is similar to that of other nymphaeaceous genera (i.e., abundant perisperm, little cellular endosperm, a haustorial nucellar "tube," and a small dicotyledonous embryo). Pollination morphology and comparative xylem anatomy support the segregation of *Cabomba* from the Nymphaeaceae, sensu stricto. The anatomical correlations between seeds and the myophilous pollination syndrome (found elsewhere in Nymphaeaceae, sensu lato), however, suggest a phyletic relationship.

Abstract

Some journals include Keywords here

Although studies dealing with the reproductive anatomy and morphology of *Cabomba* are numerous (e.g., Baillon, 1871; Caspary, 1888; Raciborski, 1894a, b; Chifflot, 1902; Cook, 1906; Fassett, 1953; Goleniewska-Furmanowa, 1970; Moseley, 1958; Wood, 1959; Ramji and Padmanabhan, 1965; Padmanabhan and Ramji, 1966; Riemer, 1966; Riemer and Ilnicki, 1968; Gregory, 1974; and Inamdar and Aleykutty, 1979) there has been little research conducted on the topic of floral biology. Tarver (1976) and Tarver and Sanders (1977) investigated the floral biology of *C. caroliniana* in Louisiana. They observed that anthesis occurs over a 2-day period with flowers opening about 10:30 a.m. and closing about 4:30 p.m. during both days. They further observed protogyny as well as changes in the floral morphology by noting that 1st-day flowers have short stamens, about half the height of the carpels, and that the carpels are bowed outward so that stigmata

are oriented toward the petals. In 2nd-day flowers, however, the anthers have been elevated to the level of the stigmata, and the stigmata are contiguous at the center of the flower. Pollen release was observed to occur about mid-day of the 2nd day. Tarver and Sanders further observed that seeds are produced only by flowers which have been visited by flying insects, for caged flowers did not set seed. They determined that the common honey bee, *Apis mellifera* Linnaeus, was the dominant pollinator of *Cabomba* in the Louisiana populations studied, though unidentified halictid bees were also seen in the flowers.

It is the purpose of this investigation to 1) collate and amplify the literature dealing with the floral biology of *Cabomba*; 2) investigate the mechanism(s) of pollination and the relationship between floral morphology and insect visitors; and 3) compare the floral biology of *Cabomba* to the floral biology of other Nymphaeaceae, sensu lato, with the possible goal of contributing to the understanding of both the evolutionary origin and adaptive radiation of the nymphaeaceous flower and the interrelationships among the genera of the Nymphaeaceae, sensu lato.

Materials and methods — Two populations of *Cabomba caroliniana* were studied. One locale was in the San Marcos River, San

Body Text

Italic (& Latin)

¹ Received for publication 7 July 1982; revision accepted 16 October 1981.

The research was supported in part by NSF Grant DEB-8102041 to the senior author. We thank Dr. D. Tuff (SWTSU), Dr. H. Burke and S. White (TAMU), Dr. J. Knutson (USDA) and Dr. W. H. Mathis (Smithsonian Institution) for their assistance in insect identifications, and Drs. M. F. Moseley (UCSB) and B. J. D. Meeuse (UW) for valuable discussions and reviews of portions of the manuscript.

Footnotes — Page #

Even the smartest librarian and the most insightful indexer can only assign code words to any present-day document based on the present day's interests. Ten or 20 years from now, or even months from now, something could happen to make an entire body of work extremely interesting again.

Researchers relying upon index information are strictly limited to the indexer's specific field of focus at the time of publication. Beyond this categorical information, the information in the source documents is not searchable.

A skilled searcher can individually retrieve documents and can individually peruse and read documents of interest. In this way, critical information may be unearthed that was never considered when the documents were being indexed, archived and filed away.

Scanned Document Management:
Access And Storage

Because image files themselves contain no data, it is critically important to assure reliable storage systems. A collection of images with no index is similar to, but worse than, a pile of unmarked microfilm rolls. A roll of film may contain a few thousand pages, while a common home PC with a 2.5-gigabyte disk might contain 50,000 images. Reliable storage is essential.

However, the heart of the matter is to ensure that index data is firmly attached to source data. A giant batch of unindexed TIFF files reduces every bit of information to a needle in a haystack. Finally, a backup of the index of large collections of image files is a critical requirement to ensure the viability of an image database.

Images are also exceptionally large files, and they usually cannot be made smaller by data-compression methods. In modems and other communications hardware, files can often be compressed during transmission. This feature allows modems to perform at greater than 100 percent efficiency. For example, a 50K text file might be compressed by 20 percent to 40K for transmission and uncompressed back to 50K on the receiving end. Thus, even though the modem ran at normal speed, 20 percent more data was transmitted. However, since images are compressed when they are created, there are few additional benefits to be gained.

These large images place unusual demands upon storage and network resources. To provide acceptable performance to the user, images should be delivered in small batches. For example, while retrieving a 20-page document, users prefer to view the first few pages while the remainder is being retrieved. This allows users to quit downloading irrelevant files before the entire document is received.

In 1995, Netscape Navigator introduced a new approach to this technique. The software downloads a very low-resolution sample of a GIF image at first, then fills in the image area with a barely recognized shape. Subsequent refreshes of the screen continue to sharpen the detail until the entire file is delivered and the final image appears. In 1996, Acrobat 3 applied this same technique to enhance PDF files, allowing more efficient access to large documents on the Web.

T Benefits of Acrobat 3

Download a page at a time over the Web

Verity SearchPDF display hit highlights in PDF on the Web

Pages download in most efficient order, text first, outline fonts, graphics, filled fonts

Getting From Paper
To Digital Format

The process of scanning and recognition is the gateway through which most
paper-based information will be brought over to the world of instantly accessible
information. It is very important to understand that the tools of scanning and recognition are not sledge hammers; they are very fine machines with subtle,
powerful controls.

typical OCR user choices

Source Page	Single Column, Multi-column, Text with Graphics
Page Quality	Dot Matrix, Normal, Auto
Output Page	Single Column Plain Text, Text with Graphics, Reproduce Page
Output Format	ASCII, RTF, PDF, Word - with or without graphics

paper to digital — basic steps

Document Prep
De-bind, remove staples, organize stacks

↓

Scanning
Flatbed or automatic document feeder

↓

Batch Management*
Control stacks of documents in process

↓

Job Tracking*
Control documents through each step

↓

Job Priority Change*
Modify order in which documents are processed

↓

Re-Scan*
If document is illegible, upside-down, etc

↓

Image Enhancement**
De-skew, de-speckle, thresholding

↓

Page Segmentation**
Choose areas of page for specific handling

↓

OCR Processing
Can be done on desktop or network server

↓

Quality Control*
Editing and clean-up of OCR output

↓

Job Status*
Overview of all jobs in the system

All functions marked with * are automated on network systems, whereas on desktop applications all of these functions are either manual or not done at all.

Functions marked with ** are optional, and may be automated through scanning controls and document templates.

Document Preparation:
The Critical Foundation

The clearest way to think about the importance of document preparation is to consider the two forms of a document. You can hold a dozen double-sided pages in your hands, you can move them around, your can turn them over, shuffle the stack, flick off an imperfection; you have total control of them.

Once you put those dozen pages through a scanner, you have a 1-megabyte file of 24 separate images. Your scanner might relate them into a single stack for you, but you now have an invisible Binary Large OBject, or BLOB, that the user has to identify and handle inside of the computer.

Compared to fiddling with a demanding set of computer tasks, those good old paper pages start looking real good. You could turn them over, you could smooth out creases, you could hold them up to the light ... yes, those paper pages sure had a lot going for them.

Users of digital documents will never have the simple powers and pleasures of holding onto paper, and it is up to the people doing the scanning and digitizing to create the best possible digital documents.

Scanning a paper document and converting it into digital form should be considered a one-time event. It's not something you take your best three cracks at like the Bell Ringer Sledgehammer on the Boardwalk.

To expedite scanning, proper procedures should be in place to:

1. **Reliably track paper documents before, during and after scanning**

2. **Use every available hardware & software option to cleanse and perfect each document**

3. **Process each image in a defined, traceable job flow, with easy fixes and error correction facilities handy**

Handling Bound Documents

To a librarian, the thought of chopping off the binding of a book is absolutely abhorrent. On the other hand, the thought of a book decaying on a shelf compared to a book on the Internet is an ever-more moving emotion.

There can only be so many books, and they will be lost over time. Users will take them out of the library and never return them. They will be so popular that they will be used up, and the bindings will fail, and pages will fall out, and eventually the covers will be lost.

Books in electronic form are not subject to such decay. A remote user can have full use of a complete and rich version of a document or volume, while the "original" is never touched. By the same token, many more users can get to these original documents than could have ever seen the paper documents.

If all of the above arguments do not make sense, there are special book scanners that allow rare or delicate works to be handled with the least wear and tear. One of the earliest models was introduced by Minolta in 1995. It included an adjustable bed on which the book was laid face up. The bed itself was separately adjustable on each side so that as the pages were turned, the left and right sides would move slightly up or down to compensate. Mounted above the book on a tall tripod, the scanner camera looked down and used auto-focus to create clear images of the pages.

This gentle machine preserves the original book and delivers excellent page images. Compared to the alternative of pressing the books themselves down on the scanner platen, or trying to squash them on a book edge copier, the book scanner is a welcome device. However, the physical labor involved in this process is quite considerable.

If, on the other hand, at least one of the above arguments about productivity makes sense, documents should be "unbound" or "debinded" before scanning. The labor savings provided by automatic document feeders is overwhelming. The least expensive sheet feeder on the cheapest available scanner will always be several times more productive than a person shuffling pages by hand.

The best way to remove the binding is to use a heavy-duty guillotine paper cutter. It is important to keep the pages as square and straight-edged as possible to facilitate scanning. The paper cutters found in commercial print and copy shops go through thick books like butter.

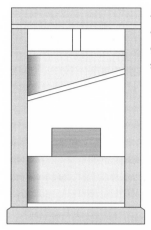

An idea that makes book afficionados cringe, the book guillotine is a useful tool for scanning in the digital world.

If the documents have been bound by less-easily-dispatched methods, more labor will be required for document preparation. The primary goal should be to make the pages ready to go through the paper feeder. This means the pages should be stacked evenly, with nothing to make the pages stick together during feeding. For example, the rough holes left by a hastily removed staple will usually be enough to keep the page more or less fastened by the paper of one page being punched through the next.

These tiny imperfections can lead to maddening rework during scanning. Document preparation is hard work, but doing it well saves time and work down the line.

Handling Single- Or Double-Sided Pages

While business correspondence documents are single-sided, published reports and other complex books are usually double-sided. Most scanners will scan only one side of the page on each pass. Software is used to simplify the process of scanning double-sided documents by incrementing the page count during scanning. For example, the tops or fronts of all of the pages are scanned first; then the stack is flipped over and scanned again. The software will count the first stack as 1-3-7-9-49; when the stack is flipped, the software will reset the counter to 50, and decrement the count as 50-48-46-2. The end result is a properly ordered set of page images from 1 to 50.

Paper Weights

Besides pages that are crumpled or stuck together, the most common concern in scanning stacks of documents is varying page thickness. Paper weight is the measure used to compare the weight and thickness of various paper stocks. A 24-pound bond paper is thicker and heavier than a 20-pound bond. Heavier paper stocks tend to have a grainier, or leathery, rough surface. Lighter stocks tend to be thinner and smoother.

The rollers in a scanner are set to the hundredth, even the thousandth, of an inch, to handle this variety. Rubber rollers are used to add another variable of flexibility. But all scanner feeders have limits in the range of paper thickness they can reliably handle. Card stock covers on reports, for example, are actually 70- 110-pound paper, or light cardboard. A single piece of cardstock is as thick as several pieces of paper and will often jam in the rollers.

At the other end of the spectrum, some paper is too light to reliably feed through scanners. Some very thin onion-skin paper, often used for typing academic papers and manuscripts, is only 10-pound stock, and much thinner than 20-pound bond. Glossy magazine pages, with their hard, slippery finish, are particularly challenging to feed through a scanner.

Fragile Handling

Fragile handling is needed for both "ancient" documents and those stored on very cheap output, such as thermal fax paper and carbon copies. Entire careers of famous chemists and physicists reside in skimpy loose-leaf binders and notebooks. Many digitization requirements become labors of love, where the work itself evokes sufficient dedication to overcome all of the difficulties.

Mixed Orientation

Any image-processing program that uses OCR can theoretically deal with mixed orientations in the scanned images. Software can look for words to determine the baseline, and thus the orientation, of the page.

Any image-processing program that uses OCR can theoretically deal with mixed orientations in the scanned images. Software can look for words to determine the baseline, and thus the orientation, of the page.

2% (OCR works)

Any image-processing program that uses OCR can theoretically deal with mixed orientations in the scanned images. Software can look for words to determine the baseline, and thus the orientation, of the page.

7% (OCR fails)

Any image-processing program that uses OCR can theoretically deal with mixed orientations in the scanned images. Software can look for words to determine the baseline, and thus the orientation, of the page.

15% (human has difficulty)

Examples of skewed text

Orientation of the page is absolutely critical in applications where there is no control over the incoming images. A fax server is the perfect example of this requirement, where literally hundreds of different styles of fax machines are the sources of the input images, controlled by unknown people. No fax server would ever be designed to expect the pages to come in right side up. However, this feature requires a lot of CPU processing power.

More expensive scanners, designed for high-production operations, offer single-pass double-sided scanning, where both sides of the page are scanned at once. These scanners are driven by software that automatically keeps track of the images being produced by each of the two sets of Charge-Coupled Device (CCD) arrays, and orders the images into a single, consecutive file. This duplex capability has recently become available on less-expensive scanners.

Charge-Coupled Devices are the eyes of modern scanners; they translate reflected light to digital information. CCD arrays are miniature rows of these light-sensitive devices that track and translate every pixel (picture element) on the page into white, black, gray or colored information.

Handling Graphics And Illustrations

To just touch upon the topic of scanning richer images, in gray scale and color, it is important to consider the combination of these images with text in the source documents.

There are several collisions between rich graphic scanning and text.

1. Rich color graphics that look beautiful on the average computer monitor are far different from text on a screen. The most common color picture format is called GIF, or Graphic Interchange Format. It's so popular that GIFs have always been handled like native files on the Web, also called inline graphics.

2. GIFs were designed to show full-color graphics, mostly scanned photographs, on the typical PC monitor. The typical VGA monitor has a resolution of about 72 dpi, so resolution above that just deteriorates the picture on the monitor.

3. Text at any resolution less than 200 or 300 dpi will produce poor OCR results.

4. Except for programs that are designed to work with HP AccuPage and other similar software, OCR requires binary images. Color images are not suitable for OCR.

You'll have to decide what features are most important when establishing scanner settings.

Scanning Techniques

Document scanners share all of the same optical and paper handling machinery used in copiers and fax machines, so the digitization of paper pages is a common and reliable technology. Because the actual "magic" of transforming black and white bits into computer images is being done on ever-cheaper silicon, scanners will be cheaper, sharper and faster with each new generation of desktop processor.

Small, Medium & Big Scanning Configurations

HP ScanJet IIIC	~ $ 1,500 (including feeder)
Resolution	200 - 600 dpi Optical resolution, up to 2400 dpi extended
Scanning Speed:	4 Pages per Minute
Comment	Clearly superior for gray & color scanning applications
Fujitsu SP 10C	~ $ 1,500 (w/ SCSI Interface)
Resolution	200, 240, 300, 400 dpi
Scanning Speed	12 Pages per Minute
Comment	Clearly superior for faster document feeding and scanning
Fujitsu 3093	~ $ 6,500 (w/ SCSI Interface)
Resolution	200, 240, 300, 400 dpi
Scanning Speed	27 Pages per Minute
Comment	Durable, productive scanner for department use
Fujitsu M3099	~ $28,000 (w/ SCSI)
Resolution	200, 240, 300, 400 dpi
Single-side Speed	80 Pages per Minute
Double-side Speed	120 Page / Images per Minute
Comment	High-speed throughput, enhanced image processing

The raw output of scanners can often be enhanced to make the finished images more suitable for specific needs. All of the following processes can be performed in either hardware or software, usually depending upon overall throughput requirements. Especially in very high-volume installations, dedicated hardware solutions may be more productive than software running on standard workstation processors and SCSI interfaces. The point is, these processes are indispensable enhancements to any document scanning and digitization system.

The most important adjustments you can make are the brightness and/or contrast settings. Brightness is directly comparable to setting the f-stop in a camera, controlling the amount of light that hits the film. In a scanner, a thin, long strip of light-sensitive computer chips passes over the image. These chips are the CCDs that measure the amount of light reflected from a given spot to determine if that spot is black or white. In color and gray-scale scanners, the CCD actually measures the wavelengths of the reflected light to accurately reproduce shades of gray or color.

Adjustments to the brightness setting change the receptivity of the CCD. This allows the user to precisely control the output of the scanner The ideal brightness setting brings out the best in the material of interest and can drop out unwanted background.

Contrast is so similar to brightness that many scanner programs combine these two adjustments into one. While brightness makes the entire image lighter or darker, contrast lets the user tune the scanner for the difference between black and white, or any other gradient of light.

Adjustments to contrast can sometimes be used to remove speckles in the image because it requires more or fewer pixels to be recognized as a speck. Higher contrast may see five or seven touching black pixels as a speck on the page image, while lower contrast might ignore so few pixels and portray the entire area as white.

Scanner Specifications And Settings

Resolution: The finest detail that can be discerned by the scanner, usually measured in dots per inch (dpi). Typical resolutions are 200, 240, 300, 400, 600 and finer. OCR is usually done at 300 dpi to provide enough detail for accurate recognition, without capturing too much detail and ending up with overly large files.

John Solomon, a seasoned veteran in the field of document digitization, won the contract for the OTA conversion. Solomon, Vice President of Input Solutions (Gaithersburg, MD), has been dedicated to the field of high-end document recognition since his years selling the first intelligent OCR machines, invented by Ray Kurzweil.

Solomon's observations on this project are very enlightening: "We tested at 200, 240, 300 and 400 dpi. One thing that we consistently saw was that higher resolution scans yielded higher OCR accuracy with Adobe Capture." Solomon is someone who focuses sharply on OCR accuracy, but he also described another benefit of higher resolution scanning. "Graphics clarity improved at higher resolutions, and moire patterns on halftones virtually disappeared.

"The Fujitsu 3099A has 100 levels of brightness, where most scanning software offers about 15 levels of adjustment. The 3099 also has 100 levels of density, and we were lucky to be able to take advantage of this extra-fine level of adjustability. We found an individual with a great eye for how the scanner would see a page. Because the typical document in this project was long and dense, we tested each book before scanning. The operator's visual judgment let us run just a few test scans to optimize performance for accuracy and speed."

Image Type: The scanner's ability to recognize binary (black & white), gray scale or color. Binary-only scanners often have the ability to dither the image to create a digital halftone of a gray or color image. OCR and most commercial document imaging applications use binary images. Scanning in gray scale and color is an art form unto itself.

Scanning Speed: The number of pages per minute (ppm) than can be scanned, usually through the ADF (automatic document feeder). On most scanners, higher resolution results in slower speeds. A scanner rated at 20 pages per minute at 200 dpi may only do 12 pages per minute at 400 dpi.

Straighten Images Via De-Skewing

Image de-skewing assures straight images through a feature called edge detection. This is a function that looks for long straight lines, most particularly at preset parameters for the page. Edge detection sees long areas of black pixels forming a long border and determines whether this border is close to the horizontal or vertical axis. The software then rotates the entire image to match the 90 degree orientation of that edge. This feature is sometimes expanded to include border removal, a process that deletes that entire area of black pixels that was seen as the "edge" in the de-skew stage.

The process of digitizing OTA reports began with the "de-binding" of the documents, accomplished by an electric guillotine slicing off the spines. The resulting stack of pages, usually double-sided, was then fed through the high-speed scanner. The Kofax 9275 Image Processor de-skewed the images on the fly, but the throughput was far below the scanner's advertised speeds at 200 dpi.

The processing of the documents was done with the Pentium Scan Station and the Fujitsu 3099A, feeding a queue on an HP NetServer, which had a 100 Mhz CPU, 64 MB of RAM and dual 4 GB drives. A Pentium/133 with 32 MB of RAM and a 2 GB Fast SCSI hard drive was designated as the Capture conversion server, running over Novell 4.1. Solomon noted that the Fast SCSI offered dramatic improvement in throughput on the Capture server. Editing and cleanup was done on 486/100s and P75s.

"Our target was 200 pages per day for our editing and cleanup operators. Our best operator hit 373 pages per day at the end. A lot depends on the source document, and a lot depends on trying hard," Solomon declares.

Five CDs, containing 23 years of pure research into technology and the future, can sit in a single tiny player. That five-disc player on a PC Web Server provides wide-open, free access to the rich reports. The Office of Technology Assessment will live on in perpetuity as a "virtual agency," mirrored on servers around the world, part of the global system that evolves from the fertile World Wide Web.

Setting Resolution

Document scanners offer varying levels of resolution when scanning, which is measured in dots per inch. Each dot, or pixel, represents the light reflected from a minute point on the page The proper resolution for each application is dependent on two factors:

  1. How the documents will be used

  2. The processes the documents will go through

Image Compression Comparisons

DPI	Bytes/Sq. Inch	Uncompressed* (8.5 inch x 11 inch page)
200	40,000	0.44 Megabyte
300	90,000	1.05 Megabyte
400	160,000	1.77 Megabyte

* Most documents are compressed in practice, but relative sizes remain fairly constant.

In actual practice, image compression is routinely employed to reduce file size, and the general rule of thumb is 50,000 bytes per image, or roughly 20 images per megabyte. The raw image file is compressed most often in an international format known as CCITT Group IV. However, a 300-dpi image will always be larger than a 200-dpi image.

Because even compressed images are such large files, the lowest possible resolution should be chosen. Lower resolution results in smaller files, reducing storage requirements on physical media and reducing transmission time and network load.

Returning to the first criteria for choosing a resolution, the user of the images must be considered. In the commercial document imaging industry, where pages are scanned into workflow and document management systems, 200-dpi images are the most widely used. The users of these documents require an easily readable reproduction of the page, and 200 dpi offers a very good copy. For example, Fine Mode Fax is 200 dpi.

Optimal resolutions are:

- 200 dpi images are fine for viewing
- 300 dpi is recommended for OCR
- 400 dpi and above is restricted to special requirements

OCR Robots Speed The Process

To make the information on the pages accessible, optical character recognition can be performed on document images, converting digital copies of text into actual computer text. OCR is a robot typist, designed to reduce the need for manually rekeying information from paper sources. OCR is always faster, and in some cases it is more accurate than human typists. Once OCR has converted document images to text, they may be searched for key words and index fields, greatly improving access to the information compared to simple images.

OCR software should be considered as more of a robot than a software program. The distinction is that a software program, like a word processor, spreadsheet or telecommunications program, is designed to automate a repetitive series of computer-based tasks. Optical character recognition exists to take in paper documents, in all their infinite variety, and bring them into the computer's digital world. OCR is built from thousands of rules, but the ultimate variable is infinite, paper documents.

In the very early Kurzweil Intelligent Scanning Systems, a number
of expert systems were used to perform character recognition. However, the system had
to be "trained" to produce the best results for each document.

In addition to the crucial Brightness settings, the operator was presented
with three choices at the beginning of each job:

Do 0 (zero) and O (uppercase O) look alike ?

This would tell the software to emphasize string-checking to assure that alpha
characters followed alphas, and numeric characters followed numeric characters.
By so doing, mixed alpha-numeric strings, such as part numbers, became
virtually impossible to recognize accurately. But at least the word "book"
would be spelled with "o" instead of "0."

Do 1 (numeral 1) and l (lowercase l) look alike ?

A "yes" answer to this question would tell the software that a serif font
was being recognized. It would also point the string-checking features to look for
unique instances where a "1" would normally be found. For example, if an
ambiguous character appeared followed by a period, "l." or "1." it would be
recognized as the numeral one. So in a long alphabetical listing, the order
would appear as a-b-c-d-e-f-g-h-i-j-k-l-m-n-etc.

Do L (uppercase L) and l (lowercase l) look alike ?

Opposite of Number 2, a "yes" answer to this question would tell
the software that a sans-serif font was being recognized, where both upper case "I" and
lower case "l" are represented by a plain, vertical line. In this case, an upper case "I"
would not appear in the middle of string of lower case letters.

Fine Tuning OCR

In the earlier section on scanner settings, we discussed brightness and contrast and how they can be used to optimize scanning. There are two types of easily distinguished OCR errors that give a clue that the brightness or contrast settings can be improved: broken characters and joined characters.

> **tip**
>
> **The adjustments that fix problems at one end of the "Too Light - Too Dark" spectrum cause problems at the other end. For example, if the fine characters in italic text are breaking up, the proper correction is to lower the brightness, or decrease the contrast. These same adjustments may cause bold text on the same page to run together. The only solution is to make a choice based on the importance or preponderance of italic or bold text.**

It is not always possible to correct OCR errors by adjusting contrast and brightness. Remember, OCR accuracy is always dependent upon the quality of the original. Having said that, hand the best possible image over to the OCR robot.

> **tip**
>
> **An old-fashioned magnifying glass is an excellent low-tech tool to double-check scanner adjustments. In situations where the problem of broken or joined characters can not be fixed after many settings changes, it can be helpful to take a close look at the original page. Many times the print on the page itself will be actually broken or crashing.**

One reliable method to determine how big to make the size of undesirable specks, to be filtered out by the despeckle feature, is to measure the smallest feature of the subject text. For example, in many fonts, the smallest discernible feature is the dot on a lower case "i." If the dots on the "i"s are disappearing, the despeckle feature is set too large and is removing more than it should from the page.

Drop-out colors are colors that the scanner does not see. Familiar forms are often printed in very specific shades of pink or green or blue, each with a particular Pantone Color. These colors reflect a wavelength of light that is not picked up by the CCD array of a particular scanner. For example, many early, inexpensive Japanese scanners used a yellow-green light for scanning. Many popular yellow highlighters would be completely invisible to these scanners.

Using the same optical wavelength trick, Kurzweil scanners designed for the office offered red drop-out. This feature allowed lawyers, for example, to mark up a contract with a red pen. The marked-up document could still be scanned accurately because the invisible red marking would not interfere with OCR. When the file went to word processing for clean-up, the typist could use the red marked-up pages to make the desired corrections.

In the section on brightness and contrast, those controls are used to perform this same trick on background colors. Paper tends to yellow and brown as it ages, and this discoloring can sometimes interfere with OCR. By adjusting brightness and contrast to emphasize the text, a form of "drop-out" is achieved by minimizing the color on the paper.

In fact, even gray-scale processing done on images is a form of "color drop-out" where all the least-informative shades of gray in the image are discarded, in the interest of presenting the best possible image to the OCR process.

Summary

The benefits of digital documents far surpass the effort required to create them. With an ever-growing array of tools, our ability to instantly access information is increasing expotentially.

footnotes

1 News Release, 2/28/95, Xplor International, The Electronic Document Systems Association

2 News Release, 2/28/95, Xplor International, The Electronic Document Systems Association

3 Gartner Group Briefing, 3/10/95, Jaime Popkin, Electronic Workplace Technologies

4 Adobe Acrobat Product Benefits Study, 9/9/94, KPMG Peat Marwick LLP

5 Source: Lawrence Livermore Labs, Coopers & Lybrand

the present:

making
existing
digital
documents

accessible

chapter two

Virtually all but handwritten documents now originate in digital form, if only for a brief time during their creation. Electronic tools like word processors, spreadsheets, electronic publishing, databases and even email now combine to form the bulk of new documents being created.

At the same time, the new universal transport of the Internet is growing with burgeoning capability. In 1996 alone, some of the major telecomm giants quadrupled their capacity. And there are now thousands of Internet Service Providers (ISP) delivering ever-widening access to the Net.

It would seem we have the tools we need to achieve instant access, namely digital documents and a global network for instant transmissions.

However, there still remains the impediment of wildly varying file formats. The situation is improving rapidly, but at the moment the majority of electronic documents are in relatively proprietary formats.

Compression schemes are a good example of the still proprietary nature of platform-specific files. How do you handle a .SIT file from a Mac friend on your Windows PC? How does he handle .ZIP files you create?

These are file formats that are universally accepted on their own platforms but require special handling to convert to something that can be opened on another platform.

For the English language version of the guide to the Egyptian Collection at the Louvre Museum, here's the link to see the Scribe, with his blue rock crystal eyes. A quick click switches to French, Spanish or Portuguese.

In person, this painted limestone Egyptian Scribe circa 2500 B.C. is entrancing with crystal blue eyes and a palpable attentiveness. By looking at him you get the feeling that his job was something like yours, only he was doing it 4,500 years ago. (Later in the chapter, see how modern monks are now scribes on the Web.)

http://mistral.culture.fr/louvre/anglais/musee/collec/colleceg.html

Why Use A Universal Format?

In the beginning, each application had its own file format. This meant you needed to run Microsoft Word to read a Word .DOC or .RTF file. These are binary files, and if you've ever received one as ASCII via email, you know they look like "garbage." Of course, viewed in Word, they're nicely formatted.

This babble of file types is addressed by forward-looking programs that allow you to import other file formats into your applications and truly share information with others. For example, WordPerfect and Word read each other's formats, allowing editing in either program. Word's RTF (Rich Text Format) is an effort to standardize file interchange between word processors.

In today's world of ever-broadening and ever-accelerating network capacity, the market demands the simplest possible methods. Based on recent progress, it seems likely that everyone will have access through the Internet to hugely varying types of documents.

Internet connections can be accomplished over every telephone line, so we have the means in place and under constant expansion. We know that an incompatible variety of applications are used to create these documents. It makes sense that there should be a format that all of these tools can output that can be read by all of the users.

Right now, there are four strategies in place for providing "universal" file access:

1. Native File Formats: Assumes user has source application (Word, Photoshop) and offers totally editable "live" documents.

2. Convert to HTML on-the-fly: Before being served up, the native format is converted to its ASCII equivalent in HTML, which degrades formatting on tables and columns but works fine on relatively plain text. Spreadsheets may become unreadable if displayed as 80-column ASCII, where word wrap distorts line length and tabs.

3. Viewer to Display Document: A viewer offers the ability to reproduce the appearance of a document but at the cost of limited annotations. A viewer by definition provides a representation of the document rather than the source itself. This means the document may be annotated, highlighted and otherwise marked up, but not edited in the traditional sense.

4. Format that is Native to the "Universe": Two file types are now popular that have been designed from the ground up to be universal: HTML and PDF.

Platform Independence Provides Easy Viewing

Both HTML and PDF allow the same documents to be viewed on all of the most popular hardware and software platforms. Web browsers run on virtually every computer, and the HTML Web pages that are designed primarily to be "universal" can even be navigated with character-based interfaces like LYNX.

HTML can be thought of as a text-enhancing programming language. It makes text references navigable through the HyperText Transport Protocol linkage. All sorts of enhancements are possible through the very flexible framework of HTML.

Acrobat PDF comes with several key enhancements on board. Because every user will be using the freely distributed Acrobat Reader to handle PDF documents, authors and readers have extensive luxury features at hand. The user can choose full-page viewing with navigation buttons for moving through the document, or he can use the Bookmarks or Thumbnail features to offer enhanced navigation.

> There will always be a difference in opinion on the "proprietary" vs. "open" nature of the PDF format. Adobe Systems, Inc. will argue (as Adobe Chairman and CEO John Warnock successfully argued for PostScript) that Acrobat is an openly published specification and anyone can exploit its capabilities. HTML purists will argue that "nobody owns HTML," as if the viability of PDF is somehow compromised by having been invented by Adobe.
>
> Beyond quasi-religious and political devotion to certain platforms, today's popular page-creation tools that are used to create books, magazines, newspapers, manuals, presentations and every other form of complex document can be better reproduced digitally in PDF than they can be represented in HTML.

Printer Independence to Retain Appearance

Excellent print characteristics are to be expected from Acrobat PDF based on its heritage of PostScript, the original "universal language" of composition and printing. The latest developments in HTML, with cascading stylesheets and other openings to traditional composition capability, are leading to ever-richer and therefore more "printable" HTML documents.

It should be noted that the $10-billion-per-year commercial printing industry is pressing for PDF as a universal standard, not HTML. At the moment, PDF has made faster progress in gaining the "linkability" of HTML than HTML has made on the "printability" of PDF. With Web links, Bookmarks, Hypertext links and navigable Thumbnail Views, Acrobat PDF provides the kind of dynamic connectedness associated with HTML documents. On the other hand, due to the wide-open configurability of every user's browser, even the latest HTML extensions still don't approach the page composition and design capability of PDF.

Integrate PDF With Text Databases

As Acrobat PDF format becomes increasingly prevalent on the Web and CD and other media, virtual universal support for the format can be expected. Some of the first information retrieval vendors to support PDF documents as fully searchable include:

Excalibur Technologies at

`http://www.excalib.com`

Fulcrum Technologies at

`http://www.fultext.com`

Open Text Corp. at

`http://www.opentext.com`

Personal Library Systems at

`http://www.pls.com`

And, as we discuss in Chapter 8, Verity's freely distributed SearchPDF Information Retrieval engine offers the means for optimum use of all of Acrobat's features for document management and information retrieval on the Web and Intranets.

The Common Archival Solution

Everyone who has used computers has experienced the "obsolescence" of formerly vital files. Either the format was unreadable because the old application was no longer around, or, even worse, the media itself became physically unreadable. Just like 78-rpm records gave way to 33 rpm, and then records themselves were supplanted by 8-track tapes, cassettes, CDs, and soon DVD, computer media have gone through comparable changes. When first introduced, floppy disks were an 8-inch format. These were replaced by 5.25-inch format, which has now given way to 3.5-inch format. Iomega's ZIP drives are on the universal horizon.

The grandaddy of all of these "universal" languages is the Standard Generalized Markup Language (SGML), which is a series of conventions that provide for data organization and text attributes to be built into a universally readable ASCII-based code. However, at this time SGML is primarily in the province of libraries and other organizations concerned with document preservation over hundreds or thousands of years.

The SGML Web Page, copyright by Robin Cover, is an exhaustive and frequently updated resource with a bibliography of more than 1,300 references at:

```
http://www.sil.org/sgml/sgml.html
```

For most users, the choice comes down to output in HTML or PDF. HTML is developing rapidly, but PDF has the huge head start of universal acceptance of PostScript in the professional page-design world. Today's PDF documents far exceed the depth of design and organizational richness of all but the most laboriously eloquent HTML documents.

Benefits Of Independence

Being free from the limits of printing devices and platforms can expand your reach and open more opportunities.

It's important to admit that we can't see the future very clearly. We can make out the blurry outlines, like the sides of the road in a blizzard, and we can thereby make our way. When it comes to new interfaces, operating systems and so on, we can only assume that certain trends will last.

HTML and PDF are built to last, and both can be generated by an increasing number of popular applications. Other formats pale in comparison, even Microsoft's cross-platform Rich Text Format (RTF), and such imaging standards at Tagged Image File Format (.TIF and .TIFF).

Documents written or "printed" in HTML or PDF will most likely have a much longer life of "readability" than previous, more proprietary formats.

In the Acrobat Reader, the author can provide the user with countless luxuries, including everything from the ability to view huge (in both length and page size) documents to built-in sound files for verbal instructions or musical accompaniment. The standard conveniences include rapid navigation, searching, easy viewing and snappy transitions.

Today's documents have many aspects, ranging from the traditional printout on paper to the rich hyperlinked world of the Web. It is desirable to create a single document designed for high performance on all of these media. The resources listed in this chapter offer inexhaustible storehouses of tools and techniques for creating universally accessible content, published once.

Sacrifices

On the other hand, you'll have to make some sacrifices for independence, including some limitations and new software implementations.

Just like PostScript, PDF is a publication format and is not designed for easy editing and manipulation. Acrobat 3 offers the Touch Up tool, which provides a rich array of controls for editing line content in a document. PDF, like PostScript, is an output file and therefore is not optimized for repagination. PDF, like PostScript, creates complete pages.

To enjoy the benefits of any of the latest media, it has been incumbent upon the user to download the latest viewer or browser. This required function will be automated soon because the user market demands it. For the time being, most sites offering PDF or other special content offer links to the required viewer.

The difficult aspect of "free" software is usually the paucity of free support. Implicit in the contract of free software is the deal that the users will train and support themselves.

This is a noble and often achieved goal in the traditional Internet community of the inspired and technically inclined. By relying upon the familiar structure of a well-designed file standard such as PDF, authors can expect a large base of PDF-literate users. This user familiarity amounts to widespread operator training, allowing many users to enjoy enhanced documents.

Kendall Whitehouse, Associate Director for Computing at the Wharton School, has a very admirable
design goal for the school's Web site: "Three clicks
and you're in to any major piece of information."

The Wharton School's home page is at:

(http://www.wharton.upenn.edu)

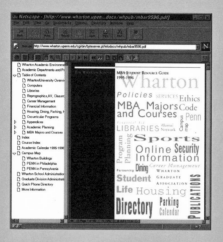

*The Wharton School's Web site may have been the
very first major site to serve up a collection of PDF documents in the winter of '93, soon after the Web was invented at CERN and NCSA. And months before even
Adobe had a Web site serving up PDF. Continuous innovation is ongoing.*

*Three maps that offer satellite-like Zoom In & Out view-
ing of the area. The user can click down through a 15-
square-mile view, to a 2-square mile view, to the few
blocks where all the buildings are labeled with their
names.*

When I ask Kendall what application these documents are created in, he declares, "We don't have a
single program, that's the great thing. These documents are created by people throughout the school
using Adobe PageMaker, Quark XPress, Microsoft
Word … it doesn't matter."

This freedom from the constraints of the particular
application seems particularly appreciated by a guy
who took it upon himself to hook up an Apple
LaserWriter to a PC back in 1985, the earliest days
of desktop machines. "I needed to learn to write

PostScript by hand to do illustrations (years before Adobe Illustrator came out). PostScript is a wonderful language. I'm still amazed by it."

The design and development of the Wharton School's Web site has been an ongoing collaboration between the students and various administrative and academic units at the school, including the Publications, Public Affairs, Alumni Affairs, Executive Education and Computing departments. "Like many other institutions, our initial Web site was developed by our computing organization," says Kendall. "But we quickly realized that if we were to be successful, we needed a joint initiative by departments across the school that understood how to communicate with the school's diverse internal and external audiences." The design elements at the Wharton School site deserve careful attention based on their chief architect's ardent beliefs and long-exercised enthusiasms. The results speak for themselves.

"Wharton's online documents emphasize PDF's navigation features," Kendall explains, "especially article threading and hypertext. Our goal is to make the online documents work successfully as interactive presentations when viewed on-screen, yet print well in hard copy."

The results of these design choices are obvious at Wharton's Web site, where many subtle and swift paths provide convenient navigation shortcuts that become obvious in the structure of the pages.

Wharton's Web site integrates PDF and HTML in a way that takes advantage of the strengths of both formats. The School's quarterly newsletter, which summarizes recent research and working papers, is a case in point.

Indices and "table of contents" pages for the newsletters are available online in HTML. Hypertext links in the HTML pages provide access to the complete newsletter in PDF. Within each newsletter, citations to Wharton research include PDF Web links to an HTML page that provides the current publication status of each paper referenced in the newsletter. "The HTML references can be easily updated over time while retaining the integrity of the original publication in PDF. It's easy to move back and forth between HTML and PDF and use each format to its best advantage. The technology behind this solution is rock solid!" Kendall Whitehouse states emphatically.

During 1996, Acrobat Readers were being downloaded at the rate of 20,000 per day, according to Adobe when Acrobat 3 was released.

On the Web, both Netscape Navigator and Microsoft Internet Explorer offer smooth integration with Acrobat 3. The early vote is in, and PDF is a majority choice for rich document format on the Web, CD and other media. The following provides a glimpse of Adobe's vision.

PostScript was a crucial component in the success of desktop publishing. What role does PostScript play on the Web?

JOHN WARNOCK: If you did all your publishing in HTML on the Web, you would find a fairly barren environment in terms of creative and graphical experience. What PostScript and Acrobat technology bring to the Web is a richer graphical experience. A document as simple as a financial statement can't be done in HTML because you can't line up the decimal points, you can't put the numbers in the right columns, you can't even do a simple spreadsheet. There are literally thousands of different kinds of documents that need to be expressed on the Web that you can't express in HTML.

PostScript brings a cross-platform, cross-architecture domain to the Web. Yet HTML is pretty much the standard at this point. I think that PDF [Portable Document Format, Acrobat's file format] and HTML will coexist. As we add interactive capabilities of PDF, many of the serious applications will have a tendency to use PDF because of its expressive character. A balance will be achieved over time. Right now, HTML is the least common denominator and it will probably be that way for years to come.

CHUCK GESCHKE: I think of the Internet as being the world's library of information, and as such, HTML does an incredible job in providing the interface, the card catalog to get you into the library. But once you decide that you actually want a book — a significant volume of content that is going to effectively communicate information — that is when you want PDF.

From "The Adobe Interview: Warnock & Geschke," referring to John Warnock, Chairman & CEO, and Chuck Geschke, President of Adobe Systems, Inc.

http://www.adobe.com/newsfeatures/warnock.geschke/page4.html

Decisions To Make

On the road to instantly accessible information, you'll need to consider a few points when contemplating a consistent digital format:

- Is PDF a more viable and enduring format than other available options? Should you use HTML in addition to, or instead of, PDF? One major answer to the first question is the way federal government is rapidly adopting PDF as a standard format. The original universal format, SGML, was never accepted as widely or quickly. Remember, many government documents are mandated to live for 25, 100, or more years. The fact that PDF is finding such rapid acceptance in this user community speaks volumes. HTML is hypertext, the ability to present lists and links to vast quantities of information. And, like the ASCII code upon which HTML is built, it is designed to be used on all computers. Perfect for a "card catalog" but less than perfect for the publication standards we've all grown accustomed to in books, newspapers and magazines. PDF offers sophisticated page composition, with much greater information density available through traditional page design and philosophy.

- Richness of PDF: Is the size of the PDF file worth the message conveyed? More information takes more space, and your audience will be deciding if your files are worth the disk space and/or downloading time.

- Do you need to use Distiller or PDFWriter? Any documents that are now being created in electronic publishing applications and output to PostScript should use Distiller to take advantage of all of the rich controls. PDFWriter is what its name suggests, a substitute printer for everyday applications such as word processing and spreadsheets. Acrobat 3 introduced Distiller Assistant, allowing simple access to Distiller for quick PDF output from desktop applications.

- How much do you want to enhance your files with sound, video and other luxuries? Are you willing to cope with the resulting size and speed sacrifices?

Working with Applications

This is not a simple topic that can be explained in a few paragraphs. One of the most amazing features of PDF is that the richness of traditional page-composition techniques are kept. You'll achieve the best PDF files from each application by following some specific guidelines for your application.

The easiest distinction is that PDFWriter is literally a printer substitute, useful to the common user who takes advantage of only basic text format features. Printing a Word document to PDF rather than to a laser printer will create a reasonable facsimile.

For any serious page layout artist or document designer working with complex images, Distiller remains the tool of choice to create PDFs.

Most automated features of document publishing are directly transferable to PDF formats. That means that advanced features of electronic publishing packages can be used to directly create enhanced, universal-format documents. The Web links listed in this chapter let you go right to the source to get the latest info on most popular applications so that you can incorporate the following features in your new documents:

Gordon Kent is the author of *Internet Publishing with Acrobat* (Adobe Press, 1996). As a dynamic companion to this comprehensive reference guide, Gordon provides a supporting Web site at:

Bookmarks	**Links**
Table of Contents	**Indexes**

`http://www.novagraphix.com/Internet_Publishing_with_Acrobat`

For the latest recommendations on creating PDF files from other applications, visit the appropriate Web site:

Application	Web site
PageMaker	`http://www.adobe.com/prodindex/pagemaker/main.html`
FrameMaker	`http://www.adobe.com/`
Interleaf	`http://www.interleaf.com/`
Quark	`http://www.quark.com/`

A book can point to the future with reliable sites that will always give you the latest information you need.

For updates on Adobe products, visit these sites:

The Illustrator What's New Page:

```
http://www.adobe.com/prodindex/illustrator/main.html
```

The Photoshop What's New Page:

```
http://www.adobe.com/prodindex/photoshop/main.html
```

The Persuasion What's New Page:

```
http://www.adobe.com/prodindex/persuasion /main.html
```

Listservs are email resources that allow software users and enthusiasts from all over the world to chat and discuss practical implementations of all this new technology. The following listserv email discussion groups let you throw questions out to the global community, and sometimes salty dogs with tons of real-world experience will toss you insights that will save you time.

As a matter of simple netiquette, you should first subscribe to or at least search the archives of these listservs before just dropping a bomb of a question on the group. The primary benefit of a listserv is that it puts historical technical intelligence into the realm of email research. But the Web offers the great advantage of searchable archives of years of expert discussion.

Still, posting your big question to a listserv will often yield golden answers. There are two ways to join the conversation of experienced Acrobat users. The easiest way is to browse on the Web to Blueworld and Emerge Acrobat discussions. You can also participate via email, even if you have no Web connection. The listserv will faithfully send you all of the posts and responses in either single emails or digest format. An email to the following address will elicit the simple user instructions for email participation in the ongoing conversation on the Acrobat Listserv.

Send email to acrobat@blueworld.com.

```
http://www.blueworld.com/lists/acrobat/
```

"and the evolution of the book"

"Since the fourth millennium B.C., scribes have created books from within scriptoria. Before the invention of moveable type, all books were written by hand, and any copies, likewise, were generated manually. The book itself has seen radical metamorphosis.

"The first writings that can be called books were made on clay tablets. The scribe, using a stylus, wrote in the soft clay, and errors could be easily smoothed over and corrected. After the clay dried, it was an indelible book. Waxed boards were an improvement over clay tablets with regard to ease of handling and storage. As with clay, errors in wax could be smoothed over and corrected, and in addition, the waxed boards could be reused later if necessary. Papyrus, parchment and paper were the next successive developments, which facilitated the creation of books closer to the form we know today." [1]

This fascinating site is the product of the same tradition that created illuminated manuscripts and preserved ancient knowledge through the Dark Ages and medieval times. The same thoughtful, deliberate, serene creativity is here devoted to writing on the new "books" on the Web.

Most fascinating of all is the exquisite use of the latest HTML techniques by these meditative artists. In the same way that ancient scribes defined the shape and structure of the earliest books and documents, these monks are creating a powerful model of evocative Web pages.

Bro URL welcomes you as you enter the monasteries.

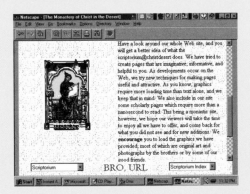

Ancient scriptorium on the Web at
The Monastery of Christ in the Desert

http://www.christdesert.org

The following URL provides a mini-manual of listserv commands is from the Acrobat Listserv at Blueworld. These commands work on most listservs.

http://www.blueworld.com/lists/acrobat/#commands

The Acrobat FAQ, or Frequently Asked Questions, file is available at:

http://www.blueworld.com/acrobat.faq.fcgi

The latest information and real-world insights on Acrobat Capture and PDF applications are available right from the user's mouth at these ongoing discussion sites. The Acrobat Capture and PDF Listservs are at:

http://www.emrg.com/ed_lists.html

Email to Capture-l@emrg.com or PDF-l@emrg.com for the Capture and PDF listservs.

Summary

In this new world of digital documents, we can view the work of multitudes of artists and craftsmen and learn through direct observation. Through a browser View Source option, we can view the HTML code of any page that catches our fancy.

Any document-creation tool that can create PostScript output can also create equally proficient PDF files for instant access.

We are at the point in time where the standard digital presentations are still being born. Not long ago, the popular formats of newspapers and magazines were developed in a synergy of technical capability and human creativity. Right now, the new pages that will be delivered on computers are being invented in the minds of thousands and millions of creative people. The key is making that information accessible through a common readable format.

This capability of a "printing press in every home" promises to yield revolutionary results in not only design, but in widespread access and distribution of information.

1 Http://www.christdesert.org/frames/scriptorium/hist2.html.

the future :

digital
documents

chapter three

I must confess it feels funny to be writing about the future of digital documents...
in a book! And not a dynabook, either.

I believe that books will outlive their original "purpose" in any case, just as we still
keep our dogs though we may not need them for hunting anymore. I think books
will be around for a long time.

But the dynabook's time is nearly upon us, and information can be better accessed
in digital format. Even in this seemingly ephemeral format of a book, if we can not
hope to view the future itself, at least we point to the places to look for the future.
Like stars on the horizon, there are reliable pointers that will last through the years.
This chapter points to those constellations most likely to continue to appear in
predictable revolutions.

The Fantastic Pace Of The Web

Ray Kurzweil is the modern-day Thomas Edison. Ray has invented machines that can
read, that can understand speech, and that have the ability to learn! The philosophies
behind his inventions of 20 years ago are applicable to digital information today in
our quest for instant access.

*"Moore's law states that computing speeds and densities double every 18 months.
In other words, every 18 months we can buy a computer that is twice as fast and
has twice as much memory for the same cost.*

*"Moore's law actually is corollary of a broader law I like to call Kurzweil's law on the
exponentially quickening pace of technology that goes back to the dawn of human
history. I mean not much happened in, say, the tenth century, technologically
speaking. In the eighteenth century, quite a bit happened. Now we have major
paradigm shifts in a few years' time.*

*"Computer memory is 150 million times more powerful for the same unit cost than
it was in 1948, the year I was born. If the automobile industry had made as much
progress in the past forty-five years, a car today would cost about a hundredth of a
cent, and would go faster than the speed of light.*

*"Moore's law is providing us the infrastructure in terms of memory, computation
and communication to embody all of our knowledge and methodologies and to
harness them on inexpensive platforms.*

"It enables us to live in a world today in which all of our knowledge, all of our creations, all of insights, all of our ideas, our cultural expressions, pictures, movies, art, sound, music, books and the secret of life itself are all being digitized, captured and understood in sequences of ones and zeroes.

"Thus around the end of this decade, a full print-to-speech reading machine will fit in your pocket.

"And Moore's law projects that our personal neural computers will match both the memory and the computational ability of the human brain - 20 million billion calculations per second - by around the year 2020.

"In the year 2040 ... In my view, Moore's law will still be going strong. Computer circuits will now be grown like crystals, with computing taking place at the molecular level.

"By the year 2040, in accordance with Moore's law, your state-of-the-art personal computer will be able to simulate a society of 10,000 human brains, each of which would be operating at a speed 10,000 times faster than a human brain.

"Or, alternatively, it could implement a single mind with 10,000 times the memory capacity of a human brain and 100 million times the speed.

"What will the implications be of this development?"

Excerpts from "The End of Handicaps," Ray Kurzweil's Keynote Address at the 1996 International Conference of the Association for Education and Rehabilitation of the Blind and Visually Impaired

Ray Kurzweil's work can be found on the Web at

http://www.kurzweiltech.com

Artificial Intelligence offers the greatest promise for automated recognition of information in unpredictable data streams. The combination of OCR and AI was coined as ICR. AI is also implicit in Intelligent Agents.

Surfing In Waves Of Information

In later chapters we discuss how to narrow down Web searches to achieve the most efficient information retrieval. We have a constant need to find better ways to navigate the ever larger ocean of information on the Web. Even in narrow fields, the Web spawns new information sources every day, and it becomes a daily, time-demanding effort to review all of the latest postings and publications.

 t i p

On the Web, geniuses and charlatans have equal access. As always, the audience and the market at large are subject to feedback. Valuable sites offer the user real content, and hype sites won't be visited twice. Intelligent agents can make the first visit and save their "masters" the time.

Before the Web search engines were toddlers, the overwhelming volume of info was recognized as a major user stumbling block. The very search engines that were taking users into this cataract of information quickly transformed themselves into brand-new vessels that could navigate the torrent.

The Web search engines were the first rafts or rowboats that allowed users to go out upon the raging waves of information on the Web and actually make some headway. When the population and density of Web sites grew explosively, the need arose to automate the search functions that people need to perform repeatedly. Intelligent agent software is designed to provide a precisely focused info-gathering robot for every user, providing searching automation to save the user time and allow people to concentrate on ideas rather than on running programs.

http://www.diglib.standord.edu/dilib/

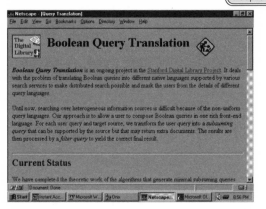

Herculean efforts are being devoted to make it easier to find information and make it less like using a computer. The goal of the Boolean Query Translation project is to create one rich language that can operate on all search engines, freeing the user from the tasks of learning many Boolean Query styles.

Intelligent Agents

The 007-ish name intelligent agent is a partial solution for the need to wade through piles of digital information. The average Web user can't and won't put in a lot of time to take advantage of the world of information on the Web. It is already increasingly difficult to keep up with the information streams pouring into the Web, and it's growing by magnitudes each year.

Intelligent agent software automates your surfing in these floods of future information, and many personal information robots are now available on the Web. Some of them can even "watch" what you retrieve and automatically retrieve "more like that." Be careful whenever this feature is available because improper use can waste rather than save time.

Never surrender categorization or gut judgment to the software; always employ common sense. Agents must be constantly tinkered with to achieve best results.

Then consider the matter of bandwidth. Those old copper wires that have been hanging from poles since the days of the telegraph still hold a lot of potential. Using currently installed copper wire, ISDN reliably delivers point-to-point communications at four times the speed of the latest conventional modems. ISDN has been available for years, and ISDN modems are relatively affordable and practical.

Through 1996, some telecomm service providers charged time-based rates. Even two cents per minute adds up when the remote work station is constantly connected, as they will be in the future, and as some are now. This ISDN service is controlled by the telco, and other than that, no network changes are necessary, except for the special modems on each end. It should be no surprise that the AT&T spin-off called Lucent makes a modem that can run data over the same wires.

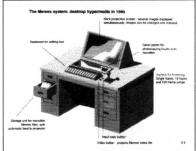

THE IDEAS ARE NOT NEW: THE MEMEX IS VISION OF WEB

Memex GIF of early illustration of imagined Info Retrieval Machine. Note the early mention "web" in Vannevar Bush's thinking.

This segment from Bush's original article presciently described the Web today:

"The human mind...by the association of thoughts, in accordance with some intricate web of trails carried by the cells of the brain... trails that are not frequently followed are prone to fade...Yet the speed of action, the intricacy of trails, the detail of mental pictures, is awe-inspiring beyond all else in nature."

Vannevar Bush, describing his fantastic Information Retrieval machine, which he dubbed the Memex in "As We May Think" in THE ATLANTIC MONTHLY, July 1945.

Service providers are being called a lot of things lately, so here's some clarification on the matter:

Telco usually refers to the phone companies, from the Bell Atlantics on down to the local providers who overcharge you at pay phones on the highway.

Telecommunications service provider is basically the same thing but refers to digital rather than voice communication, and includes everything from your local phone line to the long haul lines and backbones that make up the Internet, including Sprint, MCI, et. al.

An Internet service provider (ISP) maintains a constant link to the Internet by whatever means, from 56 KB SprintLink to leased T1, T3 lines and so on. The key is that an ISP provides a constant link to the Net, and many users can use the ISP to get to the Net.

Bill Gates, the leader of Microsoft, addressed the question of bandwidth in a very forward-looking way at Sapphire '96, the SAP User Conference in Philadelphia. Gates confidently reassured the audience that we won't run out of Internet, we can depend on it growing with demand.

"Four years ago, 80 percent of desktop applications were stand-alone, such as word processors, spreadsheets, databases and so on. Today, 80 percent of desktop applications are Microsoft Office or Professional, " Gates said.

The implications for the server software market are very clear. As Dr. Hasso Plattner, Co-Founder and Vice-Chairman of SAP pointed out in his discussion of current trends, "The majority of our applications are still running on UNIX, but NT and the AS/400 are now taking 50 percent of our new installs."

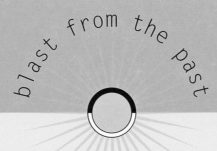

blast from the past

Before the anti-trust breakup, a nationwide network of connections seemed like a good idea. AT&T, which might be considered an artifact of early 20th century thinking that it was, really worked. Really old folks remember when there was one telephone company,
The Bell Telephone company.

Megalithic thinking has its virtues, especially viewed in light of the pragmatic triumph of the Internet.

Mr. Gates stated, "The world of personal productivity explains the popularity of PCs in business. In the past, information was just printed out, and there was no strategic use of the information. MS Office provides tools for evaluating information and doing What Ifs." All of that required more and more bandwidth.

Bill Gates predicts future innovations, stating "no time frame, but it will happen":

- Handwriting and video input

- Computers will talk, see, listen and learn

- 3D will become commonplace for collaboration

- No doubt the Internet will be the primary communications tool

You Are Not A Lonesome Pioneer

If you are going to check out only one of these global taps, try the Digital Libraries Research and Development page. Don't be shy; this page is dedicated to equal rights to information. Feel at home.

This page tracks many digital library projects, hence the "dlib" in the URL

http://www.dlib.org/reference.html

Digital Information In Perpetual Action

The best way to look toward the future is to experience it yourself, firsthand, via the Web or an Intranet or someone else's network. The following Web sites provide a fascinating glimpse of technological innovation applied to information accessibility.

The Gutenberg Project

```
http://promo.net/pg/history.html
```

"The Project Gutenberg Philosophy is to make information, books and other materials available to the general public in forms a vast majority of the computers, programs and people can easily read, use, quote and search.

"Alice in Wonderland, the Bible, Shakespeare, the Koran and many others will be with us as long as civilization ... an operating system, a program, a markup system ... will not."

Project Gutenberg Web site

The title of *www.etext.org* is Electronic Books, and this site is dedicated to a very special mission. When books go out of copyright time obligations, this group transfigures books into universal text that will live on in the digital future. To do this, they reduce everything to plain ASCII.

```
http://www.promo.net/
```

(which plays soothing background music while you are on the site)

```
http://www.etext.org/books.html
```

```
http://www.w3.org/pub/WWW/Protocols/
```

(for background on how it all started)

tip

Which three languages will be on the Rosetta stone of digital documents?

What would work at the moment? Which are the most popular and robust languages to give generations hundreds or thousands of years in the future the chance to decipher our many formats?

Right now, it's ASCII (including HTML and SGML), Microsoft RTF and Adobe PDF.

(With all due respect to the only language explicitly designed for this purpose of long-life archives, SGML is ASCII in a precise syntax.)

The Digital Library Project

"At the heart of the project is...a uniform way to access a variety of services and information sources."

From http://diglib.stanford.edu/

This arm of the Digital Library Project is linked to all of the other nationally connected branches of this future-directed initiative to move today's information onto today's and tomorrow's media. Ongoing, current information can be always found through these links. This nationally enriching research project is funded by the National Science Foundation, the source of many of the great ideas and technologies of the last 50 years.

HOW IS ALL THIS CHANGING PUBLISHING AS WE KNOW IT?

The development of extremely sophisticated electronic presses, namely today's common laser printers, allows an epochal paradigm shift. We have gone from print and distribute, to distribute and print.

Rather than fund and maintain a centralized printing facility which creates paper output, digital distribution of printable files for local paper output offers excellent cost benefits. Rather than print 10,000 manuals, give users the ability to print manuals with their own laser printers. Perhaps only 500 manuals are ever printed, because most users rely on online user guides and individually print out a few pages as needed.

When an idea such as this is embraced and espoused by everyone from Adobe to Xerox, it takes on the reliability of common sense.

NATIONAL SCIENCE FOUNDATION

The United States funds and conducts the lion's share of research and science in many fields, from aerospace to superconductors, and NSF is the government's proud masthead for these successful adventures.

http://www.dlib.org/reference.html

This site maintains clearinghouses for digital library research:

United States National Information Infrastructure Virtual Library, Library of Congress, World Wide Web Virtual Library, HyperDOC: A Service of the U.S. National Library of Medicine, and MedWeb.

For the latest research, the ACM Special Interest Group on Information Retrieval (SIGIR) maintains pointers to digital library research projects, technical papers, conference announcements and proceedings, and calendars of events.

The Electronic Journals Publishing site maintains lists of electronic journals, related projects, papers and discussion lists.

Library Of Congress

http://lcweb.loc.gov/

The National Digital Library Project is truly a noble endeavor of our government, proving that it can do some things right. This project is specifically designed to fulfill the lofty aspirations of Bucky Fuller's Education Automation Dreams. This is a very uplifting use of technology for the common good. It helps people learn by providing not only access, but also the tools to catch the fish of information. It is the idea that it's better to teach a person to fish than it is to offer a simple meal. One is transient, the other is forever nourishing.

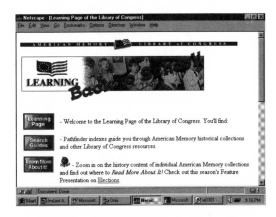

Computers are not intuitive to all of us, especially those of us born before 1980. This page leads to kindergarten through graduate school education on information retrieval on the expanding body of knowledge. To experience this first hand, visit:

http://lcweb2.loc.gov/ammem/ndlpedu/

Center For Electronic Text In Law

http://www.law.uc.edu/CETL/

At the Marx Law Library of the University of Cincinnati, an ambitious project is underway to digitize a collection of unique documents, to provide both electronic access and electronic preservation. Project Diana is named in memory of Diana Vincent-Daviss, a pioneer in these endeavors at the Yale University Law Library. Under the direction of Nick Finke, J.D., a carefully selected array of tools performs the tasks of scanning, OCR, SGML encoding and publishing on the World Wide Web.

Ignoring all of the technology for a moment, "you have to remember that we are a library," Nick emphasizes. "Our goal is to get documents to people who have a hard time getting them, and to help them find critical information in poorly indexed documents." In this effort to assist legal scholars, most of the issues of the digitization of paper information have been encountered and engaged successfully.

"We started out with the idea of preserving a precisely indexed collection of images," Nick explains, "but we came to the realization that we needed to create electronic books, not just images in a database." Working in conjunction with Don Waters and Project Open Book, it became obvious that it was critical to represent the intellectual structure of the book as well as scanned images of pages.

Anyone who has used computers for more than a couple of years has a sense for how rapidly generations of hardware and software come and go. On the other hand, documents maintain importance for years. In the case of libraries, the knowledge in books will be important forever.

"The organizing metaphor should be pages in books in a library, not pages in a folder on a desktop," states Nick Finke, in what should be a clarion call to others engaged in the task of document digitization. Producing "industry standard" .tif files is only a rough replacement for microfilm; building globally accessible libraries is another task with another set of goals. One is archival, the other is a form of re-publishing, or perhaps more accurately, re-broadcasting the data.

tip

To answer that always nagging question, "What's Legal?," this site offers an enthusiastically updated source for legal opinions, focused on intellectual property concerns. The Web and intellectual property seem to be at odds because one offers universal access and the other requires individual identity and copyright protection. The answers are hard to come by, but look here for starters.

What can I copy off the Web?

What can the Web copy off my site?

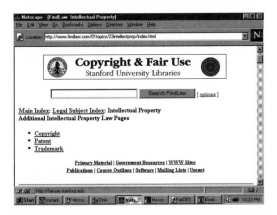

http://www.findlaw.com/01topics/23intellectprop/index.html

The law doesn't have to be a mystery when it comes to digital documents. This site offers current, continuing research and opinion on the subject of intellectual property in the new media.

The American Memory

The Library of Congress is very snazzy these days, and the American Memory Project is the embodiment of many predictions of what a World Wide Web could do. Visit the site at:

http://lcweb.loc.gov/

The Web is truly global, with supporters on all continents.

Always a good spot to check out:

"The World Wide Web (W3) Consortium exists to realize the full potential of the Web." This consortium is funded by both industry and government sources and offers updates on the latest developments in all phases of the Web."

With a gift from Ameritech, the Library of Congress is sponsoring an open competition to enable public, research and academic libraries, museums, historical societies and archival institutions (except federal institutions) to create digital collections of primary resource material for distribution on the Internet in a manner that will augment the collections of the National Digital Library Program at the Library of Congress. The National Digital Library is conceived as a distributed collection of converted library materials and digital originals to which many American institutions will contribute.

The Library of Congress' contribution to this World Wide Web-based virtual library is called American Memory and is created by the National Digital Library Program.

In the 1996-97 competition, applications were limited to collections of textual and graphic materials that illuminate the period 1850-1920 and that complement and enhance the American Memory collections already mounted in the National Digital Library.

Making Digital Documents Better Than Paper

Just as PostScript was the cornerstone of electronic publishing, enabling desktop tools to create superb creative pages, Acrobat serves this function for the documents of the future that will travel over the global Internet. Adobe PDF format offers fidelity across paper, the Web, CD and multimedia.

The Portable Document Format is much more capable of going out on its own in the broad world of unpredictable platforms than is PostScript. PostScript was a programming language that precisely defined the layout of ink on a page and had to be executed by an interpreter on the printer side.

As PDF becomes a standard page-definition language, all new printers will be able to support the rich output format (within the limits of the hardware) because no interpreter will be required on the output side.

The PDF Group is a consortium representing commercial printers who currently form a $10-billion-per-year industry. The PDF Group was formed to advise Adobe on future development of the Portable Document Format. To provide solutions for the extremely demanding requirements of this industry, which include both highest quality and highest volume output, the Acrobat family will continue to evolve.

In addition to Acrobat, Adobe Systems' other products are all evolving into both paper and digital document-creation tools. "Repurposing" is the name given to the process in which formerly print-only documents and processes advance to provide information on multiple media. PageMaker, for example, can be used to create documents intended for paper and digital form, and the digital form may be either HTML or PDF. Similar evolution is far along with Illustrator, FrameMaker and other Adobe tools.

But the real key is access. Already the Lycos and Yahoo pages reference many other full text search engines, and offer push-button access so a user can execute a query on one or more search engines.

In the commercial world of Information Retrieval, vendors such as Excalibur, Fulcrum, Open Text, Verity and many others offer the ability to execute a query on many servers and indexes simultaneously. On a Wide Area Network, a single query could interrogate all online corporate information assets. And to accommodate the user, the software blends all hits from all servers into one relevancy ranked list.

Right now, everything from handmade Java scripts to high-priced services offer the ability to run searches across multiple search engines.

The best site for managing these tools at the moment is the User. Right now the dynamic feedback and discrimination of an every day online user is superior in many ways to info robots.

To serve the user, the search engines will increasingly offer easily understood and easily reconfigurable hit lists. It is these hit lists, properly designed to convey the most important information, that will enable individuals to pick intelligent paths.

When you have become familiar with the results of searching, you get comfortable with setting up your persistent searcher, your intelligent agent.

We are on a precipice of technological development here. Artificial intelligence is not a proven commodity, not at all. We are at the point in a dramatic technology where aerospace arrived in the 1960s. In the twenty year interval between the successful employment of jets and the setting of the unbreakable speed and altitude records of the SR-71, vast advances were made. In the thirty years since, no aircraft has come close to matching that early burst of technological genius, embodied in the Mach 3 Blackbird.

We may be at a similar point in Information Retrieval, or we may not.

In any case, the vast information access now available is like the cheap air travel that arose out of all this jet testing. So we only fly 500 miles per hour from city to city now and not Mach 5, is that so bad? Compared to driving at 55 or 65 mph, air travel is in another dimension. You could never consider a one day overland trip from Philadelphia to Chicago and back. Via the airlines, it's a routine hop.

TWICE THE SPEED FOR DIAL-UP SERVICE

Lucent Technologies recently announced new chip technology that will allow PC users to access the Internet almost twice as fast as ever before. At 56 KB per second, you'll see dramatically improved use of Internet applications, especially downloading graphics, video conferencing and collaborative computing.

For more information about Lucent's technology, go to:

http://www.lucent.com/Whatsnew/whatsnew.html

Today's Web information retrieval engines offer infinitely greater convenience to learning than even jets offer over driving. You, your kids, your parents and people all over the world have access to this global library of knowledge.

Now that information has been recognized as the world's most valuable resource, we as users can expect ever better and cheaper access to information. The global spread of television is an early technological testament to human curiosity and desire for knowledge. The dawn of a library at every table will be a nurturing boost for mankind, allowing every individual to pursue their own interests and creativity.

Summary

As explained by Ray Kurzweil and Moore's Law, computers double in capability every 18 months, and this trend will continue. The computers themselves will continue to become faster, offer greater capacity and user conveniences, and either stay at the same price or drop in price.

Access to high-speed communications is likely to be as hotly contested in the future as long-distance services have been in the past. The consumer will benefit with faster connections and cheaper prices.

A few companies were poised in certain dominant positions at the start of the new media revolution, and they early on committed resources and strategic planning to the emerging trends. For example, Adobe and Microsoft have leveraged their original technology to be most effective under both current and future systems.

There are a number of projects underway on the new global information network that will track the progress of the latest developments as they are adopted by corporations, government, universities and libraries. Anyone interested in the state-of-the-art of these evolving systems and technologies can quickly update their understanding via the World Wide Web.

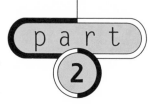

part
2

managing
digital
content

acrobat exchange:

an architecture for instant access

chapter four

Assuming that your organization or corporation has decided to provide broad online access to information in documents (or you have!), the decision moves on to what type of documents will convey the information.

Traditionally, information has been shared in ASCII appearance, as plain text in applications such as Lotus Notes, and on the Internet in Newsgroups and Listservs. With the widespread adoption of Acrobat PDF, information can now be shared online in PDF, which conveys considerably more information than plain old 80-column ASCII.

> **tip**
>
> **Design elements in written language go back to the dawn of civilization, to the elegance of hieroglyphics. Cuneiform was a simple language of lines cut into clay, of just the facts, like ASCII. Compared to the simple and limited earlier universal language of ASCII, PDF is an ineffably richer universal language.**

When documents contain almost any sort of formula, from simple math common to financial papers to complex equations found in scientific documents, PDF can provide a more accurate representation of the information than plain text can. In addition, artwork and the actual page composition are often critical to the delivery of information—all elements that can be preserved and conveyed with PDF files.

> **tip**
>
> **Foreign language documents, including European, Asian and Arabic alphabets, are often unrecognizable ASCII codes in HTML because browsers usually are not set up for anything other than simple alphabets and character sets. Any PostScript application that can use PDFWriter or Distiller can create universal PDF documents that retain their original appearance on the Web, allowing any browser to view the "exotic" document.**

Finding Aids: Author, Title, Subject, Keywords

"Meta-information" is information about information. As such, the Info fields in PDF provide a built-in card-catalog-style set of index fields to provide continuity to present information management standards and practices. Card catalogs provide information about collections of books in libraries, and most modern applications from Word to Acrobat provide these time-proven ways of handling big collections of documents, relying on a demonstrably successful method of access to information in huge collections.

One of the intrinsic features of a PDF document, whether it is a simple image or a big file, is the availability of the Info fields for tracking, managing and searching documents in large collections.

Every PDF Document Offers Four Classes Of Data

SYSTEM INFO

System-generated fields, such as Date Created and Source Application

DOC INFO

User-generated fields for Title, Author, Subject and Keywords

CONTENT INFO

Information about the content, such as File Size and Optimized status

ENHANCED NAVIGATION

Bookmarks, Links, Thumbnail Views, Articles

Because these fields are part of every Acrobat document, authors and publishers can use them to great advantage. With careful forethought, these few, simple fields can be used to provide an extensive catalog of the contents of a large digital library.

All of these fields are very large-capacity text fields, leading to the possibility of very large indexes. In a pure design sense, the main challenge would be for the publisher to decide ahead of time the top few levels of organization, and especially how to enter the data into those levels. Ideally, the terms entered should be the ones that future users will be interested in searching.

Acrobat General Info Fields:
A Foundation For Instant Access

The first four Information Fields can clearly identify the contents of a PDF file: title, subject, author, keywords.

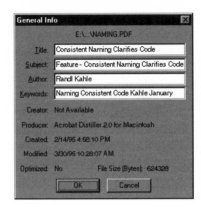

Document information fields are vital tools for quick retrieval.

Title

This is the actual title of the document, as it would appear in a paper publication. This title can be as long as the author desires, but a practical limit of about 32 characters is suggested so that users can easily see the entire title on the screen.

This is not the simple FILENAME.PDF, usually, but it can be used for that.

Subject

The Subject field should let the user browse through a simpler layer of information contained in the article than is described by the Title.

Author

In simple collections, such as small companies or single departments of companies or universities, a simple author name will be plenty. In larger collections, it is very often helpful to at least give the user the chance to sort by last name and first name to separate a particular author's contributions in the event that many authors have the same last name.

At a minimum, it is helpful that a collection follow one convention of listing authors' names. That is, whether full names or initials are used, or whether the names appear in normal or reversed order (i.e., William Shakespeare or Shakespeare, William), it is easiest for the user if the same convention is used throughout the collection.

In pure Acrobat databases, with the built-in Acrobat Exchange Text Search, the user has the ability to find information contained in a field without strict adherence to any conventions. However, a definite set of rules allows a user to enter more precise, and therefore more effective, query terms.

Keywords

Keywords should be registered as an approved and widely shared set of defined terms. An undocumented list of Keywords is the same as text searching and offers little additional finding value. By their nature, Keywords should be commonly accepted by expert users as uniquely defining some particular concept in the specific database.

Keywords can be especially useful because an expert publisher can provide additional finding aids to documents. For example, Keywords may define ideas or issues that are relevant to a particular document, even though that document does not actually include the Keyword in the text content.

A modern publisher might assign the Keyword "dynabook" to V. Bush's article "As We May Think" because that article contains historical concepts that are relevant to "dynabook." Of course, since the article was written in 1945, it does not contain this word, and therefore the article would never be found in a search for "dynabook" without the Keyword entry.

Health-ifying thousands of great recipes might be possible by adding the Keyword "carob."

All of those devil's food and wacky cakes offer plenty of good chocolate-eating fun. These original recipes for chocolate delights might be re-created with a chocolate substitute, but the original recipes would, of course, never mention "carob." By adding the Keyword, the author offers future bakers many ideas.

PDF Document Info

Then there's information related specifically to the PDF document.

Creator

The Creator field lists the program that created the document. The value of this field is that reproducible bugs will be able to be retroactively fixed, right down to the version number. It is incumbent upon authors to do their best with using the latest, legitimate version of any document creation program.

Producer

This is the actual driver or low-level document builder that wrote the file. Once again, going forward, expect that tools will come out that can automatically refine electronic document systems to make them more useful in the future.

These driver programs are destined to become history, and it will be beneficial to know their idiosyncrasies for future tweaking and translating.

Created

This is a basic file characteristic, and it enables users to quickly find the most recent files, or any file that appeared within a certain time frame.

Modified

This is another extremely basic file characteristic that allows users to make sure they are working with a very specific version of a file, whether it be the latest version or some other specific version of the file.

Additional Fields Customize Document Appearance

The five additional controls in the Document Info file allow the author to determine exactly how the document appears to the end user. The five settings areas are called Open Info, Font Info, Document Security, Base URL and Index.

These five areas are the basis for a simple digital library, and all of these settings taken together serve the purpose of a digital card catalog augmented with a number of finding aids and user convenience features. All of these fields are easily accessible to the casual user and are completely documented in the "pdfmark Reference Manual." They are widely used in managing PDF documents in third-party products such as text and RDBMS packages.

Open

This option allows the author or publisher to serve up digital documents in a designed and chosen appearance. When the user of the documents clicks on and pops open a digital document, the publisher can control the appearance of the document very directly. The document may open in Full Screen, Bookmarks or Thumbnails mode. In addition, the Page Number, Page Magnification and Page Layout can be specified.

Initial View

Page Only: This setting offers the simplest screen, and just the pages themselves are displayed.

Bookmarks and Page: This setting splits the screen and adds the navigational Finder aids of pre-defined Bookmarks. This feature allows the user to quickly browse-at-a-glance to areas of interest and click to go there.

Thumbs and Page: This setting splits the screen and adds the navigational Finder aids of pre-defined Thumbnail Views. You can quickly browse-at-a-glance to areas of interest and click to go there.

Additional Fields: Page Number, Magnification and Page Layout are additional self-explanatory fields.

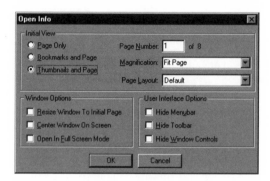

Under the Magnification Pull-down menu:

In addition to the Toolbar button choices of Fit Page, Fit Width, Fit Visible, there are multiple Zooms available at percentages of 50, 75, 100, 125, 150, 200, 400 and 800.

And, under Page Layout, the choices are Default, Single Page, Continuous or Continuous Facing Pages. The electronic publisher is faced with page composition and typesetting options, which eventually become obvious.

Windows Options

Windows options include resizing your window to fit the initial page, centering the window on screen, and full screen. Full screen takes up the user's maximum screen presentation to reproduce the original page at maximum page size settings, most closely representing the printed page in complexity and richness.

User Interface Options

User interface options include hiding the menu, hiding the toolbars, and hiding window controls and font info. Font info tells the user which fonts are included in the document, what types of fonts are being used (Type 1, True Type), their encoding scheme, and whether the entire font or a subset has been embedded in the file.

Document Security

Basic password control and access rights are built into the Acrobat Document Info structure. This level of security serves the needs of most digital library applications where access to the network itself is secure. That means that a secure library within a password-protected network will offer document security.

Document encryption and advanced security options can be added to the basic password and rights scheme of native Acrobat documents.

Index

This feature automatically opens a specific Index when a user accesses this particular document. On a Web server environment, where occasional users typically require only specific file access, this feature may be an unneeded luxury. However, on Intranet applications, the author may assume that a user of any article in the collection will probably require access to all of the articles in a certain section.

Articles:
Reading Complex Documents On A Monitor

With the Article feature in Adobe Acrobat, the author can build in the simple navigation capability that the user has with his own eyes when reading a magazine. Since a complex page is often too large to read on an average monitor, the user will typically be "zoomed in" to a magnification that presents the text in the most readable size.

The Article feature allows the user to easily follow the text of an article as it is laid out on the page. For example, the end of column one will naturally flow into column two. And the text of the article, and the information content of the article, will flow around all of the various illustrations and insertions on the page. The Article tool allows the reader to follow complex electronic text as easily as he reads the newspaper or a magazine.

Superior Navigation

Navigation is different from search and retrieval of information. When searching, the user will enter specific index criteria to identify a single file or class of files, or he will perform a text search on a collection of documents. Navigation refers to the way the user can move around within the information in an orderly fashion. Navigation is done both within a document and between related documents.

On the World Wide Web, hypertext links are the most common form of navigation, and the user must depend upon the paths built into the collection by the publisher. The Portable Document Format provides several forms of navigation that may enhance the user's access to information.

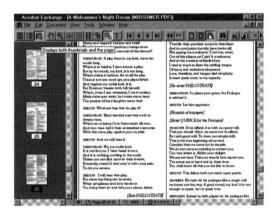

A mouse click provides quick selection of Full Screen, Thumbnails and Bookmark Views.

Thumbnail Views

Thumbnail Views are miniaturized displays of the pages within a document that are not designed to be read but instead offer a quick way to select pages for reading. Thumbnails can be automatically generated by Acrobat Exchange, and they can be viewed in a split screen beside the Page View.

Thumbnail Views are especially useful when the documents include different types of pages that are easily recognizable in the smaller pictures. For example, a technical manual often includes pages of text as well as drawings and diagrams. Rather than flip through pages one by one, Thumbnails provide an easy way to jump directly to pages of interest. Another example includes financial reports, which often include explanatory text along with charts and diagrams. Once again, the reader can quickly scroll through the Thumbnails views and jump directly to the desired information.

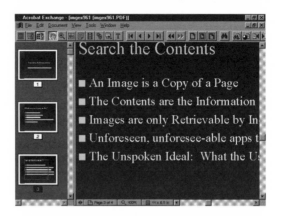

Thumbnails allow rapid navigation through recognizable snapshots of pages in a document. By clicking a Thumbnail View, the user goes directly to the fully readable Main Page.

Bookmarks

Bookmarks in PDF files are functionally similar to thumb tabs often found in large dictionaries and other reference works. In books, these are rounded notches cut into the edge of the pages, with a labeled tag at the base of each notch.

Bookmarks are provided by the publisher to allow the user to view the various topics covered within a document, and to instantly move to the desired area. These Bookmarks are selected and viewed in the same vertical window on the left of the Acrobat display.

Bookmarks can be used to indicate chapters, sections, subsections and so on, or they may be used to indicate charts or illustrations. Many electronic publishing applications, such as PageMaker and FrameMaker, can automatically generate Bookmarks from the header structure of the document.

tip

A very informative source of tips and tricks is adobe.mag, Adobe's online magazine for Web developers, online publishers and others involved in digital publishing. Its archives offer a wealth of how-to articles, and it is a great place to look before embarking upon a project. Adobe.mag is available at:

`http://www.adobemag.com`

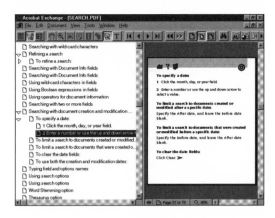

Bookmarks may be up to 20 levels deep.

Links And Web Links

Links in PDF work the same way that hypertext links work in HTML. A word or any part of a PDF document can serve as a link to any other part of the document, or to another document. With Web links, this hypertext facility connects PDF documents to any URL (Universal Resource Locator) so that the links can point out to the World Wide Web.

Web links are particularly interesting because they provide a seamless union of publishing on both CD-ROM and the World Wide Web. Assuming that the user's computer has access to the Internet, whether through a dial-up connection or through a network, a publisher can exploit the *economical publishing medium of CD* and still maintain the *timeliness of an online* offering.

A manufacturer can publish a catalog on CD, providing users with very quick access to large amounts of information. Full-color photography, lavish designs and extensive illustrations can be most economically distributed on CD, whereas browsing through the same information would be very time-consuming on all but the fastest connections to the Web. However, Web links would provide updates to the latest information and any special offers that occur from time to time.

Benefits of Delivery with PDF

The entire raison d'etre for digital documents is improved access to information. But even now, in the very early stages of the Web, the sheer volume of information is overwhelming. We already can see the need for the Intelligent Agent software that Alan Kay has been talking about for the last 20 years. Many busy people don't want to surf.

Information providers and publishers can overcome the drag of non-productive searching and link-following by structuring information in ways that are easily accessible to the users. The combined Index Fields and Text of Acrobat PDF files can be used to offer powerful and coherent organization to very large collections of information.

In most cases, the time spent in creating this organized structure will be repaid a hundredfold in the time savings of the users of the information. PDF also provides multi-platform compatibility.

There are at least a few definitions of the word "platform" in the field of computing. For example, platform may refer to the operating system, such as Mac, Windows, UNIX or DOS. Or platform may refer to the medium on which the files reside, such as Novell LAN, CD-ROM or the World Wide Web.

In the first sense, the operating system platform, Web browsers are available for all three platforms. Therefore, HTML documents written for the Web are accessible from all of these platforms and can be described as cross-platform documents. However, even though Web browsers can be directed to read files from a network or local drive, or from a CD-ROM, the practice is not common yet. On the other hand, PDF documents are widely distributed on CD and over networks, demonstrating the fact that the Acrobat format is best suited for the widest variety of platforms.

Comparing PDF And HTML Print Capability

In an announcement of Adobe PrintGear, president and co-founder Charles M. Geschke made these comments regarding the Adobe vision of the future of document printing:

> "Here at Adobe, we've been developing printing solutions for 13 years. We think we have some of the best solutions in the world for printing and imaging. We are proud to have developed some of the key technologies that have spurred changes in the market and created the market for desktop publishing.

"Looking to the future, we see a new revolution, this one driven by changes in connectivity enabled by the Internet. These changes will make the dreams of many people, of **instant access to the entire world's library of information,** *come true. (Emphasis added.)*

"At Adobe, we're creating a series of tools that will help publishers of magazines, newspapers and other sources of information make billions of pages of information simply and easily available to you over the Internet. We know that these changes will dramatically change what role your printer plays in your day-to-day life. Expect to see a series of innovations from Adobe that anticipates these changes in printing so when you buy a printer with Adobe technology, you can have confidence it's been designed to print not just the things you print today, but those you'll print in the future as well.

"PostScript is the standard printing technology for producing high-quality output. However, PostScript is both a language for describing the printed page, as well as an interpreter that resides in the output device. Moreover, there are many different flavors of PostScript based on the many applications that produce PostScript output.

"In contrast, PDF files are highly structured, and general programming constructs are not permitted. As a result, the imaging operations are usually much simpler. Each page of a PDF document is independent of the others. The apparent arbitrariness of PostScript is eliminated, so PDF provides the foundation for a print production system that can deliver consistent, predictable results."[1]

Because Adobe Acrobat software has been built on the foundation of PostScript, the PDF file format currently offers far greater promise for printing than does HTML. HTML was developed to present information on-screen, with an emphasis on individual users having the capability to control the final appearance of the pages. If printing and controlling the quality of the output is a concern, PDF is currently far superior to HTML. And because PDF comes from the same company that created PostScript, continued emphasis on high-quality output will remain a priority.

Precision: Retrieve ONLY Relevant Documents

The late Dr. Gerard Salton, formerly of Cornell University, is widely regarded as the father of Information Retrieval (IR). Dr. Salton crystallized thinking in the field when he defined the two critical measures of IR as precision and recall. The first measure, precision, refers to the ability to retrieve only results that match the query term. The second, recall, refers to the complementary ability to retrieve all results in the collection that match the query.

For more information on Dr. Salton, and his unique pioneering SMART program, try this link. Also use the root URL to get to the Cornell University Computer Science Department.

In traditional database structures, where unique pieces of information are stored in strictly defined fields, precision of retrieval is very high. Of course, applying Dr. Salton's text-retrieval measures to an indexed database is a misuse of his methodology but is informative in this context because Exchange combines traditional Index Fields with FTR.

http://www.cs.cornell.edu/Info/Department/Annual95/Salton.html

http://www.cs.cornell.edu

Dr. Salton explored the less tightly defined collections of information such as text databases and in this sense did not expect to find data in the orderly structure of a Relational Database Management System. Acrobat Search combines structured and unstructured Information Retrieval methods.

Therefore, Acrobat Search has an advantage over pure text retrieval because the query can be focused upon specific subsets of documents and would therefore be naturally more precise than text searching alone, which the criteria of precision and recall were designed to measure. The PDF Author, Title, Subject and Keyword fields can be used singly or together to identify either a single, unique document or a unique class of documents, such as all documents by a particular Author. In addition, the Date Created and Date Modified fields provide precise time sampling of the collection.

Recall: Retrieve All Relevant Documents

The difficulty in retrieving all relevant documents in a collection arises from the inability of the publisher and user to think in identical ways for classification and organization. Once again, the combination of Index and Full Text information in Acrobat Exchange provides a wide and fine net for finding relevant documents in large collections.

Annotations And Extra Links

As the name implies, Acrobat Exchange is designed for groups of users to share files on a network. The Annotations feature allows many individuals make comments on the PDF file and share the comments with the group. Because the notes are stored in a separate layer of the PDF, the original remains untouched for viewing and printing.

Annotations are represented by icons that resemble 3M's ubiquitous Post-it™ Notes, and they provide the same functionality. They convey a message that can be attached and easily detached from the original document. In Exchange, individual users can customize the appearance of their notes in such areas as color, label and fonts in the note. In a workgroup, the contribution of each individual is instantly recognizable.

The contents of all the notes of one or many PDF documents can be summarized in a separate document.

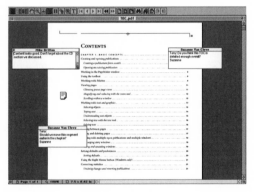

Notes can be up to 4x6 inches in size and can contain up to 5,000 Roman characters.

From Here to Multimedia—
The Create Link Tool

The Create Link screen gives the author the ability to design the appearance and action of links in PDF documents. With Acrobat 3, PDF caught up and maybe surpassed the action functions in documents available in HTML.

Each has its own place and time, of course, but the essential nature of HTML is linking, and the essential nature of PDF is presentation. PDF has made a lot more progress in HTML's field than HTML has made in the realm of PDF. No disrespect intended to the brilliant HTML designers or to the emerging capabilities of HTML that are being rapidly expanded by many vendors. Nothing promotes rapid technical advance faster than cutthroat competition on the open market, and with Microsoft and Netscape setting the pace, things happen fast.

One of the major evolutionary changes to PDF in Acrobat 3 is the new family of actions available to the author. The new Acrobat 3 capabilities in many ways mirror developments introduced in HTML 2.0 and HTML 3.0, including forms and multimedia.

Things Readers Can Do Through PDF Links

Go To View	Execute Menu Item
Import From Data	Movie
Open File	Read Article
Reset Form	Show/Hide Field
Sound	Submit Form
World Wide Web Link	

Acrobat 3 introduced a new tool under the Tools-Create Link menu, called Sound, that allows the author to add an .WAV or .AIFF sound file to a PDF document. The procedure is very simple and menu-driven, and the Sound file becomes part of the PDF file. Any sound-capable computer will allow the user to hear the voices, music or other contents of the sound file. The author can specify the action that will play the sound, such as Mouse Click in a field, or even Mouse Enter or Mouse Exit the field.

We earlier estimated a single-spaced page of text to comprise 2,000 bytes in file size, and a scanned and Group IV compressed .tif image of the same page to comprise 50,000 bytes. At normal speaking speeds, a sound file of the same page being read aloud in AIFF or WAV format may easily exceed 1 MB (1,048,576 bytes) in size.

Another innovation of Acrobat 3 was the bundling of the Apple QuickTime viewer, which had already become popular on many fronts, including such best-selling CDs as *Myst* from Broderbund. Using the same mouse techniques described above for adding sound, an author can attach video files to PDF documents. However, unlike sound files, video is always stored separately from the PDF.

QuickTime and other video files are very large. For example, the Weezer "Happy Days" video, included on the Windows 95 CD under FunStuff, has a running time of about 4 minutes and consumes about 30 MB of file storage. This poses no problem for CD publishers, but every Web and network publisher has to take a long, hard look at transmission speed and load to move a file that large.

Sacrifices

For the average user, entering the data into the Document Information Fields is like shining your shoes. Yes, they look a lot better and you're glad you did it when you're out in public. But in private, it's a nagging chore. Professional publishers add this value without fail.

Considering the benefits to be enjoyed by future users, such shoe shining should be an absolute duty. Many documents created in word processing and other office automation packages may already contain this information, and it can be automatically entered by PDFWriter or Distiller. Even when the information resides outside the format, third-party products are available to automatically populate these fields from a separate file.

Recipients Need Acrobat Reader To Use PDF

It's hard to predict how the chore will be handled in the future, but for now the users must download new versions of the Reader software as it is introduced. To the happy beneficiaries of free software, such as users of Netscape Navigator, Acrobat Reader, et al, it is a simple chore to surf to the proper URL and download the latest stuff. To the broad market, all of these technical details are unacceptable impediments to enjoyment of the online world. Therefore, to accommodate this much larger market, we can expect future software to be self-downloading, at minimum inconvenience to the user.

The basis for this functionality is already in place with the Registry function of Windows 95. When a user contacts a Web server, the server will query the user's PC to determine if all of the necessary software components are present. If something is missing, the servers of the future will automatically update the user's PC with the necessary software.

The Dreaded 'Learning Curve'

I often wondered why the best prospects for new technology always seemed to buy the stuff only after it had already been on the market for a few years. For example, major law firms were some of the last to switch to Windows. It was only after many, many years of learning that I realized they were hesitant precisely because they had already invested in earlier generations of office automation.

Not only did the stuff still work, they often had tens or hundreds of people who were skilled in the technology. The real cost of technological change has little to do with the cost of hardware and software. The cost of change is in training and learning, the cost in people time to transition to a new technology. Imagine if we had to totally relearn how to drive our cars on totally redesigned highways every five years. Delays would be expected.

The larger the network or number of users, the more difficult and expensive it becomes to move to a new way of doing things. A second level of chaos is introduced if the changes are partially phased in over a large network because different versions of files inevitably clash in all but the most meticulously designed transitions.

The great advantage today is that the leading software environments are designed to be cross-platform. Windows designs to be cross-platform by being the only platform, Mac finally designs to be cross-platform, UNIX is widely revered.

The two leading universal document formats, HTML and PDF, are being handled by millions of users on the Web. Both formats are designed to blend into the woodwork, and both run smoothly and familiarly on Windows and Mac PCs. Because these document types have been designed from the ground up to run on all popular platforms, it is likely that the learning curve will be drastically reduced. People will be familiar with the technology, and in society's eyes Instant Access will be more like programming your VCR than programming a computer. A little complicated, but anybody can do it.

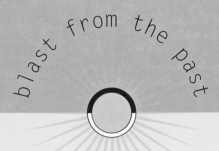

Present And Future Readers

Anybody who has been using computers for more than 10 years has old files lying around. They might be Wordstar documents on 8-inch floppy disks that were written on CP/M computers, or they might be 5.25-inch floppy disks with Xywrite files written on an old DOS PC. All of these digital files have something in common with earlier generations of files that were stored on 9-track tape in IBM's old EBCIDIC language; what they have in common is that both the media and the file formats are virtually inaccessible now.

Like PostScript, PDF developed a rapidly building undertow of support. Its adoption as a standard comparable to PostScript is already a foregone conclusion. Modern technology in the form of telecommunications has given us the ability to rapidly move and preserve our files, virtually freeing us from the dead end of hardware changes. And PDF offers a stable, standard format that will generate the self-propagating support necessary for long life.

What to Index for the Future

At Biological Sciences Information Services, they have been publishing both citations and abstract information on the life sciences since 1926. In their case, the Keywords assigned to certain articles may not even appear in the articles, but the Ph.D.s who will search this information will be pursuing certain concepts or trends, and the Keywords will bring certain articles to their attention. At Biosis, Ph.D.s actually do the Keyword coding!

The emphasis must be on serving future users. If lawyers are going to be handling this collection, use legal conventions. If biologists are going to be using it, organize the info the way the scientists will use it.

In other words, use only those data fields that are most helpful, but be sure to exploit these fields to the fullest extent.

See Process Map on page 100 for a step-by-step guide.

Decisions To Make

Let's not reinvent the wheel when it comes to designing digital documents because paper documents have a half-millennium of traditions and lessons learned. But we must not fail to give our future readers every possible advantage of the new document. It is at this nexus, where paper information becomes digital, that we have the historic and singular opportunity to offer our users a new way of reading, researching and learning.

Perhaps in the future, a society at home in a digital world will think more along the lines of Bucky Fuller than Aristotle. Bucky often said that he could not afford to remember anything he could look up in a reference book. He wanted to reserve as much of his considerable mental processing capability for creative and synergistic thinking, and he zealously strove to focus his mentality on the most productive processes.

Perhaps the just-in-time philosophy of total quality management will be applied to knowledge and learning in the future, as it is now applied to manufacturing where parts and material only show up when they are required by the production process.

In this scenario, people in the near future will come to trust and rely upon the availability of information, and they will free their minds to concentrate upon the creative tasks at which human thinking excels, and which no computer to date can accomplish. The computers do their jobs, we do ours.

In looking forward to such a world, it is the duty and burden of every publisher of digital information to offer up products that lend themselves to these new and as yet still experimental approaches to using data and knowledge.

Sometimes the rate of change outruns the sensibility of change. The examples are myriad. In the auto industry, when automatic transmissions became available, many people became convinced that manual transmissions had been rendered obsolete by automatics. In the '60s and '70s, manual transmissions became a special option on American cars. Of course, manual transmissions are a lot more fun to drive and give you a lot more control of the car. When the imports arrived in the '70s and '80s, manual transmissions reassumed their rightful share of the market.

This allegory concludes with the observation that the forms and conventions of digital documents are in a state of vibrant flux right now, and sometimes valid traditional forms are ignored for trendy but unproductive presentations. Every digital publisher and digital librarian should see the new media not only in the light of what it can do that paper cannot. Every new media presentation should also be judged on what it doesn't offer that a book containing the same information does.

As an example of the rate of change of new media, consider the 3-D visualization software called the Virtual Reality Modeling Language (VRML). The prototype VR browser appeared in a sort of game called Labyrinth, which was produced by Mark Pesce and Tony Parisi. Labyrinth came out in February 1994, and by October of that year VRML 1.0 was recognized at the Second International Web Conference.

Silicon Graphics stepped up and took responsibility for VRML 1.0 as a standard, published programming environment and released its VRML development environment called WebSpace in April 1995. The recently introduced Cosmo from SGI takes VRML thinking and capability to new dimensions and new forms of object interactivity.

The lesson learned in the example of VRML is that it went from dream to reality in less than two years! Technology cycles are intensifying and shortening in quantum leaps. In this mystifyingly rapid evolutionary cycle of new Web technologies, we must try to put documents into the most stable formats. The documents themselves must be ocean-going canoes with outriggers with oars and sails that can ride through oncoming waves of technology changes.

How Much Is This Info Worth To Convert?

Books are sitting on shelves, chockful of meticulously organized and presented information. I'd like to think digitizing all of the books on library and university library shelves, all the rare books in the world, all of mankind's accumulated visions of truth...but I know that business and legal documents will be the first afforded this royal treatment.

There are several digital library projects currently active on the Web, and the trend is in place for future global libraries, as originally envisioned by Vannevar Bush and Bucky Fuller and Alan Kay and the rest. But this technology will first be embraced by

Because the idea of a universal document seems so natural to most people, the technical details are usually overlooked. Because of the way computers were presented to us as a society, we assume computers can do all jobs better than all previous means. This is a thought bubble that pops almost as soon as you begin to really try to use a computer on the Internet.

In the old days, there was only one standard: ASCII. The standard 128 characters of basic ASCII were almost universally shared by all the BUNCH. In the early days of big computing, there was IBM and the BUNCH, comprised of Burroughs, Univac, NCR, ControlData and Honeywell. The BUNCH shared the language of ASCII for files, while IBM used an expanded language called EBCIDIC for files, which has since receded into history. ASCII, that limited set of characters derived from typewriters and telegraph machines, has prospered. HTML is ASCII.

commercial publishers and businesses that have a real stake in the information and can see the value of instant access in their profit & loss statements.

Every potential user will look at a bookshelf full of information and ask himself the simple question: How much can I afford to spend to make all that knowledge available on my Web?

Sometimes gross measures help to put the new media in perspective. A brochure or white paper published on the Web is instantly accessible, and the end user can choose to incur the cost in toner to print the document for his own use. For the user who really needs the information, the cost of paper and toner at a couple of cents per page is certainly worth it. The primary advantage is that only qualified prospective clients get the marketing materials.

Not only are printing costs virtually eliminated, but the intellectual density of the piece can be increased because of the very focused audience that will read it.

The Process

Any author or publisher can easily migrate to the new world of universal format publishing, and the most important consideration is carrying forward all possible benefits of the present processes. Most often the only step that needs to be changed is the output option. Everything upstream of output is secondary, unless the publisher can take advantage of one or more advances in digital publication to add navigation or index value to the published information.

In an ideal world, every author has filled in all of the document information fields in the source applications, and field data can be translated directly into the PDF Info fields or perhaps into HTML Meta tag fields. The primary directive is to capture as much information as possible from the original document.

Meta Tags: Definable fields in HTTP headers that can add traditional index fields in document collections. Organizations that have defined specific Meta tags include those that serve math, physics and computer science disciplines. These Meta tagged documents are the HTML equivalent of other indexing schemes, with virtually unlimited variations on Author, Title, Subject, Keyword, Accession Number, Citation and all of the other traditional fields.

Of course, to be useful, these fields should be openly published and accepted in the target user community. Carrying on the conventions of paper journals makes sense.

If the original document lacks this information, it is still important to enter as much data as possible before committing the PDF document to a widely published collection. Of course, the value of this added information vs. cost of acquisition should always be considered. The only hard and fast rule is what will best serve users in the future.

There are software products available that can apply a set of data fields to a set of documents, whether they be PDF or HTML.

For batch scanning purposes, a data entry sheet could be devised that would include the Author, Title, Subject and Keywords fields. The sheet would be either typed or handwritten, and either a person or an OCR program would capture the data.

This sheet would either be retyped by a data entry operator or converted by OCR into the Author, Title, Subject and Keywords fields. The result of these processes would be an ASCII file that could then be read into the fields in the Acrobat PDF files by a third-party product from Ambia, Inc. or some other developer.

process: secondary publishing

Journals and other source documents come to BIOSIS;

↓

Specialists review journals and select articles;

↓

Modify document info fields, or use as they appear;

↓

Adobe Capture and enter selected info into database;

↓

Publish in access-enhanced online collection.

Summary

The key to building any new collection of documents is to accommodate the needs of our future users. What is the nature of this information? Most important, how will people be led to just what they are looking for?

How can you lead the users to information when the they don't know what they are looking for? The publisher must take the traditional lead and proceed as if he knows what the future user needs.

The work put into a digital document should not exceed its practical worth. If a set of documents will never be accessed by more than a single field of data, two fields of data are an indefensible luxury.

What does it cost to make all of the information instantly accessible?

All of these concerns can only be answered for each specific application. General recommendations are guidelines, common sense questions that might avoid silly mistakes.

1. PDF for Production Printing, Adobe White Paper, March 1996.

footnotes

acrobat
catalog:

creating
the keys
to instant
access

chapter five

Transforming Vast Collections Into Retrievable Information

Acrobat Catalog is the indexing process that converts a large collection of electronic files into a coherent and searchable database of documents. The process itself is simple: point the Catalog application at a directory or a set of subdirectories of PDF files, and the software does the rest.

The end result is an index of the entire collection that can be accessed by the Search program. The index and the files can reside on a network or Web server. Or the entire collection, along with a licensed copy of the search engine and Acrobat Reader, can be published on CD-ROM.

Acrobat Catalog and Search employ Verity text-search technology to index and retrieve information in PDF collections. This means that a single desktop user of Acrobat 3 can create very large libraries of files that can be searched with all of the information-retrieval capability of the Verity search engine. And this single user can publish collections on networks, CD-ROM and the Web. Compared to typical HTML hyperlinked collections, large indexed databases offer more stable long-term performance because there are no links to be broken. As long as the index is not changed, large collections will be reliably accessible through both index and full text-search and retrieval.

These simple Include and Exclude Directories boxes allow many directories and subdirectories to be Catalog-ed into one searchable .PDX index.

The indexes created by Catalog offer a full set of features for searching the document collection. On the Web, most document collections are organized into somewhat hierarchical arrangements, and the publisher provides links among the documents for ease of surfing the information. For example, the Adobe Home Page at http://www.adobe.com provides a number of paths from the top page.

This very simple screen has powerful effects on future searching of this collection. For example, if none of the Word Options was checked, future users would not have access to these search enhancements. Another testament to total user control of the database index is the "Words to not include" menu, which allows the publisher to declare certain terms to be of no value for searching.

The home page of a Web site is the first page that is presented to a user. In most cases, this top page contains links to many other sub-pages, which comprise the bulk of the contents of the site.

Acrobat Catalog adheres to common file structures.

The limitation to this approach is that there is only one way to find things, which is the fixed set of links designed by the Webmaster who manages the site. For this reason, most large commercial Web sites include a content search facility, often available through a button on the top page. The content search engines are free for the asking on the Web. Adobe started using the Excite! engine in early 1996. The limitation of such content-based search tools is that inexperienced users often have trouble writing a productive query that retrieves all relevant documents and only relevant documents.

By combining the limiting effect of Document Info and Date fields with full text retrieval, Search provides a simple interface for creating well-focused queries. Verity began shipping its free SearchPDF Engine in mid-1996, which is specifically designed to handle Catalog-indexed collections of PDF documents on the Web.

Document Management 101

Many people lose track of the files on their own PCs as time goes by, and this tendency increases by a couple of orders of magnitude when many users share the same files on a network. Every user has felt the frustration of looking back over old directories and mentally kicking himself for not remembering what the file was called or where it was saved. Most modern applications, from Microsoft Word to Adobe Acrobat, offer users the ability to add Meta-information to their files. Thus, we hope in the future that many paths of inquiry will lead to lost documents rather than confound the user with the silent opacity of forgotten or too-often-used file names.

The key to feasibility of this scheme is that someone makes sure to take advantage of the built-in structure by filling these value added fields with intelligently organized information.

The PDF structure offers many of the core elements of document management information. Documents are specifically identified through these multiple fields, and future users of these collections will be able to assemble very specific subsets of the collection for a unique purpose or audience.

T Elementary version control, one of the key functions of traditional document-management systems, is available in the Date Fields that show when the document was Created and Last Modified.

Combined with the Security feature, a basic document-management system is built into the Portable Document Format. Two primary functions of document-management systems are available: Access to the document is limited to password-group individuals, and version control is determined by the Date Fields.

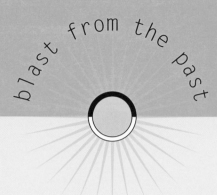

Document-management software grew up around network word processing. Some of the heaviest word processing users are law firms, where one of the primary products consists of words on paper, in the form of legal documents. As most of us know all too well, legal documents tend to be long and complex and evolve through many versions during their lifetimes. In a law firm, the factory where these intricate devices are fabricated, many individuals are involved in the process, and many subcomponents are assembled in the final product.

When typing moved to word processing, the individual operators still had physical control of the documents and components, if only on floppy disk. When word processing moved to the file-sharing environment of a network, a critical requirement arose to control all of the versions of the documents and subcomponents. An entire niche industry grew up known as document management, and the early leaders included SoftSolutions, PC Docs and Saros. These document-management systems brought traditional controls to the potentially chaotic world of electronic files.

On a global contract, many offices will work with the same set of documents. It becomes vitally important to control each document in the physical sense, restricting access of certain users to reading, copying, editing and so on. More fundamentally, it is crucial to maintain the integrity of the final document and all of the sources and versions that contribute to the ultimate document.

Acrobat Catalog in action, charging through a collection of directories.

Full Text Retrieval For Total Access

Full Text Retrieval (FTR) technology corresponds to a sort of Popular Mechanics view of using computerized information. Once the stuff is in the computer, most users assume they should be able to just enter their question and get their answer. It's hard to argue with that premise because we all wish that everything would be as simple to use as Star Trek led us to believe. "Spock, give me all the information we have about life forms on this planet," Captain Kirk would command. In seconds, Spock would come back with all the relevant data.

High expectations, fueled by sci-fi, are almost realized through the FTR engines, especially on the Web. A seeker of truth can really learn a lot by pursuing certain ideas through several queries because the varying results of each query can be incorporated dynamically into a more precise query. However, while the results are spectacular, they are never achieved with the ease of Spock because most users are still limited by a lack of knowledge of all of the power of the available tools. But it won't be self-limited for long thanks to the user-friendliness that is increasingly engineered into the Web search engines, as well as the "intuitive" techniques woven into the desktop operating systems. Some day soon, a commonly accepted query language will be adopted as a standard, and information retrieval will be as simple as math and algebra.

The harder you work, the luckier you get.

Index searching and FTR, the two polar extremities of document searching, are perfectly complementary. Full text searches tend to return too much content that is irrelevant, whereas index searches tend to miss relevant material because the user is not familiar with the index structure. Referring to Dr. Salton's criteria for measuring retrieval effectiveness, precision and recall, Acrobat Exchange offers the potential for great performance by giving users tools to directly adjust both parameters.

FTR = Full Text Retrieval, refers to a user's ability to search the contents of the documents rather than just the index.

Precision = Retrieve only those documents relevant to the query.

Recall = Retrieve all those documents relevant to query.

Acrobat Catalog creates an elegant, multifaceted document database that can be served up on the Web. With Verity's freely distributed SearchPDF server software, a breakthrough in rich, searchable collections is expanding quietly on the Web.

At a time when most Web sites offer either preconceived hyperlinks or some loose search capability, Web sites with large collections of PDF documents and SearchPDF offer a very organized, stable structure. Acrobat PDF and Verity combine to form a very strong alloy of technology.

Full Powered Boolean Search, Without the Hassle

Boolean search is popularly depicted as uncool, as a first-generation approach. New engines promise concept searching and natural language interfaces to very large collections of information. They encourage a "just type in whatever might relate to what you are looking for" approach.

The fact of the matter is that today's concept engines do a great job at expanding the query, which means they tend to retrieve a ton of documents. This is often counter-productive because the user now must plow through tons of "hits" to find information of real value.

Anyone who has tried to use FTR search engines productively will admit Boolean queries make a lot of sense. The drawback, or sacrifice, is that the user must make the effort to learn a little simple arithmetic to begin to appreciate the full power.

Concept search engines are simply automating basic Boolean search operations. The concept search engines rewrite the user's query by expanding the original terms. Obviously, semantic and statistical concept search theory represent some of the leading developments in this field, but most business applications will be very well served by the simple yet powerful Boolean search capability available in the Search feature.

	For Greater Precision **Refine The Search**		For Greater Recall **Expand The Search**
①	**AND**	A AND B AND C	**OR** A OR B OR C
②	**PHRASE**	"A B C" (in that order)	**Wildcard**
③	**NEAR**	A NEAR B NEAR C	**Word Stemming**
④	**NOT**	A, B, C NOT D	**Thesaurus**
⑤	**FIELDS**	(Title **Contains** Acrobat)	
⑥	**Combine Terms**	A AND (B OR C)	
⑦	**Review Results**	Refine Terms for New Search	

Field/Full Text Search Combined

The limit of success for searching a specific field index database is the user's knowledge of the field structure and contents. If the user does not know the specific appearance of the query target info, in terms of exact spelling and particular field location, it is impossible to reliably find information in a traditional field specific database.

At the same time, a full text retrieval search will often be far clumsier than an index search. It is difficult for the user to guess at the proper terms as they might appear in the text, and query expansion techniques often return large numbers of irrelevant documents. The time spent wading through large hit lists is counterproductive in the information-seeking process. The combination of using document information fields and text search in a query is the most productive way to use this knowledge-expansion technology.

(t i p)

The answer to the question of how to index a document data-base is always: "As many ways as possible. I have no idea how future users might use this collection!" But still, this question must be asked: Do you want to sacrifice labor and overhead to add more accessibility to your collection?

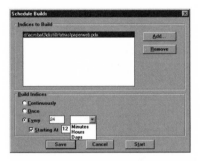

"Builds" or new indexes can be created according to the users' needs. A Build re-indexes all of the PDF files in a targeted set of directories and can be scheduled to be performed at all intervals from just Once to Continu-ously, with Minute, Hour and Day frequency definitions available.

For ease of operation, it is helpful to have all of the related files in one directory
to get the most out of Catalog and Search.

Optimizing Build Options

Because index size directly affects performance speed, and because this issue is by far the most important issue for the end user, it is vital to understand the Build options. There are two options that remove words and numbers from the index. And there are three options that provide query expansion through wildcards, word stemming and thesaurus; and two that refine a query through case match and proximity.

All of the Build options affect index size and, therefore, performance speed, and the end user's needs should determine which options to employ. Features that are un-likely to be used, or unlikely to provide useful help, should be discarded.

Full-featured information-retrieval systems are resource-intensive, and adequate hard-ware and bandwidth are required for optimum functionality and user approval. This is not the type of application to be dropped willy-nilly on an already-busy network server.

Individual Builds, or index-creation processes, can be designed to include and exclude an array of directories and network drives. Builds can be scheduled to occur Once, Continuously (careful!), or on a time schedule to accommodate resource availability.

To assure best performance, a Purge should be performed on an index before each new Build. This can be accomplished by simply deleting the nine subdirectories, or subfolders, under the index directory or folder.

For ease of purging, and also for moving and backing up to other media, it's best to keep the index and nine subs together: assists, morgue, parts, pdd, style, temp, topicidx, trans and work.

The Process

The process for creating and maintaining the Catalog will vary depending on the scope of your digital document collection. Again, preparation is critical for creating an ongoing dynamic collection that makes information readily available.

> **tip**
>
> **Encourage the use of the Author, Title, Subject, Keyword and Date Fields because they make the contents of big collections much more accessible. If you're searching a set of articles or memos, you want to be able to narrow the search down to the smallest subset you can define. If, for example, you want all the memos authored by Bucky Fuller that concern the keywords tensegrity principles and spaceframes, written between 5/47 and 5/74, this type of re-fined search will be much more rewarding and will illustrate the real speed and power of instant access to information.**

(1) Determine user requirements and areas of improved access to information:

Publish an author's guide to proper and accepted use of Doc Info Fields;

Options that affect Index Size, Speed and Search Features:

List of Excluded Terms

Include or Exclude Numbers

Case Sensitive

Sounds Like

Word Stemming

(2) Carefully estimate required resources for Catalog and Search:

(Do Not Scrimp HERE!)

Processor resources should be generously allotted to this intensive task;

Disk space for documents PLUS 50-80% overhead for index.

(3) Create a new index in Catalog:

Create Index Title and Description;

Choose Directories, or Map Network Drives,

where PDF collections are stored;

Schedule the Build (Index Creation Process) for Once, Continuously

or Timed;

Choose Options based on User Requirements for Exclude Terms and

Numbers, Case Sensitive, Sounds Like, Word Stemming.

(4) Document Index features and options in effect to help future users be most efficient.

Summary

The two prime approaches to information retrieval, which are fielded index and full text searching, are available with Acrobat Catalog.

Index retrieval through the Document Info fields provides specific access to individual files through traditional document-management methods.

Text Search offers the ability to query the entire contents of the files, in addition to the Document Info fields.

Combined index and text queries offer the synergy of both techniques, as long as the end users are familiar with the data likely to be found in the Document Info fields.

To take fullest advantages of these capabilities, all authors should add Document Info to offer another means of navigation, potentially as helpful as Bookmarks and Thumbnails.

Document database architects and publishers (such as yourself) should always provide simple guides suitable for first-time users that tell them what they can expect to find in the Document Info fields and text of the collection. A few simple hints can point the best way to success in each particular index and text-retrieval collection.

decisions in

ndexing

chapter six

Having a pile of digital documents isn't any better than having paper if you can't instantly retrieve the information you want. To achieve instantly accessible information, you'll need to carefully consider your indexing plan to accommodate the needs of both current and future users. With tools like Acrobat Catalog, you can establish consistent and effective indexing criteria.

How Will Future Users Access the Collection?

Future users will experience your document collection in many ways, and it is important to consider all of their goals when creating indexes with Acrobat Catalog. Though it is tempting to check off every option and take advantage of every possible feature, overall user satisfaction has to be considered. Just because your car can go 120 miles per hour doesn't make it a good idea to take advantage of that capability in every situation. By the same token, not every capability of Acrobat Catalog should be used "pedal to the metal."

> **tip**
>
> **While UNIX, Mac and Windows 95 all support "long file names," the large number of users and computers out there still make this old convention a serious consideration.**
>
> **Remember, to handle any files with this currently dominant convention, all long file names are truncated. When "My Documents" is reduced to "mydocu~1," information retrieval capabilities may be severely degraded. Therefore, it is still a good idea to use conventions like FILENAME.EXT file names.**

All of the word search options come at the price of overhead in the index, which affects everything from overall index and collection size to the response speed of the search engine. Although users may not care about the former, the latter is a paramount concern.

If future users will rarely or never use certain options, you should not burden your collection with them. If the Case Sensitive, Stemming or Sounds Like options aren't worth their weight, they should be ignored.

Effects Of Options On Index Size

Index Size compared to Text Collection	*10-30%*
Remove up to 500 Stopwords	*10-15% Reduction in Index Size*
Remove Numbers	*10-20% Reduction in Index Size*
Remove Word Stemming	*10-20% Reduction in Index Size*
Remove Case Sensitive	*05-10% Reduction in Index Size*
Remove Sounds Like	*05-10% Reduction in Index Size*

Stopwords

Stopwords are words that are not indexed, and therefore not searchable, in a text database. The reasoning for stopwords is that they convey little value for the burden they place upon the database. Typical stopwords include articles like "the," "a," "an," as well as prepositions such as "to," "in," "from" and other common words. By removing them, not only is the text index smaller, but the number of irrelevant retrievals is often reduced.

However, if your users will be searching for "From Here To Eternity," they would get hits only on "Eternity." Or if they were searching for "On The Road," they would find every document with the word "Road."

On the other hand, if your database includes terms that are simply too common to provide any search value, the Stopwords function allows database customization.

Meta-information such as Index Title and Description is entered here, and all of the Index Options are available as pulldown menus. The Build button creates the Index.

Numbers

In the modern world of brand names and revision levels, it might be difficult to choose not to index numerics. For example, it wouldn't be possible to search for "Windows 95" or even "July 4."

There may be certain disciplines where numbers will never be used in queries. For example, searching for taxonomic classifications may never require numbers. And if there is an alpha-only primary field or key in this index, searching numbers may be superfluous.

Options

Case Sensitive, Stemming and Sounds Like Search options require a certain amount of overhead in the index. This overhead affects both the speed of searching and the size of the overall indexed collections. If future users are not going to enjoy significant, outstanding benefits from these enhancements, they should not be larded on to the system. For details on these search features, see Chapter 13.

Dynamic Or Static Collection - How to Manage Updates

In the ideal system, every new document is instantly incorporated into the index. The Continuously option provides for this luxury. A folder can be constantly watched or be in perpetual processing, with Catalog grabbing every PDF file that shows up and adding it to the Searchable Index.

It is yet another one of those "common sense" feelings about computers: They should naturally have this ability. At this point, the software can do it, and the hardware is rising to the challenge, doubling in speed every 18 months while staying at the same price.

However, as collections grow in size, even the fastest computers run a little slower. It will always be a tradeoff between user response and timeliness of database updates. In the fields of finance and war, timeliness is everything. In more conventional fields, other measures may apply.

Updating Once would be used by publishers who wish to distribute pre-organized, enhanced collections.

Using the Every menu option is the conventional way of doing database updates, popular on every platform from the earliest mainframes to every type of online host platform. Usually, these scheduled builds interfere the least with users because they are scheduled for off hours.

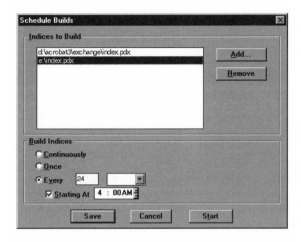

For these choices, consider the effects on server loading compared to the value of updates to the users. Information currency vs. access speed is a question that arises at the busiest sites.

Naming Conventions

Standards are a godsend, allowing developers to concentrate on meaningful issues rather than try to invent new publishing media. Now that virtually every PC ships with a high-speed CD-ROM drive, this media has achieved universal acceptance. It's cheap, it's easy, and it works on every platform.

ISO 9660 is in large part responsible for the fabulous blossoming of this new media. By providing one stable standard format for all CD-ROM, the cheap real estate of that 650 MB universal media on a sturdy plastic disk became the de facto standard of physical distribution.

**Scan 70,000 Pages
Per Week
At 99.985+ Accuracy**

An Interview With Dave Abbott Of Reed Technology Information Services

The Government Services RTIS has held the data-entry contract for the Government Patent Office since 1969. This demanding contract specifies extremely high accuracy and a rigid production schedule. ICC has consistently exceeded the specifications by always seeking out and using the most effective techniques and technologies.

Since joining International Computaprint Corporation (now RTIS) 15 years ago, Dave Abbott has been a driving force in developing world-class data-capture systems. "We are always aiming to increase productivity so we can increase the workload," he declares. By employing the most effective systems, "Resources can be allocated to intelligence and information development."

A review of Dave's production methods over the last 15 years provides a unique history of the scanning and OCR industry. The contract involves data entry of legal, approved patent applications into the GPO's typesetting system. "We still use a term called 'brown bag patents' to refer to very long patents," Dave explains, "going back to the days when all the patents were keypunched onto paper tapes. The tapes for a 1,000-page patent would have been moved around in a shopping bag."

From those early days of paper tape, ICC moved on to key-to-tape and key-to-disk operations in the early '70s. However, the first breakthrough in data-entry productivity came in 1983 with the adoption of Dest OCR scanners.

Dave smiles with satisfaction at a technology investment that paid for itself 100 times over. The Dest 246, perhaps the most successful OCR scanner of all time, accurately read a limited number of popular typestyles at a rate of 15 seconds per page. Having recently retired the Dests due to lack of maintainability, Dave estimates, "Our cost on those scanners was down to the hundredths of a cent per page."

Though the Dest was limited to about a dozen typestyles, 75 percent of patent applications were typed in those styles. As Project Director for the patents contract, Dave developed a custom interface to the error-correction and composition systems. "We expect our typists to produce eight pages, or about 10,000 keystrokes, per hour," he says.

For scannable patents, the Dest 246 could potentially outperform a data-entry operator by 30 to one. And the scanner's accuracy was equal, often superior, to data entry. That bench of Dest 246's ranks as one of OCR's greatest implementations ever.

In the last year, Dave has raised the standard again. "With the new system," he says, "our scannable documents have increased from 75 percent to 95 percent of our work, up to 70,000 pages per week." In effect, ICC has increased the number of documents processed by more than 20 percent while decreasing the time to scan them by a factor of three.

Dave scans the documents at 400 dots per inch rather than the more common standard of 300. "It only adds 20-25 percent to the file size,". he tells us. "And I have never heard of accuracy *decreasing* by going from 300 to 400 dpi."

"OCR accuracy is around 98 percent," states Dave, "or 2,000 errors per 100,000 characters. Our contract calls for 15 errors per 100K, and we do better than that." Though spell checkers are a common means of document correction, Dave is "cautious about using dictionaries. Humans have a better overall frame of reference, so we only use dictionaries with human review."

"We have found self-directed work teams to be a tremendous source of innovation," Dave explains. "We have scheduled training courses in Object-Oriented training for both our operations and programming staffs because learning is the foundation for innovation. We want to provide our people with intellectual tools as well as hardware and software tools." Dave's devotion to understanding and using technology is obvious as he says, "We are constantly streamlining our processes through these tools. They are all enablers."

David K. Abbott is Vice President for Reed Technology and Information Systems in Horsham, Pa.

The Process

The actual process of indexing your collection is straightforward if you've already assessed your user needs.

steps

1. **Gather PDF Files For Your Collection** ⇒ *Keep Relative Paths*

2. **Finalize Document Information And Navigation Requirements** ⇒ *Bookmarks, Hyperlinks, Thumbnail Views*

3. **Help Users To Grasp The Collection** ⇒ *Document Site With Maps, Search Options, Descriptions*

4. **Use Catalog To Build The Index** ⇒ *Use Fast Machines For Servers Set Preferences For Peak Performance Optimize For CD-ROM Purge For Efficiency*

5. **Serve Your Index On A LAN, Web Server Or CD**

Gather PDF Files For Your Collection

The best way to build an Acrobat Catalog collection is to put all of the files into one folder, with all related files in subfolders. This conventional directory tree structure provides both efficient file access performance and convenient portability.

Acrobat Catalog directs its indexing function at pre-defined file structures that are specified in the index definition process. The subsequent index and the nine support directories should ideally be stored in the same folder with all related files in the collection.

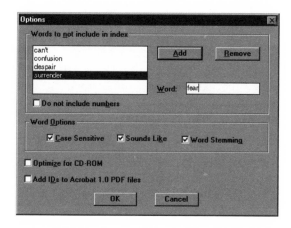

Sphinx-like simplicity of interface offers extensive database tailoring choices.

The beauty of keeping all of the documents and organization files in one folder structure is that the entire collection is easily portable. This means that the hyperlinks within a Catalog-indexed collection will maintain their full functionality when they are moved to new media, whether that be a CD, a new disk array or a Web server.

Finalize Doc Info And Navigation Enhancements

Like everything else, the work you do is equal to the value you create when it comes to building a Catalog Index. To be truly better than paper, our new documents must take advantage of all of the built-in potential for advanced functionality.

At a bare minimum, the Title, Author, Subject and Keyword fields should be filled in to provide future utility to any and all potential users. The System fields of Date Created and Modified and so on will be automatically indexed.

All bookmarks and hyperlinks should be finalized before the Catalog process, although they can be added later. The value of one agreed-upon version of a document collection can not be overstated, and multiple versions of an index inevitably lead to confusion.

Help Users Grasp The Collection

In addition to employing effective design rules in building your collection, you can help the user by explaining the rules you have followed. These rules include the type of information in each of the document info fields. Specific usage should be described, and any custom fields must be explained.

For example, the doc info fields could be used for legal documents

Author	*Lead Attorney*
Subject	*Client Matter #*
Title	*Client Name*
Keywords	*Related Parties*

Any use of Catalog options should be explained, to help users understand the search techniques that will work in this collection. If stopwords are used, it would be helpful to include a list to avoid wasted queries. Certainly, if numbers are not included in the index, the users should be warned.

Following the example of many advanced Web sites, the folder structure might add to user convenience with a description of the contents available for top-level browsing. This approach gives the user a bird's-eye view of the entire collection before he begins to search and retrieve.

tip

Always design collections to emphasize user convenience. All the information in the world is useless if no one gets to it.

Building the Index

Never make the mistake of choosing your information retrieval server as the place to save money just because it is actually just a big computer sitting in a room gathering dust and generating heat. Large text database collections should be hosted in environments with lots of free random access memory (RAM) and fastest possible bus connections to large-capacity storage.

The Acrobat Catalog User Guide suggests having at least 10 times the amount of RAM as the file size of the largest document that will be indexed. For example, 24 MB RAM is recommended to index a document of 2.4 million words.

Compared to the earlier examples in this book of 333 words per single-spaced page, 2.4 million words could be estimated at a nominal 7,200 pages. Since most of the new PCs come with 32 MB of RAM, a 9,600-page document should fit into memory comfortably on a midrange PC for speedy Catalog indexing.

Nominal pages as defined in this book are 2,000 characters per page, or 333 words per page, equivalent to solid, single-spaced typing. This is a relatively dense document format, somewhat less dense than books but much more dense than most common business and legal documents.

The moral of this story is that the capacities are at once incredible and still realistically limited. The Intel P7, the PowerPC and the Ultra Sparc, fast memory buses and cheap RAM may minimize all of these concerns in the immediate future. Performance is, of course, enhanced in high-powered operating system environments. Still, economic design choices never change. If no one will ever use the frills, don't waste the space.

Set Preferences For Peak Performance

Even for those of you who never touch .ini files, let alone consider editing them, please do consider it just this once. The Acrobat.ini file contains the parameters that precisely control the Catalog indexing functions, and they can be tweaked with just a little effort. The .ini file is ASCII, so it can be easily edited in Notepad or DOS Edit.

These simple adjustments are explained for Windows and Mac users in the Catalog 3.0 Online Guide. They allow the publisher to best serve the users, whether it be a dynamically updated database or a tightly streamlined index for CD-ROM distribution. It's worth learning because it serves the primary goal: making the information easily accessible to the user.

Optimize For CD-ROM

This option organizes the files so that the index information is optimally accessible, providing for the quickest possible searches. This option is only one step in creating a collection that is optimized for CD-ROM.

The 650 MB capacity of a blank CD seems gigantic, but multimedia such as sound, and especially video, will consume large chunks of storage. The rich graphical content of new documents also creates big files, and the search and navigational capabilities add their required space. Plan ahead!

According to the Catalog Online Guide, the "GroupSizeForCDROM=4000." In English, this suggests that 4,000 documents is the maximum number that will be reliably indexed under the Optimize for CD option.

If you are writing large numbers of short documents, you should consider using automated bookmarks and links to provide alternative navigation and retrieval methods.

Purge For Efficiency

The Acrobat Catalog indexing process is incremental, so if a collection is being re-indexed as new documents are added, the file space consumed by active and inactive indexes grows continuously. To improve response time and to provide additional disk space for new information, it is important to Purge the indexes as often as necessary to always arrive at the most efficient system.

"A faster way to purge an index is simply to delete the nine subfolders of the index folder: assists, morgue, parts, pdd, style, temp, topicidx, trans and work."

Such a "purge" could be accomplished with the DOS "DEL-TREE" command from the Index Directory on down.

Courtesy of the Acrobat Catalog Online Guide

Serve Your Index

The Catalog-indexed collections can be served on most media. The mix of Acrobat products available includes

LAN *Multiple User licenses of Acrobat 3*

Web *SearchPDF on Server, Acrobat Plug-in on Browser*

CD *SearchCD and all Acrobat Readers on disk*

Managing Folders And Drives

Keep your file hierarchy consistent when using indexes, otherwise your system won't be able to find the original files to retrieve. The whole idea is that you can just pick up the top folder and move the whole collection elsewhere (even to other drives), keeping the relationship of the contents intact. The idea of subdivided but cohesive files is actually just like the hanging Pendaflex folders full of manila file folders full of paper-clipped documents that we all know and use.

Summary

The key to accommodating the needs of our future users is providing a speedy and productive means of retrieval. The nature of this information should determine the way it is indexed.

- Is pure speed of retrieval likely to be more important, or should utmost flexibility be built in for future researchers?

- Is this collection designed for ongoing, dedicated users who will learn all of the available functions, or is this information meant to be available on a hit-or-miss basis to casual users?

- Is file space or bandwidth a consideration, such as on a network or a Web site? How many CPU clicks can be devoted to option-enhanced text searches?

The best answer is generally not the "kid in the candy shop" response. The publisher must consider the way the information is currently accessed, and how that access can be improved in terms of response time and information retrieval options.

searching
digital
content

acrobat
search

chapter seven

Acrobat Search employs Verity, Inc.'s text-searching technology, as do many other popular products. It is very important to consider the real-world presence and staying power in the fluid timescape of software development. By pursuing the very effective strategy of getting onto the most desktops, Verity is following in the footsteps of Microsoft, Netscape and even Adobe, which decided to offer the Acrobat Reader free over the Internet. The advantage of building a base of millions of users proves the efficacy of giving software away free. Verity technology is embedded in Adobe Acrobat, Lotus Notes, the Netscape software family and other extremely pervasive products. The real benefit to the digital author and librarian is that these products achieve a life of their own because millions of users depend upon them.

"With SEARCH'97, content providers and corporations will have a powerful and ubiquitous search platform," says Phillippe Courtot, chairman and CEO of Verity. "Content providers will be able to make their information personalized and searchable and deliver it to the enterprise. Corporations will be able to link their multiple sources of information and create their 'corporate memory' and make it easily accessible by their employees as well as customers."[1]

Why Use Search?

The vital key to Courtot's statement is Verity's unswerving focus on becoming "ubiquitous," and commitments from leading industry players ensure that Verity will remain a safe standard for building your organization's search engine.

The Verity capability built into Acrobat 3.0 and the Verity SearchPDF Web search engine are designed specifically for information retrieval on PDF collections. Additional modules add more features, such as Verity's Search '97 Agent Server Toolkit, to search collections of many other types of files, including HTML and common office applications such as word processing, spreadsheets and email. Also, topics, or pre-defined searches, can be stored and executed on demand. There are even third-party products that offer entire sets of topics that can be selected from menus, putting extremely sophisticated search capability within the reach of the average or occasional user. The Search '97 Agent Server Toolkit can be configured to "watch" and retrieve specific information from many sources, including Web servers, databases, newswires and netnews.

All of the above growth and flexibility options offer plenty of development paths for the future. However, there are other full text retrieval engines that can also search PDF, HTML and many other forms of information, so the PDF author and publisher is not limited to Verity. Other text-search engines that currently support PDF include Open Text, Excalibur, Personal Library Systems and Fulcrum.
(See Chapter 13 for details.)

For more information on search engines, see the following Web sites

```
http://www.opentext.com
http://www.excalib.com
http://www.pls.com
http://www.fultext.com
http://www.verity.com
```

Basic Text Searching Via Exchange

The Portable Document Format is an "encapsulated" document format that contains significant amounts of information about the file, as well as the contents of the file. The fields described in Chapter 4 can combine with text search to take advantage of these built-in features of PDF files.

Adobe Acrobat Exchange is a database for collections of PDF files that provides the capability to extensively search the collection using a combination of techniques. On the most elementary level, documents can be retrieved via specific fields. Alternatively, the contents of the document themselves can be queried via text-search techniques. These two techniques can be combined to perform very sophisticated queries. For example, to retrieve all files by certain authors published during a specific time period, you would combine Author and Date Created fields. Within this defined subset of documents, the user can search for specific words, terms or phrases within the contents of the text.

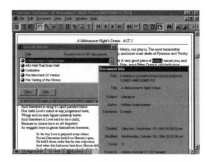

On the left, a compound search of the Shakespeare Collection on Acrobat CD.
On the right, the multi-level organization of the Catalog database: the Source Doc, the Source doc Info, and Rank.

Adobe Acrobat Catalog is required to build the index for these collections of PDF documents. Acrobat Exchange is then used to query and retrieve the documents on a network or Intranet, and *Acrobat Search for CD* can be used to query and retrieve collections that are published on CD-ROM. A combination of these packages can be used to publish collections on both CD-ROM, to take advantage of the large storage available on CD, and on a net, to take advantage of frequent updates.

Web links in PDF files allow information on CD-ROM to be linked to complementary files on the Web or on an Intranet. For example, a tech manual published and distributed on CD could be used on an individual workstation. By clicking on a Web link in the CD text, the user would be linked via his browser and communications connection to the Web or Intranet.

For example, this book contains many references to products that are current as of this writing but that will undoubtedly be updated as time passes. By making Web links of all of the references to products and companies, the information would stay current by always connecting to the dynamically updated information on the Web.

In general terms, any text search follows four basic stages:

First, the query terms are entered and joined as necessary.

Second, the query terms can be expanded or restricted.

Third, the search is run and the results list is presented to the user.

Fourth, the user can then view the documents containing hits, or refine the search based on the results list.

As we will see below, and in Chapter 13 on Advanced Text Search, these simple steps can be greatly automated and enhanced by the text-searching software. It is important for users of digital libraries to become proficient in searching because of the tremendous access such skill provides to the information within digital collections.

The user has an option to display the document with other info in the search screen.

The Exchange search screen illustrates the steps between simple and advanced text searching. The three Action buttons on the right side, including Search, Clear and Indexes, are the primary controls for issuing a query. Search executes the query based on all of the information entered on this page. Clear empties out all of the query fields for a new query, which is very important because variables left over from previous searches will often cause the incorrect data to be retrieved. The Indexes button allows the user to choose between several databases upon which the search will be performed. Many separate indexes can be searched simultaneously, and the responses will be delivered in one ranked list of hits or results.

The user may review Index Information to determine the likely relevance of a particular document. The following information is available for each Acrobat Exchange Index:

Title	Name in the Index Selection dialog box
Description	Publisher or author description of the index
Path	Full path location and name of .pdx index file
Last Built	Date of last update when new and changed documents were added
Created	Index creation date
Documents	Number of PDF documents in the collection

In a digital library where there may be a great number of subcollections, each with its own index, this feature is very helpful for the users. There are many reasons for the creation of a number of separate indexes, including operational efficiency, disparate and unrelated collections, and multiple sources of collected documents.

Upon selecting one or more indexes, the user can conduct a search by creating a query. In the first field the user can Find Results Containing Text by entering the actual words or terms of interest.

Even when searching for a simple word, this is a different function in a text database from that in a word processing file. The Find feature in a word processor will only find the one, single word or term that is entered in the particular document that is open. In a text database, such as that created by Acrobat Catalog and used in Acrobat Exchange, the query will search an index of all the documents in the collection. Usually, the results will be reported back as a list of documents ranked by occurrences of the query within the documents.

Building More Extensive Search Queries

A query begins with a single word or phrase, and a simple query will retrieve a set of documents containing that word or phrase. This method works perfectly well as long as the single word or phrase is relatively unique in the database. If the word or phrase is relatively common in the database, or if it is likely to appear in irrelevant documents, the query will retrieve too many documents to be useful.

For example, if you were searching for information on the famous aircraft designer Kelly Johnson, you might enter the term "Kelly" or "Johnson." In any moderately sized collection, this query would retrieve any document with the individual words occurring

within them. However, in a big collection, you'd probably get a results list that is too long to comfortably peruse—a major disadvantage of searching for a single word.

To improve upon this example, you could search for the phrase "Kelly Johnson" in quotes instead of the individual words. Now the results list will contain every occurrence of the entire phrase, but will miss "Clarence Johnson," which is his given name. It will also miss "K. Johnson" and "Johnson, Kelly" because they do not match the phrase in quotes.

Boolean logic is the method used in text searching to combine multiple query terms. The three primary Boolean Operators are And, Or, Not.

To improve the results of a text search, the user is encouraged to use more than a single word or phrase to describe information of interest. Boolean logic allows the user to build a query that contains many terms used in combination. It should be noted that many text databases reduce the size of the index and speed the search and retrieval by removing the "stopwords." Such stopwords include common articles and prepositions, such as "of," "the," "by," "for" and so on. Because the removal of such stopwords may limit the user's ability to search for specific phrases, this feature is optional. In creating some text databases, including Acrobat Catalog, the author has the option to decide to include some or all of the words in the index.

Below are a few search examples:

Query	Finds documents that contain
1. price **And** discount	Both "price" and "discount"
2. price **Or** discount	Either "price" or "discount"
3. price **And Not** discount	"Price" but not "discount"
4. (total profit) **And** "revenue" or "income"	The phrase "total profit" and either (revenue or income)
5. "profit and loss"	The phrase "profit and loss"

Examples 1-3 above demonstrate the self-evident functions of the Boolean operators. Example 4 introduces another convention derived from mathematics, namely the use of parentheses as a symbol of grouping. In a text search, as in math, the entire contents within the parentheses are considered one result. In this the case, the parentheses define a term (total profit) made up of two words, and a combined OR term (revenue OR income).

In the fifth example above, quotes are used to define a phrase that overrides the Boolean And operator and simply treats the word "and" as a query term. This means that both parentheses and quotes can be used to form phrases, but the double quotes are required when the phrase includes search operators, like Or in this example.

Another way that Boolean text-search logic corresponds to mathematical formulae is that queries can be comprised of a great number of related elements. And these numerous elements can be grouped or "nested" to virtually any depth within layers of parentheses.

By default, the Boolean And operator is evaluated before the Or operator. The Not operator is evaluated before either of the other two operators. This is logical because And more precisely defines the search than Or; and Not still more precisely defines the search because it specifically excludes certain matches.

Parentheses can be used to change the default order of evaluation of the Boolean operators and can dramatically change the results of a query. For example:

The query "(darwin or origin) and species" would find all documents that contain either "darwin" and "species," or those that contain "origin" and "species."

The query "darwin or origin and species" would return all documents that contain "darwin" or "origin and species." You could get documents that contain "darwin" but do not contain "origin" or "species."

The potential length of such complex queries is suggested by the size of the box under the prompt Find Results Containing Text in the Acrobat Exchange search windows. In the hands of a skilled user, precise queries can be built that will search vast databases and return only highly relevant information. This is increasingly true in direct relation to the user's knowledge of the contents of the database.

Expanding Your Search Terms For Better Results

Straightforward Boolean searching as described above depends upon the user knowing the specific appearance of the term as it occurs in the database or databases. Remember, Boolean searching was designed for simple logic systems where the only values are 0 and 1.

This means that the spelling in the query must exactly match the spelling in the occurrence. The query term "search" will not find "searching" or "research." To overcome this severe limitation, many methods have been developed to make text searching more flexible. As we will see, Term Expansion includes a wide range of techniques that cover not only alternate spellings of query terms, but even various meanings of the terms.

tip

Acrobat Exchange ignores punctuation in query terms and searches because many relevant hits would be obscured by punctuation. For example, if punctuation were not ignored, the query "Johnson" would not find the word at the end of a sentence because it would appear as "Johnson."

Wild Cards

Wild cards are symbols that can represent any character or any string of characters within a query statement. This same feature is available even in simple operating-system-level functions. For example, a simple DIRectory command in DOS can contain wild cards. The command "dir *.doc" will return a list of every file in a directory that has the ".doc" extension because the asterisk stands for any string of characters.

There are two types of wild cards available in Acrobat Exchange, and they are single-character wild cards and string wild cards, symbolized by "?" and "*" respectively.

Below are a few wild card examples from the Exchange Help file:

Wild card	Matches
geo*	words such as geode, geodesic, Geoffrey, geography, geometry, George and geothermal
*nym	words such as antonym, homonym and synonym
?ight	words such as fight, light, might, right and sight
555-????	all seven-digit numbers with the 555 prefix
pr?m*	words like premature, premeditate, prim, primate, promise and promontory

In the first two examples above, the two sides of the problem are covered. In some advanced text-search descriptions, these two functions are referred to as left-hand and right-hand truncations. In the English language, these functions are very helpful in handling prefixes and suffixes. For example, the query "*fill*" will retrieve all terms using the root of "fill" including such words as "refill" and "filling."

A more precise version of this right and left truncation is accomplished by the single-character wild card, "?," which substitutes only one character in the search string. This can be very helpful in applications where the user is searching part numbers or file names that are predictable in length if not in content.

Word Stemming

Word stemming offers a way of expanding query terms in the most relevant directions. Rather than randomly replacing each character as if it were a simple 0 or 1 in a logic argument, word stemming uses actual language resources to determine the core word in a query term. Word stemming is the default option from Exchange Search dialog box.

Using word stemming, query terms are stripped down to their linguistic antecedents, such as their Latin or Greek root words. For example, when the word stemming option is applied to "build," such words as "building" and "rebuild" will be found.

Sounds Like

Sounds Like is another expansion option in the Exchange search, and it is similar to the Soundex method of most spell-checking programs. As the user types in a word, character by character, the Sounds Like expander displays a list of words that are somewhere near the query term in the alphabetical listing in the database. This

method of expansion should be very carefully used because of its gross level of association. Much more than the above methods, Sounds Like can add an inordinate
number of irrelevant terms to the query.

On the other hand, the Sounds Like option can give the user an instant preview of the
terms as they appear in the database that is being searched. When used this way, as a
preview of good search terms, Sounds Like can be extremely helpful. The benefit to
the user is twofold. First, the search terms can be restricted to only those terms that
appear in the database. Second, and more important, the Soundex may suggest
forms or alternative spelling of terms that had not occurred to the user.

Getting Help From Computer Intelligence

In the previous section we considered a number of techniques for expanding the individual terms entered by the user. Further help is available from computer intelligence, which comes to the aid of the user by suggesting additional query terms.

Where a term expansion varies the spelling and extensions of a *particular string* entered by the user, a query expansion varies the meanings and emphasis of the entire
idea of interest.

Thesaurus

The Thesaurus expands the search to find words that bear some semantic resem-
blance to the search terms you enter in the Find box. For example, searching for
"begin" finds "start," as well as "attack," "produce" and many other terms.

Of all the query expansion techniques, Thesaurus has the greatest potential to expand
the search to irrelevant topics. To help the user manage this tendency, Acrobat Exchange offers the Word Assistant to allow a preview of the expanded terms before
they are included in the search.

Individual Observation And Creativity

By individual observation, the user will notice certain words and features of the most
interesting documents returned on the hit list. On the Web, for instance, you'll find
that certain sites seem likely to contain the most interesting content through your
prior experience. The labor required to gain the advantage of such perfected searches
means that the user must read or review the documents returned by the hit list.

Advanced Text Search includes the ability of the software to "read" documents and
"understand" them based on the concurrent appearance of certain words or phrases.
For details on the most advanced technique described, Search by Browsing, see Chapter 13.

An individual user can quickly inspect the articles as they appear in the Relevancy Rank listing. A first pass through the search reveals the first results list, so the user can read only the articles of greatest interest and then choose terms from the most interesting of the articles to build a new search. This feature is discussed later under "Refine Search."

Variables to Restrict Queries

Proximity

The Proximity option instructs the search engine to find occurrences of two or more query terms that are appear close together in the document. In Acrobat Exchange, the terms must appear within a few pages of one another for the Proximity option to take effect. Without the proximity option, two query terms related by the And operator may appear anywhere within a document. The reasoning behind this option is the common sense logic that says if the words appear close together, the passage in which they appear is more likely to be of interest.

The effect of the Proximity option is demonstrated in relevancy ranking of the documents. Not only are documents with the highest number of hits found, but also most closely occurring hits, or clusters of hits, are ranked higher. And the greater the proximity of the hits, the higher the ranking.

Match Case

Match Case allows the user to specify such items as proper names, initials and other case-sensitive terms. For example, using the Match Case option to search for the chemical symbol for helium, "He," would not find the male pronoun "he."

The Match Case option allows the user to restrict the search to only those items most likely to be of interest, and to minimize the number of irrelevant hits. Match Case does not work with Word Stemming, Thesaurus or Sounds Like options because they are all term expansions.

Word Assistant

The Word Assistant offers the users controls to refine the expansion options. The user is presented with a dialog box where a query word may be entered and the effect of Sounds Like, Word Stemming and Thesaurus may be previewed. All the words that will be found when a certain option is used are listed. From this list the user can selectively cut and paste suggested terms to the search box.

Without this Word Assistant, the Sounds Like and Thesaurus would often expand the query term to the point where many irrelevant hits would be returned. This option allows the user to enjoy the full benefits of expanded search without the downside of imprecise queries.

The user can select only the best terms in thesaurus list.

Narrowing Your Search Using Document Information Fields

All of the text-search capabilities described above can be directed to act upon a specific subgroup of documents by using field values to restrict the search. Through the combination of Text Search and Field Values Search, the user can take advantage of simultaneous unstructured and structured searching. Most important, the user is given finer control over the entire process of searching for information within a digital library.

For example, if we were searching a library for post-war American writers, we could specify "Vonnegut or Kerouac or Pynchon" in the Author field. By concentrating on this subset of authors, we could get an alternative view of World War II compared to a wider search that would include history and newspaper stories and so on.

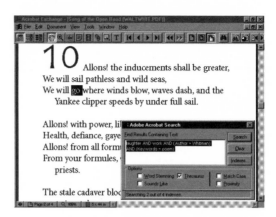

Boolean expressions can be used within the document info fields to select certain groups of documents. This means that all of the inclusive and exclusive terms described above can be applied to the following.

The **Document Info fields** displayed above are separated into different types of info:

The standard **Document Info fields** are **Title**, **Subject**, **Author** and **Keywords**.

The **Date Info fields** are **Created** and **Modified**.

The **File Info fields** are **Path** (to hit document) and **Found In** (Index Title).

The **Score field** is the numerical ranking assigned by Relevancy Ranking.

---

t i p

Document Info field searches will retrieve documents with or without terms in the Text Query field. In this sense, the Document Info serves as an advanced card catalog, or a free-standing Citation Index.

Authors and publishers of PDF files are not required to enter the information in the Standard Document Info fields, and these fields may be empty. The information in these fields is automatically captured from other applications that use such fields, such as word processing files.

Since these fields can affect the relevancy rank listings, it is usually desirable to enter the information into these fields. Acrobat Exchange allows editing of these fields for manual updates. In Chapter 9, Advanced Navigation, techniques are discussed for automatically filling in these fields for batches of PDF files.

Single-Field Search

If the user does not enter any words or terms into the Text Search field, and uses only the Document Info field, any and all documents that contain the value entered will be retrieved. For example, using just the Keyword field, a user could find every document that the publisher has determined to be relevant to the topic of Search.

ActiveX: ActiveX is the branding name for Microsoft OLE (Object Linking and Embedding) Controls. These controls allow programmers to use embedded functions within Microsoft environments to perform specific functions. This means that Web applications can take advantage of all of the programs in the Microsoft Office and Professional suites that are on 80 percent of all desktops. This is part of Bill Gates' strategy to offer the Microsoft Explorer as the universal interface to digital documents, whether they reside on your hard drive, LAN or the Internet. (It should be noted that Microsoft also licenses Java, which is similar in intent of small, fast program applets that work on all platforms.)

The best place to learn about ActiveX is http://www.microsoft.com, which is an extremely busy site. At this time, the "ActiveX, Activate the Internet" page can be found at

http://140.116.72.228/xxjyh/ActiveX/Overview.html

The effectiveness is determined by the nature of the material within the collection. For example, a very large collection of documents related to engineering and manufacturing documents could be managed with just the Document Info fields.

In this case, the documents themselves tend to be specifically identified by Work Order, Part Number, Purchase Request and similar information. By agreeing to a convention to entering specific information into the Title, Subject, Author and Keyword fields, documents could be retrieved by any one piece of information in any one field.

Multiple-Field Search

Continuing the previous example, engineering documents are often changed through many versions, and the Date Info fields could be used to track the latest and all historic versions of a document in which the only field that changes is the Modified Date.

In this case, if the user knows one of the Key fields, he can retrieve all of the versions of the file or a specific version of the file. By adding a Creation or Modification date, the user performs a simple two-field search to retrieve a specific document.

All of the Document Info fields can be used to perform combined searches. In collections where much of the field info is repetitive, such as a collection where a single author has a large number of documents, very selective retrievals may be made done on subsets of the documents.

Wild Cards In Fields

The wild card characters function in the same way within fields as they do in full text searches. Both the single-character wild card "?" and the single-to-multiple character wild card "*" are available. Therefore, the query string "Sm?th*" will return occurrences of Smith, Smyth and Smythe.

For example, if Part Number or Purchase Order or other such data is stored in a field, the user could perform wild card searches to retrieve information even when he has only partial data to start with.

A page called "World Wide Web Robots, Wanderers and Spiders" by Martijn Koster offers a WWW Robot FAQ and a list of known robots

Bot: This slang form of "robot" refers to almost any program that performs tasks similar to those done by a human. In other words, a bot is a program that runs on its own, performing tasks that involve decisions and discrimination, and does it in an unattended mode. The big search engines use such bots to update their Web indexes automatically. The Eliza program is often considered the first bot because it acted like a human.

http://info.webcrawler.com/mak/projects/robots/robots.html

Beyond Document Info Fields: Expert Searching

In any field of study where there are frequent updates or regular series of articles, these simple fields can be limiting. Of course, with the wealth of data available here, anything is possible! But in less stringent applications, where the end user is not expected to be an expert in query writing, the document info needs to be expanded.

Chapter 14 describes full-featured Relational Database Management Systems to organize document collections. In this case, documents can be cross-referenced ad infinitum, and a powerful body of meta-information about a digital library is available to expert users.

Expert users of information include many academic and commercial professionals who follow extremely dynamic fields of development. Due to very high volume of information in these fields, it is a necessity, not a luxury, to provide improved finding aids and access controls.

A citation database serves as an example. The same author may write on the same topic in many different journals, with different emphases appropriate to each journal.

You might want to find all examples where John Dvorak (author) has discussed "interactivity" (query term) in Boardwatch magazine (keyword), but you may not be interested in the same author's comments on the same subject in other publications, or in articles published before a certain date. In a customized database, all of these elements can be tracked and valued separately, and the digital library user can choose a very specific set of documents to view.

Java: The Java™ Programming Language Platform from Sun Microsystems can be thought of as the HTML of programming. Just as HTML documents are designed to run on many hardware and software platforms, the Java language is designed to allow developers to write an application with the same freedom from constraints.

An excellent starting place to learn about Java is "The Java Language Environment" White Paper by James Gosling and Henry McGilton at

http://java.sun.com/doc/language_environment

Even further, a citation applet could be written in Java or ActiveX. This bookworm-bot would allow the raw results of a database or text search to be returned to the user for further investigation. Along with the results, a customized applet would pop up to allow instant sorting, reviewing and reporting on all of the fielded information. The user could then retrieve this carefully selected subset.

In this way, the remote user of a database can intelligently examine the contents of the library. Precise retrieval of information is the goal of this theoretical applet.

> **tip**
>
> **Whenever you attempt to access a specific URL, such as those listed above, and find that the page no longer exists, it often helps to simply back up to the base of the URL and try again. For example, while the White Paper at Sun in the last example may change and get updated over time, it is likely that "http://java.sun.com/" will always offer relevant information on the same topics.**

Range Searches: Creation And Modification Date Fields

The system-generated fields of Creation and Modification dates provide the user with an elementary version control capability. In addition to the ability to include these Date fields in the arguments described earlier, the user may directly access these fields through the Search screen.

Because the user can search for both before and after, as well as exactly equal to or exactly not equal to, the user can easily specify a range of files by date.

Sometime last year I read a neat set of criteria for determining true portability, as envisioned in the dynabook idea. The author used something like "The Three B's: Bed, Bathroom and Beach" to identify the obvious advantages of books over current portable computers. The problem is, I can't remember the author, title or any other information about the book. And a text search for "The three B's: Bed, Bathroom and Beach" is nonproductive because it's not an exact phrase and the terms themselves are uselessly common.

However, these common terms applied to a short date range may be more productive. Since I remember when it was published, I can focus my search by date and have a better chance or finding the document.

Relevancy Ranking In Results List

A document's relevancy ranking presents an orderly list that starts with the documents most likely to be of interest. Acrobat Exchange uses five icons to indicate relevance, which range from a full circle to an empty circle, with 3/4, 1/2 and 1/4 as the three middle gradations. A full circle indicates the most relevancy, an empty circle indicates the least.

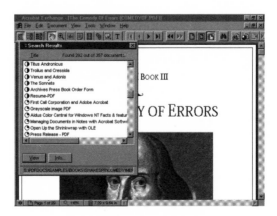

Unlike a library, the user views catalog and book at once.

The actual method used varies somewhat according to the type of search, but in general there are four rules for ranking the documents:

Occurrences Of All Query Terms In One Document

When two or more query terms are associated with the OR operator, documents that have more of the query terms are ranked higher than those with fewer of the query terms. This method gives greater relevance to documents that contain every term, compared with documents that contain many occurrences of a single term.

Total Hits

In a single-term search, the documents with the greatest number of hits will have the highest relevancy ranking. All other things being equal, namely that all of the query terms appear in all of the top documents, total hits will generate higher rankings in multiple-term searches.

Proximity of Hits

When the Proximity option is selected, documents containing occurrences of the query terms appearing closer together will be ranked higher than those with more dispersed hits. This ranking is only in effect for occurrences that are within a few pages of one another.

Hit Density

Finally, the number of hits within a document is compared to the number of words within a document to determine hit density. Of two documents with same number of terms and hits and the same proximity ranking, the shorter of the two documents will be ranked higher due to the higher hit density.

Views Of Search Results

By default, search results are listed as document titles in order of Relevancy Rank Score. The software is trying to help the user by following a simple set of relevance rank rules. However, the user may want to look at the documents according to a different set of criteria other than this so-called relevancy rank.

The user can rapidly re-rank the Results List.

The Search Preferences dialog box allows the user to specify exactly the way in which documents are sorted in the results list. Once again, through a very simple interface, the user has access to techniques of Relational Database Management Systems. In a traditional RDBMS environment, each of the various "views" of the data that the user is able to generate by simply choosing the Sort variable would have been Custom Reports, in the sense that the user could specify the appearance of the output.

The user can sort the results list by the various info fields:

Author	**Created**	**Creator**
Keywords	**Modified**	**Producer**
Score	**Subject**	**Title**

In effect, the user can choose the primary sort field for the results list, and thereby generate dynamic views of uniquely clustered hits. In this case, the word "dynamic" means that the user has great control over the view of the data and can easily change the report structure of the hit list without redoing the search.

The power of this technique cannot be overestimated, and an extremely sophisticated digital library can be built on this architecture that will serve the needs of a wide spectrum of users.

The least sophisticated, first-time user can achieve successful searches on the same database that allows the most sophisticated, hardcore users to generate extremely focused retrievals.

Adjusting The Highlighting Of Hits

In Acrobat Exchange, the user can choose three levels of highlighting within documents:

Highlight	Movement in Documents
By Word	Each click moves back and forward in highlighted hit terms
No Highlighting	No highlights, each click moves back and forward through pages
By Page	All hit terms highlighted, page movement same as above

The highlighting of terms attracts the user's most intense interest, so it is a very important consideration in the design of any electronic document system. For example, the last choice above, Highlighting By Page, offers an instantaneous, visual relevancy ranking function to the user. Any user can pop up a screen full of text, concentrate on the highlights, and very quickly decide the relevance of the document.

The effectiveness of user-level enhancements such as highlighting cannot be overestimated. However, too much highlighting and emphasis can be distracting, so discretion is advised in customizing these elements for each application.

Building On Previous Retrievals

The Refine Search feature allows the user to perform a new search upon a previously retrieved set of documents. This capability can be very productive because the user can educate himself with a quick browsing of documents retrieved by a wide search. After reading a few returned documents, a sharp user can get a good feel for the nature of the documents in the collection. Based on this understanding, the user can build a much more refined query by simply including and excluding certain terms, authors and so on.

Any new set of search terms may be entered, including document info, date info and full text. Since the new search is restricted to the results of an earlier search, this process can be continued and the user can "drill" down through a collection to the most interesting documents.

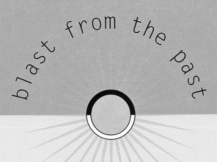

Way back in 1979, a revolutionary one-piece word processor made the cover of Time Magazine. With the screen, keyboard and disk drives all molded into one sleek console, the Lanier No Problem looked quite futuristic. But what was even more revolutionary than its appearance was a slick user interface that was built upon function keys and mnemonics.

At that time, the dominant competition were earlier generation models from IBM, Wang and Xerox [and others, like Jacquard, NBI (Nothing But Initials - old inside joke), and so on, found only in history books, now]. All of the dominant early models offered a menu-based user interface.

Part of the appeal of Natural Language interfaces is related to this ease-of-use idea of dumbing down the system for the inexperienced users. In this case, rather than using menus or function keys to replace commands, simple language is used to replace complex query language. At the annual TREC convention, where the most intrepid information retrieval vendors line up in open competition, the queries are intricately crafted equations that are far from Natural Language.

Back in Sydney in 1979, where I worked for Lanier Australia P/L, when confronted with the so-called ease of use of menu-oriented systems, we would offer the following argument: "Menus are like training wheels, which are great when you are learning to ride your bike. But after you know how to ride, they just get in your way." We would then point out that these menus were mostly impressive in sales demonstration, when the potential user was seeing the system for the first time. Most people soon came to see menus as a slow, repetitive way to use a computer.

Limitations of Acrobat Searching

Acrobat Searching is a powerful way to access information but there are limits to its present functionality.

Searching Without a Natural Language Query Interface

Natural Language Query Interface means the user can just enter an ordinary question, with no special structure to the query.

Following the common wisdom (wish!) that simpler is better when it comes to computers, it seems like a great idea to be able to perform complex information-retrieval operations by asking common, everyday questions. Expectations tend to be deeply influenced by science fiction, such as the dictation machine in the movie "Being There," upon which Peter Sellers, in the role of Chauncy, watched his master write his last will and testament by speaking to the device.

These devices do work, they just don't work like that! And the common perception of Natural Language interfaces to text databases is similarly simplistic. By surrendering precise control of the query to a generalized program, the user loses a certain amount of precision. As always, the author, publisher or digital librarian must concentrate on the needs of present and future users and provide the best tools for that clientele. If future users will probably come back and use a collection over and over, it is to be expected that they will spend a few minutes learning the elementary query language and commands because they will be self-motivated to become more efficient.

That said, the allure of Natural Language search capability is still very powerful. After a user has exhausted all of his ideas for query terms and fields to search, it is great to have the option of throwing his ideas to the computer for help. The greatest adventure on the Web is finding ideas and information that you never knew existed. Because you were ignorant of its existence, you could not know how to search for it.

The glory of Natural Language text searching is that your query terms are modified and expanded, syntactically and statistically, to find new information that you would probably never stumble upon by traditional methods, limited as we all are by our own ignorance. This process of discovery is something no stone-and-mortar library could ever make so easy.

No Fuzzy Search

Fuzzy Search may be thought of as a form of automated wild card searching. Fuzzy Search is designed to find imperfect occurrences of the query term, and this is accomplished by a very smart software algorithm that substitutes wild cards for each of the characters of a query term.

A Fuzzy Search for the term "search" might be thought of as multiple wild card searches such as "?earch," "s?arch," "se?rch," "sea?ch," "sear?h," and "searc?." Such a multiple wild card search, which will find every occurrence where any one of the characters in the term is missing, is equivalent to a Tight Fuzzy Search. Correspondingly, a Loose Fuzzy Search would make allowances for more missing characters in the string.

The value of Fuzzy Search is that the user doesn't have to enter a different search term for each exact occurrence the target term.

In Fuzzy Search, there is often a setting for Degree of Fuzziness, which has the effect of including more or fewer wild cards within the search terms. If the previous example, where a single wild card substitution is made for each character in the term, a "fuzzier" search might include two or more wild cards within the string.

As shown in the example of wild cards and Fuzzy Search, advanced text-search techniques are very often simply automated versions of basic text-search techniques. The same discipline is applied on the character, word and document level, in terms of variable definition of what constitutes an acceptable and recognizable version of the shape, character, word or idea.

For demos of Fuzzy Search on the Web, try

http://www.zylab.com
http://www.excalib.com
http://www.pls.com

Customization Is Somewhat Restricted

The document info fields can be customized through the Acrobat Software Development Kit, but a certain amount of technical effort is required. For example, the average user may be familiar with creating new fields in a desktop database such as Microsoft Access and would find such Windows-based functions easy to modify. In the case of Acrobat, the user must declare the custom fields in win.ini, which is an area that is not difficult but rarely dabbled in by the everyday user. However, while it's not a pick-and-click process, it is not exceedingly difficult for any programmer or technically oriented user.

Report Generation Is Limited

The advantages of full database functionality within digital libraries for selective re-trieval can be invaluable. Advanced listings and presentation of particular sets of files, including analysis and report generation, offer an unprecedented opportunity to cre-ate new ways of using very large, complex bodies of information.

In Verity's Topic™ product line, very specific, complex queries, called topics, can be stored and run against dynamically changing data. Because the data is always struc-tured in a predictable format, these topics can generate very specific results or reports on the database. The capability in Acrobat is somewhat limited in this regard, and Verity provides an upgrade path to add such capabilities.

There are many third-party approaches to this function, as well as other databases that can manage PDF collections. This requirement is highly specific to each applica-tion, and many creative techniques can be applied to these areas.

Boolean Query Is Complex

To many part-time users of online information, it will seem to be a burden to learn the basic language of Boolean text searching. It is with the utmost charity and best wishes that any publisher or Webmaster can understand this complaint. It is the user's traditional role to always hope for more, easier, faster access to information. If the content is valuable and deep, users will happily learn the simple syntax because it of-fers quicker, more direct access to the collection.

Summary

All of these potential enhancements come at a cost, of course.

- Document info fields must be considered a bare minimum requirement to offer the most possible value, at the least possible effort.

- To include the word stemming or thesaurus capabilities, the database publisher adds a significant overhead to offer these search enhancements.

- Thumbnails can be generated automatically, but if the pages are indistinguishable in these small views, they serve no purpose.

- Bookmarks make online manuals seem familiar.

- Hyperlinks are proven productivity boosts.

- Keywords can be used for database fields, Cust#, Inv#, Serial#, etc.

- Article reading allows use of current document formats online.

All of the above items are overhead and must be very carefully weighed between their value and the effort required to create that value.

footnotes

1 Press Release, September 12, 1996, "Verity's Search'97 product family brings single user interface for searching across personal data, the Internet and the Enterprise,"
http://www.verity.com/PR/960912um.html.

enhanced
PDF
collections

on the

web

chapter

eight

The concurrent releases of Adobe Acrobat 3 (optimized files) and Verity SearchPDF combined to create a watershed of digital document distribution technology. Richly enhanced collections can now be served up on the Web with a luxurious set of search features.

The non-intuitive market strategy of the Internet has led to many free search engines. The Excite engine from Architext is a prime example of powerful software technology given away free. It doesn't seem to make sense, but consider the Acrobat Reader, the Netscape Navigator, the Microsoft Internet offerings; they have all been free.

And the most remarkable feature of the free products from the big commercial vendors is simply the fact that they are being offered by commercial, most definitely for-profit corporations. But the Web itself was born of free software, the NCSA and Cern servers, and the Lynx and Mosaic browsers.

The single biggest problem with free software is that users are required to download and install new versions, and to a large extent support themselves. (Adobe experiences 20,000 to 30,000 downloads of the Acrobat Reader per day!) A free, fuzzy search engine may offer little value to users of a collection because a commonly accepted organization is lacking. If users don't understand how the data is structured, their searches are just shots in the dark.

From a Web operator's point of view, the most common failure is in hardware and software support. But from a user's point of view, the major concerns are rapid response and useful results.

A person seeking information is probably fired up, motivated, and therefore impatient. A search that takes a minute or more to process is simply insufferable to many online users.

A carefully constructed Catalog-indexed collection will offer excellent performance from the user's point of view. The motivated user will always enjoy the best that any information collection has to offer. Search aids and descriptions of the indexes will help more users become expert users. Searches that specify Document Info fields such as Author, Title, Subject, Keywords and System Info Fields (Creator and Producer, Date Created and Date Modified) will be very fast and productive.

The search capabilities available in Acrobat 3 to query the entire database offer a uniquely disciplined and organized Web resource. Directed to the needs of a specific audience, there are few if any comparable packages for creating a digital document database at off-the-shelf prices.

Full Power Searching On The Web

Version 1.0 of Verity's SearchPDF for Web servers offers three standard user interface screens for entering queries. They are Simple Search, Standard Search and Power Search, and they appear to be dead-simple easy.

Through the Simple Query entry window, the extremely sophisticated text-searching technology is fully available. All of the logic operators are available to be entered into the Query field, including the Evidence, Proximity, Relational and Concept Operators. This means that this free software can serve the needs of a supremely demanding audience for information retrieval. The only caveat is that the users must learn how to use the system to appreciate its advantages.

> **(t i p)**
>
> **The two measures of information retrieval are precision and recall. If a query recalls every document in the database, the user will never find what he is looking for. On the other hand, if the user can't specifically identify the query term exactly as it appears in the collection, relevant documents are lost.**
>
> **However, in large collections, the first problem is usually most difficult, where too many irrelevant documents match the search criteria, leading to a failure of precision. Just a few operators can enable a user to be tremendously more productive, more precise, in searching text collections, by narrowing down the retrieved documents to only those most likely to be relevant.**

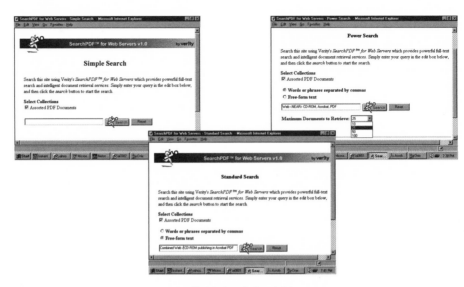

Simple Search (top left)

If additional collections of catalog-indexed collections
were available, they would be listed under the Select
Collections in a check box list.

Standard Search (center)

Standard Search offers enhanced options over Simple Search, allowing for more complex queries.

Power Search (top right)

All of the Verity topic query operators and syntax may be exercised through Power Search, and the user may
select the maximum number of documents retrieved.

The Basic Boolean Operators

Since the dawn of full text retrieval, these functions have been the building blocks of
information retrieval from unstructured databases. Because these concepts go so deep
to the core of free text searching, many users expect these functions to work on every
database. Through many variations on a theme, information seekers naturally gain
proficiency in these Simple Search techniques.

Brackets should be used to join query terms and operators into a single search argument. Boolean operators are:

And	**< Near >**
Or	**< Phrase >**
Not	**,**

((Kelly Near Johnson) Or (skunkworks))

Near (Phrase "faster than a speeding bullet")

Or (blackbird, aurora, stealth, SR-71, U-2, F-117)

Not (thrush, borealis, ninja)

Prefix And Infix Notation

"Words that use any operator except evidence operators (Soundex, Stem, Wildcard and Word) can be defined in prefix notation or infix notation.

Prefix notation is a format that specifies the operator comes before the words to be used with that operator. The following example means: Look for documents that contain a and b.

   And (a,b)

When prefix notation is used, precedence is explicit within the expression. The following example means: Look for documents that contain b and c first, then look for documents that contain a.

   Or (a, **And** (b,c))

Infix notation is a format that specifies the operator be between each element within the expression. The following example means: Look for documents that contain a and b or documents that contain c.

   a **And** b **Or** c

The logic of infix notation is that each operator appears between each element, which means that the section "a and b" (where "a" and "b" are the elements and "**And**" is the operator) is executed before the next section in the statement, which contains another operator and element ("**Or** c").

When infix notation is used, precedence is implicit within the expression; for example, the **And** operator takes precedence over the **Or** operator."

Quoted from the Verity SearchPDF online documentation.

Evidence Operators

The evidence operators provide term expansion, which takes advantage of the Word Stemming, Wildcard and Soundex options of Acrobat Catalog. The author or publisher of the index must include these features during index building, or they will not be available for SearchPDF queries. Evidence operators are:

Word	**Wildcard**
Stem	**Soundex**

Proximity Operators

Proximity operators allow the user to specify that the query terms must appear within a certain distance of one another to constitute a highly ranked hit document. For example, the Near/N operator can specify that terms appear within a specific distance of one another in the text. Proximity operators are:

In	**Paragraph**
Phrase	**Near**
Sentence	**Near/N**

---

example

A query delimited with the **Near/N** operator can find related terms in multiple orders:

The query "Kelly **Near/2** Johnson" finds Kelly Johnson; and Johnson, Kelly; and "Kelly" (Clarence) Johnson.

The query "Kelly **Near/2** Johnson" will not find the following relevant article because the Query Terms are too far apart:

> Clarence *Johnson* is the legendary designer who visualized the most advanced aircraft in history in his head, and then he managed a cadre of engineers in the Lockheed Skunkworks to build them. In the case of some of his inventions, he had to build the factories that could build the planes. The peerless SR-71 Blackbird had to be fabricated in titanium to survive the performance regime that *"Kelly"* envisioned. Titanium had never been worked before, and all new tools and procedures had to be created to handle this unusually strong element.

The previous paragraph contains interesting material that is very pertinent to the user's intended query, but it would never be retrieved with the narrow proximity operator of "Kelly Near/2 Johnson," which requires the two terms be within two words of one another. Some search engines offer proximity operator of within sentence, within paragraph, within "X" words and so on. A **Within Paragraph** operator would find this reference.

Relational Operators

These operators are designed to take advantage of the preparation of the files in the collection by providing the means to selectively use the information in the Author, Title, Subject and Keyword fields. Relational operators are:

Contains	**Starts**
Matches	**Ends**
Substring	

(tip)

Don't forget the extra operators:

? Single character wildcard

* String wildcard

' Single quotes initiates word stemming

" Double quotes finds only exact matches

Concept Operators

Concept operators are the glue that congeal many query terms into a model of an idea, or a "topic," in Verity-speak. Very precise arguments, or query statements, that have been built with the evidence, proximity and relational operators can be synthetically combined into one large search "equation." Concept operators are:

And

Or

Accrue

---

tip

Verity SearchPDF is just the tip of a family of information-retrieval tools called topic (with a lowercase t). SearchPDF is a sophisticated and very effective teaser for the rest of the software tools. There are a couple of key limitations or enhancements available in the free SearchPDF package. While all of Verity's extensive search and retrieval functions are available, they only work on Acrobat Catalog-indexed collections of PDF files. Verity's engine can actually index and search hundreds of formats, and users who enjoy searching PDF documents may feel a need to have the same search power over other formats. That's where the rest of the topic family comes in, offering the ability to search virtually all digital documents.

Another key capability reserved from free offerings like SearchPDF is the ability to reuse queries. In fact, the product name topic refers to the ability to precisely define a concept, or topic, that embraces a complex question. These topic queries can be stored and executed on schedule or on demand. Expert queries can be adapted and reused indefinitely on dynamically changing data.

A topic persistent query can constantly interrogate data sources, such as stock tickers, wire services and many others, and then generate timely reports of new information that appears relevant to the information seeker's interests. This is called the topicAGENT.

Intelligent agents, persistent searches and other automated information-gathering techniques offer viable means to surf the overwhelming deluge of information coming online.

Modifiers

Modifiers allow the user to put a particular spin on each of the search terms. These modifiers give the savvy user the tools to create queries that can deliver traditional reports of results, including the "order" modifier. Modifiers are:

Case   For word & wildcard searches

Many   Density of term vs. length of document

Not   Exclude "thrush" when searching for "blackbird"

Order   Specific order of terms in sentences, paragraphs or proximity

> **The Verity topic products provide for storage, reuse and flexible deployment of these pre-defined topic queries. Very advanced information-retrieval techniques are available to tailor Web topicAGENT software robots to roam the Web or specific databases and bring back the most desirable and valuable information.**

tip

Many times, an initial search on a database will provide clues on which terms to exercise the NOT operator. For example, if you were searching a news database for the "blackbird" spy planes, you would like to avoid mention of the English blackbird, which is actually a common European "thrush." By excluding this term, you would avoid mentions of blackbirds in nature and birdwatching articles.

Density refers to the number of hit terms as a fraction of the entire document (hit terms/total terms). Logically, if the hit terms comprise the bulk of the document, it is likely that the hit terms are the most relevant subject of the hit document. This feature is specifically designed to overcome frequency errors. For example, a 400-page manual will probably contain a greater number of hits on a certain term, but the information will be more diffused than a 400-word post that contains a lesser number, or frequency, of hits.

For example, to search for the best solution for both paper and online publication, you might query for:

"Best fonts and point sizes for both paper and online publishing"

An authoritative 200-word listserv posting on PDF-L will mention the terms in logical order with very little extraneous data. Therefore, the ratio of search terms to all terms in the individual posted document will be very high. The answer to the original question is likely to be given in this type of hit.

On the other hand, a long document, or even a list or index, may contain many more instances (frequency) of the hit terms, but at a much lower density. The user is more likely to find information in the shorter, "denser" document. Of course, if not, the longer documents offer another option.

tip

The Many modifier directly affects relevance ranking. If the new user were to learn only one "extra" command, it should be the Many operator. In most texts, this will lend extra importance or weight to a particular term.

"<MANY> supersonic AND stealth" would retrieve all information about supersonic and stealth aircraft, and would present supersonic stealth aircraft at the top of the heap.

Check out SearchPDF for yourself on the Web. Excellent documentation is available on all search features:

http://www.verity.com/demo/index.html

Simple Search

The only options presented here are the ability to select collections for searching, and the Query window. The zen of this interface is that the entire organization of the database is accessible through that simple view. An experienced user can enter the most highly structured queries into the elementary screen.

A list of hypertext links is returned as the hit list of a Simple Search,
with documents ranked numerically by relevancy rating.

For Simple Search, Standard Search and Power Search screens, see the first section of this chapter.

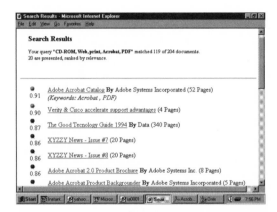

The Standard Search hit list returns document information such as Author (By), File Size and Keywords.

Standard Search

The Standard Search screen offers two pushbutton qualifiers for the terms entered into the Query field. The default choice, "Words or phrases separated by commas," is the approach taken in the Simple Search above. The other choice, "Free-form text," offers the user an unstructured interface that interprets the information entered into the Query field.

Power Search

Power Search offers control of the number of documents retrieved by any query. There is no need to clutter the user's mind, the network's bandwidth or the server's CPU with excessive file transfers. This option provides economies on every step of the info-transfer process by simply limiting the number of documents referenced and handled for retrieval.

> **(tip)**
>
> **Remember, while you are searching for words or ideas, you are actually retrieving documents. The best query retrieves the most relevant document by prioritizing the overall concept — through careful use of search operators.**
>
> **Every query should consider relevancy ranking because that determines the order in which the retrieved documents will be presented. Once again, it's the question of precision and re-call. By weighting queries toward precision, the desired information floats to the top for easy retrieval.**

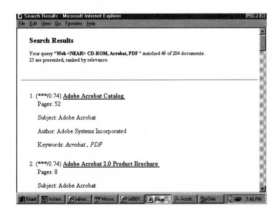

Power Search retrieves document info that could be exploited by a careful author or publisher who knows the needs of his users.

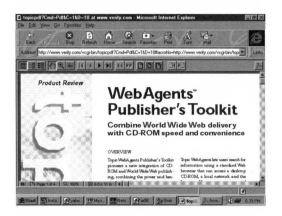

When a PDF document is selected from the HTML link in a results list,
the Acrobat Plug-in automatically views it within Netscape Navigator
and Microsoft Internet Explorer, as shown here.

Web Servers and SearchPDF

Verity's strategy for this great freeware is consistent with the Internet model, so
SearchPDF is designed to run on the most common and popular server software platforms. Version 1.0 runs on NCSA, O'Reilly's WebSite, Netscape's Commerce Server
and Microsoft's Internet Information Server.

Search Results In HTML

The Search Results page includes a relevancy ranked list of documents that match the
search criteria. A numeric relevancy grade is displayed, as well as the contents of the
Keyword field from Document Info.

This simple combination offers the best of both worlds: Relevancy is computed in the
software as it analyzes a document, while the Keywords let the author or publisher
specify relevant interests in the Keyword field for each document.

The PDF documents themselves are available via hyperlinks in the hit list. It is very considerate of the Webmaster to note the number of pages in the file. You might have time to grab a 4-page PDF, but you'd have to carefully schedule downloading a 400-page file.

The Power Search Results page of SearchPDF returns the hit list with the following helpful fields:

Relevance Rank, Hyperlink Document Title, Author, # of Pages, and Keywords.

Experience teaches users to instantly recognize patterns and information in the hit list, and this presentation provides for efficient browsing of the hits.

Help the User by Explaining the Organization in the Collection

For example, a manufacturer offering digital documentation might provide online users with these helpful Hints on the home page:

Reminder - Always use the "Contains" operator in Field Searches for widest possible retrieval. That is, use Parens to include Field Names with Contents, as in (Subject ~ WidgetX3). These searches will retrieve all documents with your search term in a particular field.

Reminder - We use each Info Field as follows:

Title - Document Name, including such useful search terms as Install Manual, User Manual, Online Help, etc.

Subject - Product Name, Product Number

Author - Product Manager, Corporate Contact

Keywords - Acronyms, Nicknames, common references, etc.

Multi-Platform Access

Operating systems mirror the primacy of platforms on the Internet and in corporate America. Windows NT is the fast-growing "new install" by far, while a significant part of the installed Client/Server environment runs on Sun Solaris, HP-UX and IBM AIX. SearchPDF runs on all of these platforms and is compliant with any Web server that supports a Common Gateway Interface (CGI).

CGI allows otherwise static and one-way HTML pages to provide dynamic interactivity. The basic Web browser is designed to follow links and display pages. CGI scripts are the links between these hypertext pages and all other complex online processes. They are programs that run on a Web server, and they are initiated by a Web-linked user. Any anonymous surfer on the global Web can run a program on a remotely linked server through these commands. This facility is universally exploited on the Web to offer enhanced functionality.

Today, Java and ActiveX offer the next generation of dynamic functionality originally provided by CGI scripts.

Acrobat 3 provides extensive, fluid access to the PDF content online, including the display of hit terms in the retrieved documents.

Verity's SearchPDF is specifically designed to work with indexes built by Acrobat Catalog. SearchPDF does not offer traditional Verity text-retrieval capability on other collections, such as all the word-processing files on your hard drive.

Sony Electronic Publishing
Services Tackles Large Jobs

Bob Marsh, of Sony Electronic Publishing Services, a division of Sony Disk Manufacturing, has mastered techniques for handling one of the largest CD-ROM publishing applications to date. In the spring of 1995, SEPS won the contract from the Institute of Electrical and Electronics Engineers to convert over one million scanned images to Acrobat format and publish the entire collection on CD-ROM.

The collection of .tif files going back to 1986 included conference proceedings and colloquia, standards and journals, and was housed in a proprietary viewing system and directory structure. The project included re-mastering 220 CDs.

"We had three primary goals in the project," Bob explains. "First, we wanted to upgrade to a non-proprietary environment, and we chose Windows. Secondly, we decided to use the Verity Search engine. Finally, we wanted to move from scanned input to electronic source material."

"We decided to use Acrobat at the outset. We now use Acrobat on everything we do for several reasons. It's a cross-platform format that is efficient for the widest range of users. We can integrate scanned and electronic source material in a way that is totally seamless to the end user."

"The converted images are searched through the meta-data provided by IEEE, which is tagged ASCII in their INSPEC database, which is widely used by technical libraries. We created our index from the ASCII and attached the images."

"The project included three systems we developed for the conversion, production process and retrieval tools. We provide retrieval through a VB wrapper on top of the full Verity engine and Acrobat serves as the embedded Viewer. The path to the articles is through a hierarchical browser, which works through a tab dialog system."

"We use Verity to search the INSPEC data which indexes the database of images. The index requires two CD-ROMs, and the collection of a half million articles is published on 240 CD-ROMs."

"For simplicity's sake, we decided to deal with only scanned images, and provide the means for users to take advantage of the meta-data professionally compiled by IEEE to search and retrieve documents. Going forward with monthly updates, we now take electronic source in PDF directly into the system, eliminating the need of scanning and image conversion. The collection appears as a seamless whole to the end user."

— Thanks to Bob Marsh
of Sony Electronic Publishing Services

Visit the web site at: http://www.seps.com

Summary

One author using Acrobat 3 can convert many forms of paper and electronic documents into PDF content. Very large collections of files can be processed by Catalog so that a single, comprehensive index offers instant access to information content.

Verity's free SearchPDF allows for up to four indexes, providing the potential for information-retrieval capability over literally millions of pages.

A Webmaster should publish a directory of the conventions used in the collections so that even newbie users could efficiently peruse the information.

The full Verity text-search functionality conveys dynamic research functionality upon any large collection of PDF documents on the Web.

Offering such capability on either the Web or an Intranet should not be taken lightly. As always, user satisfaction must be of paramount importance. It is always a good idea to overbuild every aspect of a Full Text Retrieval database, including the CPU, disk drives, communication interfaces and available RAM. Remember that the cost of the server is spread over all of the users of the system.

advanced
navigation
for
superior
information
access

```
chapter  nine
```

The main point cannot be over-emphasized: the most important advantage of digital documents over paper documents is the *superior access to the information* in the documents. Depending on the nature of the information and the user's needs in handling the information, there are many techniques that add greatly to the value of collection. The publisher can *empower* the user through more *efficient organization* in published digital documents.

The following are currently available features available to expand the navigation capabilities of PDF files.

The point of this section is that documents must at least *equal*, but should intend to *better* the user's access to information in digital collections as opposed to libraries of paper. The plug-in tools listed here are remarkable for the functionality they provide for publishing and researching your information. A dozen are included free with Acrobat 3; others are sold by third-party developers.

Some plug-ins are included on the CD that ships with Acrobat. Adobe also offers a frequently updated collection of free plug-ins that enhance Acrobat Exchange:

Acrobat 3 Plug-Ins

```
http://www.adobe.com/Acrobat/Plug-Ins
```

AutoClose

This option is similar in function to a Web browser in the sense that it closes pages that have been accessed earlier and are still stored in memory. When the 11th document is opened, the last accessed document is closed. It's *always important to conserve* RAM, storage and communication bandwidth.

AutoIndex

The AutoIndex function immediately opens an associated Catalog-created index when a page with this feature is accessed. It's based on the thinking that if the user has found a hit in the Getting Started guide, he is likely to soon need information in the User Manual and Tutorial and other files. This option immediately fires up the appropriate index and allows easy navigation to related information.

Capture

Capture performs multi-level recognition of page images, converting not only the text content, but also the appearance of the page. This process involves substituting fonts and font attributes to match the source document, as well as rebuilding the document in the exact dimensions of the original page.

> **tip**
>
> **Capture offers two primary output options:**
>
> **PDF Normal reproduces the page with recognition;**
>
> **PDF Image & Text offers original image with hidden text, which allows content searching.**

EPS Links

A collection of recipes and examples is available for merging traditional design logos and elements with links.

ExecMenu

Digital documents don't get much more dynamic than this. This is where sound, movie and all of the other multimedia capability enter the PDF world.

A site that will always be dedicated to faster, richer, better online experiences is the virtual reality guys at:

example

With the Execute Menu feature enabled, a PDF link to a virtual reality world could be viewed with Silicon Graphics Cosmo shareware VRML.

`http://www.sgi.com/Products/cosmo/`

Virtual Reality Modeling Language (VRML) allows representation of objects in interactive 3-D. In a technical manual, for instance, in addition to explanatory words and graphics, virtual working models of mechanical systems can offer a far richer experience.

A VRML lesson on replacing an electronic component might begin with a photo or simple schematic of an aircraft. Choosing a particular part would cause that part of the plane to glow, and the user could easily "walk under" that spot. "Looking up" a couple of screws might appear, and when you touch them, the mouse becomes a screwdriver and opens the access hatch. When you "look into" the hatch, you have a *better than video view* because you can see through physical objects to see how they might be connected on the other side. Through a well-designed VR interface, entire procedures can be practiced and referred to even while doing the job.

The U.S. Air Force is already in prototype development of such systems, with hip pack computers and displays built into lightweight goggles. A crewman could walk out to the aircraft, triple-check everything through the VR-assisted procedures, and confidently and efficiently perform complex tasks.

Forms

> **tip**
>
> **The Forms feature of Acrobat 3 offers significant efficiency gains over HTML Forms because only the variable data is transmitted back to the server. Compared with HTML, which transmits back the entire form, this Acrobat technique is demonstrably more effective than previous means.**

The Forms functionality in Acrobat 3 includes a number of classic design elements and also provides for online creation of dynamic files with elements served up from the Web server. This feature is demonstrated at Adobe's Web site. It is fairly amazing that custom forms can be built online based on the initial responses of the user.

Import Image

This is the doorway for many popular images to enter into the bigger world of PDF files. The files being imported are all widely used in their particular fields, but upon becoming PDF, they achieve universal status.

The importable formats include BMP, CompuServe GIF, PCX and TIF. These formats represent, respectively:

BMP: The Windows bitmap format

GIF: The most widely distributed online image format universally incorporated in HTML

PCX: The original Paintbrush and Paint formats

TIF: The industrial standard of fax and document imaging

> **tip**
>
> **The Acrobat viewer technology is in widespread use, exceeded only by Web browsers in number of users. These numbers include many who never use the Web at all.**
>
> **By importing a traditional image into PDF format, the image becomes universally accessible on all platforms, hardware, software, online and CD media, because it is the first rich viable universal format.**

Movie

This is a Windows version of the Apple QuickTime movie viewer, the one used in Myst and other popular multimedia publications. Using the Movie pull-down tool, it is very easy to create a link to a QuickTime or AVI video file. By activating the link, the user calls up the externally stored movie and QuickTime plays it. QuickTime offers a range of effects to size or even distort the movie presentation.

QuickTime movies are very large video files. The Weezer "Happy Days" video on the Windows 95 FunStuff disk has a running time of about four minutes and a file size of 30 MB. New users should always be informed of file size.

For this reason, video is always stored external to a PDF file, so extra care must be used in maintaining these links.

OLE Server

This feature brings PDF documents into the mainstream desktop applications by allowing *inline viewing* of Acrobat files. Lucky users of *Lotus Notes* might find rich PDF documents online and can immediately view, search or print them in their full-featured presentation. Microsoft Access applications can query a database and easily retrieve and view PDF contents.

Optimizer

The key technical breakthrough in Acrobat 3 is the ability to Optimize PDF files. For Web-accessible files, the most dramatic feature is the ability to take advantage of byte-serving Web servers to deliver only certain pages rather than entire documents. This can provide great economies of transmission speed and response time for online users.

Repetitive elements in pages are consolidated and reused, such as background images, text and line art. This leads to significant reduction in file sizes, the key to speedy transmission of information.

PDF Type Utility

This is a Mac applet that makes Mac-created Acrobat files more accessible to Windows and UNIX Acrobat users.

Scan

The Scan module includes the ISIS drivers for most popular scanners, as well as the TWAIN interface. ISIS drivers can be selected from the pull-down list and provide instant functionality for scanners as varied as the inexpensive Fujitsu ScanPartner 10 and the 120-page-per-minute Fujitsu 3099 family of duplex scanners.

⊤ ISIS Scanner Drivers

ISIS Scanner Drivers are software creations of Pixel Translations, which was acquired by Cornerstone Imaging in 1995. As more and more scanners are connected by standard SCSI connections rather than the traditional proprietary scanner interface cards, most applications that require scanning now include the ISIS drivers. This means that the user can simply choose from a pull-down menu to select a scanner, and the ISIS driver will allow the application to run the scanner.

A driver is a piece of software that translates all of the functions of the scanner to a common set of controls that can be exercised as buttons, bars and so on in the application software. This means that Acrobat Capture and Watermark and other packages that include the drivers offer freedom of choice on scanners.

Search

The Search features available in PDF collections are extensively covered in Chapters 7 and 12.

SuperCrop

SuperCrop provides the ability to eliminate unnecessary white space around PDF documents to improve viewing characteristics. This new crop tool allows rubber-band box selection of the area to be cropped, which is considerably easier to use than the Standard Crop arrow buttons. Users of Acrobat Exchange can also automatically crop to the bounding box of the page.

SuperPrefs

The SuperPrefs plug-in allows the user to tailor the function of Acrobat Reader to meet specific requirements. The options include:

- File Open Behavior
- Acrobat Always on Top
- AutoSave Currently Open Docs
- Replace Rotate Dialog: Replaces standard rotate dialog to include 180-degree rotation and cancel
- Cleanup Bookmarks: Removes Bookmarks referring to pages that are deleted
- Hot List: A Menu Item listing your favorite files
- Auto Tiling: Choose your layout of multiple open files

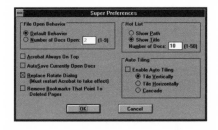

SuperPrefs creates a new set of preferences for user convenience.

TouchUp

TouchUp is the tool for editing PDF single-line character strings, ideal for editing the results of Capture-created documents. This allows users to clean up and modify the output of the recognition process by modifying text, attributes and other components.

WebLink

A WebLink is the PDF equivalent of an HTML hyperlink, and WebLinks function across the World Wide Web in the same way hyperlinks do on the Web.

The WebLink plug-in allows the user to add World Wide Web hyperlinks to PDF documents. The Acrobat Exchange Link tool is extended with this plug-in so that a URL can be specified as the target document.

When a WebLink is clicked, the user's Web browser is launched if it's not already running, and the Browser follows the link. WebLink is compatible with Netscape Navigator, Microsoft Internet Information Server, Spyglass Mosaic and Quarterdeck Mosaic.

The user can specify the appearance of links and specify one of a broad array of actions that a link will perform.

Re:Mark for Digital Annotations

The most obvious difference between digital documents and paper documents is that *it's a lot harder to write on digital documents as opposed to paper documents*. A paper page can be changed and emphasized with a wide range of desk drawer tools.

Handwritten notes and drawings can be scribbled with any number of pens and pencils, areas can be circled and pointed at in bright redlining, words or sections can be highlighted with broad strokes of yellow.

> **Digital movie-making tools can be used to add visual content to PDF files. Adobe Premiere is designed for digital video editing and production, an excellent enhancement tool for PDF information collections. Searchable, rich multimedia collections on the Web are simple to create.**

Since the introduction of Magic Markers by Carter's Ink in the 1960s, business documents have been augmented, annotated, highlighted, and updated with a variety of colors and writing implements. People have become accustomed to a thrilling array of annotation tools, from highlighters to spray paint.

Digital documents often lack any means for such reader input. Simple e-mail, for example, can be easily copied and quoted, but direct *paper-like comments* are very limited.

Re:Mark, published by Ambia, brings these *markup techniques*, tried-and-true and widely relied upon, to digital PDF documents. The original business process relied on all of the pen-based means of document comments and emphasis. All of these markup features were *required* to make the digital documents match the functionality of the paper documents.

Acrobat users have a wide range of tools for adding emphasis and comments.

Re:Mark's Markup Capabilities

As described above, this set of tools allows the publisher and even the readers of documents to add dynamic input. With paper documents, this number of easily understood comments would be impossible. Markup tools like this allow groups to use
digital PDF documents far more dynamically than any paper system. Groupware applications are enabled by this simple ability to add rich "paper-style" markup features
to digital documents.

In a way that no paper document could equal, many unique and individual user comments and annotations can be color-coded for immediate identification of the source
of the comment. In this digital document, the reader has selective access to *just some*
or *all of* the added comments.

The notes should be minimized for clear viewing of the original document, and they
are clicked for reading the contents of the notes. The markups can be rendered into
the PDF documents so that the commentary can be shared without the need for all
users to have Acrobat Exchange.

Underline

The oldest form of text emphasis is to underline words. Underline is one of the two
text emphasis features shared by many handwritten styles and most early machine
printers, like typewriters.

Strike-Out

The other original text emphasis feature is to strike out words. Just as underline pro-
moted the importance of certain words and lines, strike-out deletes certain words and
lines from consideration. Even cuneiform in ancient Babylon used strike-out on mistakes and edits.

Highlight

Though the inspiration for highlighting may hark back to the miraculous dawn of illu-minated manuscripts, the function as illustrated here is closer to Magic Marker high-lighters.

Comment Pop-Up

The author of any of these Re:Mark items can insert a simple text comment about the markup itself. For example, the author of a Highlight or Underline may offer an ex-planation for the emphasis added to the original document.

Draw On The Digital Document

This ink-drawing tool mimics the simple ability to write on a piece of paper. Of course, if this feature is going to be used extensively, a pen tablet would be an excel-lent input as it is difficult to write with a mouse. However, even a mouse is sufficient for simple cross-outs or pointers that are used in text and page editing.

File Attachments

The file attachment feature offers capabilities similar to MIME attachments in e-mail. Any file may be attached to the PDF file, including spreadsheets, word-processing documents, and pure binary documents such as bitmap images, sound and movies.

One of the great benefits of the way this feature works is that the attached file be-comes part of the PDF file (except for video and other extremely large files). Since only one file needs to be shipped and retrieved, the danger of lost and missing files is avoided. The end user can then view the Acrobat file, and the attachment can be extracted and viewed in its native application.

For the storage, retrieval and transmission of compound file types, such as a PDF that contains word-processing or spreadsheet files or other binary types, *this method is equal to the best of the MIME-capable e-mail systems.* This *single-file format is simpler* but similar to the methods used to handle compound files in document-management systems.

Multimedia Attachments

Sound annotation allows verbal comments to be incorporated in the document and played on the increasingly common multimedia workstations.

Color-Coded User Input For Digital Personality

All comments and annotations are color-coded to represent the author of each note. In this way, the reader instantly recognizes the probable purpose and importance of a particular note based on previous knowledge of the author.

Review

All of the above modifications and comments can be gathered together from many users. Comments can be filtered by author and annotation type, allowing quick consensus and input aggregation.

All of the input from many sources, identified by User and Note Type, can be viewed in one Master Document. The Master can be reviewed by one editor or shared with the entire group for dynamic access and development.

The contents and comments can be created on either a Mac or Windows platform, and the results are useful for users on either platform. All of the comments and annotations can be rendered into a standard PDF file, viewable with the standard Acrobat Reader.

Extraction

The Re:Mark Copy Table to Clipboard feature allows the extraction of complex tables in spreadsheet format. This software analyzes the layout of the rows and columns and attempts to rebuild the structure as cells in a spreadsheet.

A PDF-to-RTF converter provides for the transformation of PDF files into the Rosetta stone of word-processing programs: Microsoft's Rich Text Format. The resulting RTF files are widely supported by competing programs and can usually be efficiently loaded into word-processing, spreadsheet and other applications.

Compose

A recurring theme in this work is that digital documents should be better than paper documents in the way they deliver information. Given the oft-stated 500-year head start that paper books got on digital books, it is usually a good idea to try to reproduce the proven techniques of history in today's digital forms.

Given the fact that digital documents can be text searched and recalled en masse via broad retrieval commands, it would seem that superior access is a given with digital documents. However, simple practice shows that the ancient book organization of documents is essential and critical to navigation in search of ideas.

Compose, published by Ambia, attempts to restore the organization and structure of paper documents to digital documents. Text searching is not enough; it is important to be able to navigate by page numbers, indexes and the table of contents.

Automatic Bookmarks And TOC

A great technique called Bookmarks By Example searches for all particular format elements to identify chapter and section markings. By recognizing a combination of font, size and format that is used for a certain heading, multiple-level bookmarks can be automatically generated.

These bookmarks, based on repetitive markup of headings, can also generate an extended table of contents.

It must be noted that the "automatic" quality of this process is limited to the consistency in the source document. If an entire collection of documents shares the same style sheet, it will be possible to perform a highly automated conversion to an orderly digital library form.

If, on the other hand, the documents are inconsistent, this process will require hands-on correction and quality control. For example, files converted by Acrobat Capture may not always assign exactly the same point size or weight to a particular font. Such variations are common in scanned documents. In this case, quality control will be required to generate a predictable and reliable index and table of contents.

Hyperlink Index And TOC To References

The index and table of contents of any document can, and perhaps should, be hyperlinked to the chapters and sections listed. The Page Linker uses page number recognition to automatically build hyperlinks.

This will give the reader the ability to use these traditional Finder Aids with digital efficiency. After locating a topic of interest in the index, a simple click will take the reader directly to the reference within the body text.

Automatic Hyperlink Copying

Repetitive links throughout a document are very helpful to the document user, so they should be used generously in the publication of digital documents. The Copy Link tool allows links to be duplicated and populated throughout a long document, providing the utmost in navigation for the user with the most efficient effort by the publisher to add this valuable feature to the digital document.

The most common use of such repetitive links are simple "next page," "previous page" and "table of contents" buttons, which allow users to quickly move through documents even if they are not familiar with Acrobat's buttons.

Link Auditor

The Auditor checks the entire PDF document and fixes broken bookmarks and links.

Chain Linker

The Chain Linker creates links between every occurrence of a word or phrase. This is like the ultimate index, where every single instance or mention of a certain term is listed. Applied sparingly, this tool can be extremely effective in offering shortcuts to related information. Used profligately, this feature will be so tedious that users will never touch it and its index will just be excess baggage in the PDF file.

Multi-Document Composition

This feature works just like the Master Document feature in word-processing packages in that it allows the user to build large documents from collections of smaller documents. The smaller documents may be input from several authors, collections of earlier published documents, or conglomerations of several input sources or news wires.

This feature also allows the page numbering of the original documents to be removed, and a common page-numbering scheme is built for the new, compound document. In addition, customizable page headers and footers can be added, which may include document name, date and time fields, page numbering and other components.

Master Table Of Contents

Hundreds of individual documents can be linked in one title page so that an entire collection can be easily accessed.

InfoFill

This tool is used to automatically populate the General Information Fields in collections of PDF documents. For example, a simple ASCII file of information can be merged into all of the Title, Subject, Author and Keywords fields. This capability may be exceptionally useful when documents that have already been indexed in another scheme are being converted to PDF and Acrobat Exchange database format.

When used with the above Table of Contents Builder, very large numbers of PDF documents can be quickly linked.

Navigate By Title And Author

This feature allows users of large collections to browse by actual document Title and Author rather than by the cryptic file names found in simple directory listings or FTP-style hierarchical UNIX directories. PDF Launcher allows the user to immediately view the files chosen from the Title and Author listings.

Aerial

Ambia offers an add-on document navigation tool for Adobe Acrobat called Aerial, which provides many of the common functions of paper documents, such as index searches, page number browsing, and a couple of handy tools for page marking and printing. Aerial reproduces many of the functions that users are accustomed to doing manually on paper documents.

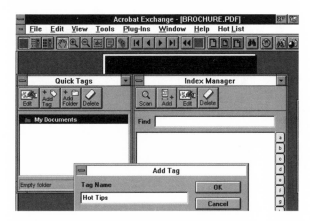

Aerial enhances user cruising through PDF documents by bringing paper document techniques such as page number browsing and paper clip notations to PDF documents.

Page Number Navigation

Many everyday documents have page-numbering systems that don't match Acrobat's sequential order. This feature restores that ancient Gutenberg facility to Acrobat documents. With its ability to recognize most page-numbering schemes, Aerial effectively upgrades your Go To Page button.

In any project that deals with traditional complex page- and section-numbering schemes, this feature is extremely helpful. Because of the complex nature of the information presented in the source documents, many complex page-numbering schemes are encountered. It is the norm rather than the departure for these documents to include title pages, prefaces, chapter numbering, appendices and so on.

Aerial can recognize page numbers in a variety of formats, including Roman numerals and double folio styles such as 5-15 and so on. In this way the reader can use the Go To Document Page tool to specify an original page number.

Of course, similar functionality could be added on at the time of creation of the digital document through the use of bookmarks or links. However, this tool brings this functionality to virtually all Acrobat documents with page numbers.

Search Document Indices

The most common value-added navigation or finder/helper in a document, not counting the table of contents, is an index. All but the simplest books or manuals contain an index to guide the user to the information in the document.

An index in a digital document can often be more productive than a full text search. When a reader is looking for specific information, an index allows direct access to the place or places where the information occurs. A text search may produce too many hits, potentially causing the user to review irrelevant pages on the path to the correct page. In addition, an index can help a user find the proper spelling or usage of a term as it appears in a particular document.

The Aerial Index Manager is a Soundex listing, like the Windows Help dialog. As the user types in the letters of a word, the system automatically scrolls to that region of the index. The user can then click on a choice to visit that page.

The index feature can be used to create more refined text searches. By displaying occurrences of terms as they appear in a particular document, an advanced text search user can dispense with Wildcards, Thesauri and Word Stemming to avoid extraneous hits. As documents get larger, ever more precise text searching is highly desirable.

By choosing particular terms to include in an index, an author or editor has ranked the important information in the document and excluded the least-valuable terms and words. For this reason, it is often a very effective value to add hyperlinks from the index to the references of a document. Readers will appreciate this improved accessibility. Most readers probably expect it because they intuitively expect digital documents to be better than paper documents in every way.

Tag Frequently Referenced Pages

Occasionally we have to admit that paper documents do offer some conveniences not always available in digital documents. When we put a physical book down, we can fold a corner to mark our place. The next time we pick up the book, we can flip directly to our marked spot or spots. Digital documents often aren't as easy to mark.

The Aerial Quick Tags tool provides this feature. Very similar to Netscape Bookmarks, the tags are stored outside the Acrobat documents themselves. Just as Netscape allows the user to click to visit favorite sites on the Web, the Quick Tags allow the user to immediately jump to a particular page.

In many projects, important documents maintain their relevance over a period of time. Previously published information must often be compared to newly arrived documents. Analysts and reviewers find this Quick Tag feature to be an almost absolute necessity. Without such features, a growing digital library can become unwieldy, and research and retrieval can be slowed. Once again, this feature restores a functionality familiar from books on shelves.

Clip Pages For Quick Reference

Perhaps nothing is more annoying to the user of a digital document than losing his place. It's a common occurrence, however, during the process of tracking down a question, to find answers in separate, unrelated places. Following the train of thought often causes a user to lose track of earlier locations.

In a paper document, the user can stick a finger in related pages or put a pencil in the book. The Aerial Paper Clip tool gives the user this handy ability with digital documents. The user can quickly click back through marked pages for ease of reference.

Users and analysts of large collections of data often have the need to flip between charts and explanations on widely separated pages, and the Paper Clip tool makes this process simple and quick. This feature is essential for every task from a two-part brownie and icing recipe to a brain surgery text. And as usual, users seem to intuitively demand this instant access to information that is expected of digital documents.

Print Selected Page Portions

Digital documents include all of the special pages of other complex documents. From the simplest oversized spreadsheet to the most complex map or schematic, oversized documents are common and must be accommodated in digital documents.

When it comes to viewing the document on-screen, the Zoom and Pan tools can be very useful and efficient. However, printing oversized documents on common-size printers can result in documents that need to be read with a magnifying glass.

To accommodate the user, who happens to be a human who has eyes that can't zoom in to pixel view of a piece of paper, it is important to be able to print documents in a useful size. The Aerial Print View tool allows users to print parts of pages or print pages in sections for full-size reconstruction.

Like many differences between paper and digital documents, you never know what you're missing until it's gone. Single-page digital documents fall short on even simple dual-page documents, where a headline or illustration might span the left and right pages in an open book. The ability to print documents at their original dimensions once again rises to meet the functionality of old-fashioned paper.

Sys-Print

Sys-Print software, published by Sys-Print, Inc., automatically converts high-volume print streams to fully bookmarked PDF documents. This product is aimed at current high-volume printing applications and is therefore designed to accept mainframe output and traditional print languages.

For example, in one demonstration, a 213-MB input file was processed on a 486/66 PC in less than three and a half hours. The resulting PDF file was 61 MB, including bookmarks and reports.

As Jim Ware, VP of Sales & Marketing and co-founder, explains it, "We all come from a publishing background, and we are aiming for completed automated database publishing." The Sys-Print product offers very sophisticated processing of the input streams to produce customized PDF output. We transform SysOut data directly into a bookmarked PDF.

For example, in a payroll application, multiple levels of bookmarks can be generated based on the structure of the mainframe data. Top-level bookmarks might represent regions, second-level bookmarks might represent departments, and third-level bookmarks might represent Social Security numbers.

Compared to traditional greenbar and laser print reports, the user has an infinitely better tool for quickly accessing data.

And for archived data on tape, Sys-Print offers a Data Mining tool because this data can be output as intelligently organized PDF collections, indexed by Catalog for text searching, perhaps printed to CD for distribution, and made available for access in an electronic document system via an Intranet.

Emerge:
Lessons Learned in an Acrobat
Capture Service Bureau

As manager of the Emerge Acrobat Capture Service Bureau, Glenn Gernert has faced and conquered most of the challenges that any potential user may encounter. In this conversation Glenn graciously shares a wealth of practical knowledge:

"One of the first considerations in any job is whether to use PDF Normal or Image + Text format, and when there are any legal ramifications we always recommend the latter. In terms of cost, Image + Text is about one-quarter the cost of full clean-up in PDF Normal. Of course, I+T files are 80-100K per page, while PDF Normal files are about 10K or less per page. So of course, anything going on the Web, we strongly recommend PDF Normal.

"We use a guillotine for de-binding, and we never scan more than 100 pages in a batch. We normally scan at 300 dpi, but below 8 pt. text we consider scanning at 400 dpi. Our process starts with document preparation, which includes debinding and fixing any mutilated pages. We count out 100 page batches and assign a name to the document during scanning, and we all check the process for 100 page batches. We use four or five character names, and use and underscore to separate the sequential numbers. If we have grayscale images to scan, we scan the entire document in binary and then insert the grayscale images by replacing pages in the directory, and then Capture processes the entire document.

"To prepare for clean-up, we stitch the batches back together in Exchange. We feel it's very important to have a single ACD file for editing, rather than try to assemble the pieces at the end of the process.

"Ambia's Compose is worth its weight in gold! On clean documents, Compose makes it very simple to add Bookmarks with the Bookmark by Example feature. Another dynamite feature is the Page Linker for an Index or Table of Contents. The Info-fill features is great for automatically entering all the Document Info fields by merging the files with an ASCII delimited file of information.

"We typically output on CD-ROM, because it is cheap and easy. It's a good idea to create a hybrid CD that can be read on Windows, Mac and UNIX rather than the standard ISO 9660 format. Now that Acrobat 3 includes the Reader with full Search capability, it doesn't make sense to create a CD without using Catalog to create an Index."

Glenn Gernert's Basic Clean-Up Procedures Overview

Each page is comprised of two basic elements: Text and Graphics. Establishing a base for each is the purpose of this help sheet. The following are methods to increase efficiency and accuracy.

Step By Step

I. Establish your base font.

> Before beginning a new document, browse through it and take note of formatting.
>
> Note all column headings, their font/size and bold/italic state.
>
> Note switch of font sizes and styles that are consistent.
>
> Once base font is established, be consistent in its use throughout the document.

II. Clean-up of Text

> Select all text with your short cut key. (CTRL + A)
>
> Set base font for page. (Change ALL text on page to base font)
>
> Set base font size for page. (Change ALL text on page to base font size)
>
> Bold on/off. (Change ALL text on page to bold, then non-bold)
>
> Italics on/off. (Change ALL text on page to italic, then non-italic)
>
> Re-establish any special font size changes and characteristics to the page.
>
> Page numbers and Table/Figure headings should always be text.
>
> CTRL-TAB through highlighted words as final task. (No highlighted words should remain on document, unless specifically placed there.)

III. Dealing with Graphics

> Take note of the graphic elements on the page.
>
> Replace Bullets, Squares, Dashes, and other organizational headings with graphic boxes. (But not numbered paragraphs.)
>
> If spending more than a minute or two deciding how to handle a specific page/graphic, ask for help immediately.

NOTE: Keep in mind that this is a basic outline of how each page could be handled. There are documents you will not be able to use these methods on but overall, this will decrease time spent on proofing and checking each page.

Thanks to Glenn Gernert, Acrobat Capture Service Bureau Manager, EMERGE - http://www.emrg.com

RAELS

The Rapid Access Electronic Library System from Loral Space and Range Systems offers an Acrobat Exchange plug-in called the RAELS PDF Links. This product was developed specifically to save time in creating hyperlinks within very large documents.

Loral estimates that on one task of hyperlinking 250,000 hotspots in a series of related repair manuals that totaled 6,500 pages, almost an entire person-year was saved through the use of PDF Links.

The approach of PDF Links is different from a "link by example" system because it is based on rules rather than examples. The user creates rules in a script that specifies how information is to be connected. For example, complex documents might have several rules to define relations between TOC, illustrations, appendices, footnotes, text and other documents.

The software ships with a Philosophy of Rules to help the user understand how to write simple and effective rules. There is a rule checker that verifies the integrity of user-created scripts. These rules are reusable and can be used on any number of new or updated documents.

Once the rules are created, the PDF Links software automatically applies them and creates links throughout the document and recompiles it to PDF format. PDF Links is also capable of generating automated bookmarks for top-level navigation.

Complete information is available from Loral at:

http://www.loral.com

The user manual is intended to educate the user in rule writing and includes plenty of samples to start with.

PDF Reference Manual: 2nd Edition

Insert link to this epochal document, which is so cool it hardly needs to be updated, just like the pdfmark Reference Manual. Standards don't wiggle like Jell-O, unlike other technology fads.

```
http://www.adobe.com/supportservice/devrelations/PDFS/TN/PDFSPEC.TXT
```

Many of these products are available on the Web for free evaluation. The best places to start looking for commercial Acrobat plug-ins is:

```
http://www.emrg.com.
```

Summary

Every potential new user of the new media comes to the keyboard expecting better access to information. Beyond all the economic and process efficiencies of the new media, every individual user judges it in terms of, "What have you done for me lately?"

A world full of creative page and document designers is nimbly evolving into digital document designers. We can expect to see brilliant innovation in the near and ongoing future.

Business projects and procedures are being automated in this new media, and more efficient information-delivery mechanisms are already working and doing a better job than earlier ways.

Automation of digital document-building techniques and procedures can enable rapid site development. These tools allow automatic navigation building and free the Webmaster from tedious, repetitive tasks of meticulously linking interesting info. These tools can build table of contents, index and other links automatically. This is truly enhanced and improved access to information.

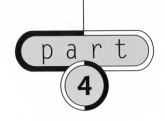

part
4

using
digital
content

organizing digital documents

In this chapter we examine techniques for organizing files to enhance the user's ability to find and retrieve information—almost instantaneously!

The documents themselves are electronic files, and they physically reside on some storage device, whether it be magnetic disk, CD-ROM, optical media or some other form. As files on storage systems, all these documents have file names, such as FILENAME.TXT. For any collection of documents, the limitations of such short file names, or even long file names such as those permitted under UNIX, Mac and Win95, soon become apparent.

To achieve instant access, there is a critical need for a better way to organize files than using simple directory listings of file names.

The ability and tendency of HTML documents to provide dynamic links to other documents is the key difference between Web-centric documents and other document types. As stated earlier, the breakthrough of HTTP links between all of the servers on the Web offers unlimited access to data and knowledge resources. This universal linkage of resource defines the philosophy of Web-centric documents.

This limitless branching, which led to the description of a "Web" originally, presents the contents of libraries as an ongoing succession of lists of hot links. A "normal" Web page looks like a pyramid, or river delta, of previously organized folders of files. The branches of the streams, or lists of files, are the points where hypertext links are connecting separate documents or separate parts in one document.

> **(t i p)**
>
> **The most important understanding of simple HTML linked collections is that they are the products and offerings of a specific author or group. For every link in an HTML document produced by traditional processes, some individual author or editor has made a decision to link two points on the Web. Even in the case of automatically bookmarked files, at some point a decision on the orderliness of the documents has been made. It is for this reason that text search is so important for collections of electronic documents.**

Such singular decision presupposes a singular path and may one day leave a file or a collection of files out on an unconnected island. This dependence upon a single author or publisher is one of the weak links of the Web.

The long-term utility of individual collections can be assured through offline backup of the files. Future researchers will be able to use data-mining software to sift through large collections and retrieve valuable information. But the intent of this book is to create digital collections that have orderliness built in and offer far greater access to the contents than has ever before been possible.

The goal of the Web, whether on Internets or Intranets, is instantly accessible information. On the communications level, this fantastic goal has been achieved. On the user level, the great advantage of HTML is that the linking of files and great collections can be organized through anchors and links.

On the file level, it is very important to consider the contents of the file and what resources will be required on the user's end. Users coming into the Web via modem can't easily handle gigantic files.

Using HTML Documents To Organize Files

The definitive source of information for the structure of HTML is the IETF HTML 2.0 specification. The URL (Universal Resource Locator) of this document is: http://www.w3.org/hypertext/WWW/MarkUp/MarkUp.html. Any user on the Web can select this URL in his browser and view the documentation.

In an HTML document, the name can be marked up as the anchor, and the corresponding link will be the URL. Any user with a Web browser can now retrieve the document by clicking on the marked-up text.

For example, the first paragraph of this section could be modified with one such anchor and link to accomplish this click navigation:

"The definitive source of information for the structure of HTML is the _IETF HTML 2.0 specification._"

The rest of the paragraph is assumed by the user because of the convention of _underlining and highlighting_ text to represent a hyperlink. So, a familiar Web user immediately recognizes the "hot text" of the link as a pointer.

When the HTML source, which is the ASCII characters that make up the HTML document, is viewed, the linked statement appears as:

"The definitive source of information for the structure of HTML is the < A HREF = "http://www.w3.org/hypertext/WWW/MarkUp/MarkUp.html" > IETF HTML 2.0 specification." < /A >

Most HTML editing packages provide a graphical user interface (GUI) that allows statements such as the above to be created with word-processor-like simplicity. For example, selecting a portion of text to serve as the anchor is as easy as selecting text to add bold or underlined attributes. The user is then prompted to enter the linked file or text. For the purposes of explaining the hypertext linking, the ASCII shows the nuts and bolts.

> **(t i p)**
>
> **HTTP Anchors Turn Text Into Links**
>
> **Technically, just like bold or underline, the anchor code is an "attribute" of the highlighted text that serves as the clickable link in the document.**

In HTML, an anchor is defined as an element that points to:

- A specific location in the current document
- Another document
- A specific location in another document

In the previous example, the separate parts of the Anchor are:

Begin anchor (A) element: < A

Hypertext REFerence: HREF =

URL of the Link: "http://www.w3.org/hypertext/WWW/MarkUp/MarkUp.html" >

Highlighted text: IETF HTML 2.0 specification."

End anchor (/A) element: < /A >

The separate parts of the above URL are:

Access method: "http:" means to use HyperText Transfer Protocol

Server name: "//www.w3.org"

Top-level directory: "/hypertext"

Subdirectories: "/WWW/MarkUp"

Linked document: "/MarkUp.html"

It is important to note that in addition to http, other Internet communications functions, or schemes such as ftp (File Transfer Protocol), gopher, and even e-mail through the "mail to:" function can be used to access files with a properly configured browser. Files on a local file server use the scheme called "file" and are accessed as "File:///" in the Browser Location window.

Popular Web home pages are more like magazines than any other publication. Everything is new every week or month. The Adobe site maintains an immediately understood layout, while changing the contents, just like magazine cover pages.

Running the mouse over the varying geography of the image maps (see details on image maps later in this chapter) displays the many geysers of information under the home page.

Anchor Link To A Specific Location

The author or publisher of an HTML document can provide the reader with preordained paths through the document. For example, in a traditional book, this is the equivalent of taking the table of contents and turning it into an instant page locator.

Or, in a word-processing document, every chapter or section heading could appear in a list, and the reader would be able to instantly jump to that area by clicking on the list item. This basic theory of ordering documents is used throughout many sites.

> **tip**
>
> **The outline feature of popular word processors can be easily converted to HTML equivalents. With a little forethought, print and HTML design easily merge.**

This is a core hypertext technique, and it is successfully employed not only in Web documents, but also in many of the online Help files that are included in popular software. In fact, a short review of one or more familiar Help files will provide tips on how professional electronic publishers take advantage of this feature. Most Help files offer two types of navigation, contents and search. In this case, contents is an example of hypertext organization.

However, without any advanced word-processing or electronic publishing tools, it is easy to create HTML files that offer this feature. For example, many FAQs (Frequently Asked Questions lists) follow this format.

There is FAQ for Acrobat 3 at

```
http://www.adobe.com/Acrobat3/acrobat3.html
```

Of course, this means that the document *acrobat3.html* is in the subdirectory (or server) called *Acrobat3*, and it is on the main Adobe Web site at *www.adobe.com*.

The first page of the document consists of a list of hot links, which are arranged in about 10 categories. To make it very simple for the reader to find what he is looking for, the text of each of the anchors is a simple phrase describing the content of that section. In fact, as we see when we read the rest of the document, the anchor text represents the section headings for the rest of the document.

Integrate PDF Files

When the user clicks on a link, he is instantly taken to the chosen point in the document. Clicking on the link below would present the relevant or related text.

```
What do I need to do to serve PDF files a page at a time?
```

There are four pieces to the Acrobat-on-the-Internet picture:

- The Acrobat 3 Reader for integrated viewing of the web
- Web servers that can "byteserve" optimized PDF files a page at a time to the Acrobat Reader
- Optimized PDF files that offer many common-sense advantages over megalithic mega-files: progressive display and maximum file compression
- Web links to connect your PDF files to other content on the Web

This example of a well-prepared HTML document provides many insights about advantages to the user, the most important of which is the ability to quickly find and retrieve the information of interest. Other advantages for both the author and user include ease of construction and efficient transmission.

In Adobe Acrobat, the Bookmarks feature offers the equivalent function to this intra-document organization and provides the same quick navigation features.

Anchor Link To Other Documents

The keystone of the Web is this ability to create source links in a document that point to target links in another document, either as a whole or to a specific location. It was this hyperlinking capability combined with HTTP network communications that created the World Wide Web.

By using the same structure as described above for links between sections of the same document, a page of links can refer to an entire collection of documents. These pages can be organized in several different ways according to the type of documents and the needs of the users.

Simple Lists

The needs of digital document collections may be met by simple lists. This is particularly true in technical and scientific fields, where the information is pre-organized by the subject of the documents.

For example, a manufacturing company may have a series of documents for each of its products. No matter how many manuals are involved in the entire collection, they can be presorted by the subject. All manuals that go to Satellite X are in one list, all that pertain to Rocket Y are in another, and so on.

For example, many times the "patch" software offerings provided by vendors are presented this way on the Web. The reason for this is that users who want these files are highly motivated to find them and don't mind scrolling to do so.

These types of applications lend themselves to simple list organization, and this requires the least amount of effort to organize the files. However, significant value can often be added to the collection if these simple lists are combined with other forms of navigation.

Most professionally produced home pages of big and popular Web sites contain extensive identifying information about the site, some hints on how to use the site, and only a few links. These few links immediately take the user down one of a small number of easily recognized paths.

For example, a software vendor's page will often have the following elements, or categories, each of which offers particular information or services:

What's New!

Software

Upgrades

Support

Hot Stuff!

Another example of this is found on home pages where there may be entire discrete categories of documents. For example, on the Adobe Home Page, it is necessary to present the user with a choice of platforms, so an early branch in the list might be:

Macintosh

Windows 95 and Windows NT

Windows 3.1

OS/2

By choosing one of the early branches, the user is then directed to only the body of files relevant to his needs. This greatly reduces the number of files that the user would otherwise have to review, thereby speeding up the process of locating the desired information.

Mingled Lists

There are many applications where there are many references among the documents that contain links to the same pages. The simplest examples are the marketing pages, where many of the original branches eventually lead back to an order form.

In the above example, "What's New," "Hot Stuff," "Software" and "Support" could all ultimately refer back to the page for "Upgrades," where the user can purchase any or all of the above.

A mingled-list approach can produce an extensively cross-referenced database of HTML documents. The depth and functionality of such mingled lists are limited only by the author's creativity and labors.

Annotated Lists

The following example shows construction, but also more important, *contents*. This annotated list shows how useful short comments can be in finding interesting information. It also shows the early state-of-the-art of this list with the relatively recent dates of some of the oldest electronic text sources on the list.

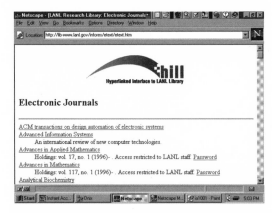

Annotated lists allow rapid browsing through large collections. Note that both public and password-protected files appear.

When reading an online document, you can simply copy the text of a URL address and paste it into the location field on your browser. With a single carriage return, you go right to the copied link.

The Los Alamos Research Library provides an annotated list of electronic text sources at this site:

http://lib-www.lanl.gov/infores/etext/etext.html

To access the Administrative Manual, you need to have Adobe Acrobat installed on your system or local server. For more information, contact the LANL Index Project by sending e-mail to index@lanl.gov. The following are hyperlinks.

| Los Alamos Administrative Manual |

The Los Alamos Research Library contains these references:

| Discover Magazine |

Table of contents to current and back issues with some full-text articles.

| Fortune |

Tables of contents and some full text since Sept. 1996. (sic)

| Internet Resources Newsletter |

A monthly newsletter of links to new Internet resources.

| Macweek |

Full text of articles beginning with January 1995. Some of the articles may contain hypertext links.

| New York Times |

Today's New York Times. Registration is required for free access.

| Optical and Quantum Electronics |

A trial subscription.

| Science |

Summaries/abstracts of items in Science since October 1995, with full text of This Week in Science: Research Highlights. Contents only for June 30-September 19, 1995.

| U.S. Code |

Experimental searchable version of the entire U.S. Code (with amendments through Jan. 4, 1993).

| U.S. News & World Report |

Online version with top stories, etc. Includes the annual College Fair with rankings.

| Directory of Electronic Journals |

Gopher and URL addresses for electronic journals and newsletters; list is maintained by Association of Research Libraries.

"Speed Dialer" Links

To speed up access to very long lists, "speed dialer" links can be built into the document. For example, in a list organized alphabetically, users can be prompted to click on a letter of the alphabet to move directly to that section of the long list.

By providing this simple toolbar, rapid navigation is available:

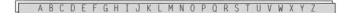

A B C D E F G H I J K L M N O P Q R S T U V W X Y Z

Eliminate scrolling through long lists with Pushbutton Dash. The same techniques can be used for other long, orderly lists such as date order lists or numerical lists.

Special Uses Of Links

Hot links can be used for many other functions to make the document more accessible to the reader. For example, a series of buttons can be used to perform the handy functions of Page Forward and Page Back. In this usage, the hot link takes the user to a specific page or to the previous or following page.

The well-rendered HTML version of "As We May Think" demonstrates this type of functionality. The buttons are unobtrusive but still allow smooth full-page turning as an alternative to scrolling vertically through the pages.

An authorized copy of this spectacular, future-predicting article from Atlantic Monthly 50 years ago is available at:

http://info.cs.vt.edu/AWMT/

This approach can also be used to allow instant access to any special pages in a document. For example, every page can offer a button to go to the table of contents, or to an index, or to any other frequently visited page or function set.

Building Organization Into New Documents

It is always a good idea to capture as much structural information from a file as possible. The simplest example is capturing the Document Information fields from a word-processing file, including everything from the author's name to the source application and system information. Ideally, as much of this baseline information as possible should be accessible via search techniques.

Title, Subject, Author and many other standard fields might serve as great hyperlinks for future users, and they are easy to include.

The Meta field in HTML files may be adapted to carry this type of information. In "encapsulated formats" such as PDF, much of this information can be readily captured from the source applications and fully exploited in a Web database.

Using Images to Organize Files

During the first week of May 1996, Adobe Systems introduced a new Web page that takes advantage of all the latest extensions currently available on the Web to present at once an attractive visual page and a highly interactive hyperlink menu.

Any graphics program, such as Illustrator or Photoshop, can be used to create graphically rich and appealing presentation pages. These attractive pages can then be used as image maps, which allow the user to navigate by clicking on a certain area on the page. Image maps function by watching the position of the cursor and assigning a specific URL to specific areas of the page.

In this way the most gorgeous traditional graphic pages can be used as a precisely defined grid of "pushbutton" hyperlinks in HTML. From the most mundane usage, where a schematic drawing may be hot linked to each component in the drawing, allowing a user to click on a certain point in the graphic and be instantly linked to relevant files...to the very attractive and pleasant-to-use file folder metaphors common to Windows applications ... image maps offer a very friendly navigation style. To view the HTML code for an image map, simply chose View Source Code from your Web browser.

Converting to HTML Structure

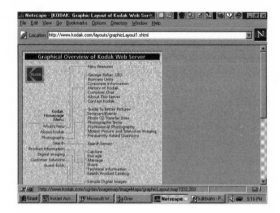

This page offers a graphic layout to a large, complex Web site through a simple image map
of a conventional organization table.

It is completely feasible to mimic the current organization and present the user with a
series of ordered lists of the contents. Just as in a card catalog, the user can search by
author, title and subject.

Of course, every digital collection will face a unique set of challenges, and many will
only have file names to start from. Assuming that the files contain the common word-
processing fields of Title, Author and Subject, all of this document-management information can be reused when moving to HTML pages.

Separate lists for each of the three categories would provide instant links to the source
files. A simple automatic process could link the same source file, via its unique URL,
to each of the Index fields. This allows the user to retrieve files through all of the traditional Title, Author and Subject fields.

> **tip**
>
> **By viewing a list of files, the user can simply click to read a
> chosen file and then click Back to view the list again.**

Convert your directory listing (DIR) to an HTML structure with hot-linked file names by copying names to a home page. Most home pages are stored under a specific server and top-level directory. This means that the base directory appears after the primary URL.

The key is to convert each directory to hyperlinks under the following convention:

```
http://www.ISP.com/HomePage/Index.html.
```

By not renaming your home page, you can shorten your URL to the first term after the home server.

Directory list		Universal Resource Locator List
filenam1.htm	=	http:\\www.ISP.com\HomePage\filenam1.htm
filenam2.htm	=	http:\\www.ISP.com\HomePage\filenam2.htm
filenam3.htm	=	http:\\www.ISP.com\HomePage\filenam3.htm

In the above example, filenam1.htm and so forth are directory names. By converting directory and file names to hypertext links, hierarchical sets of files can be automatically generated. For example, filenam1.htm might refer to all Acrobat files, filenam2.htm might be all Photoshop files, filenam3.htm all PageMill files and so on. The point is that entire directories can be converted to branches on hypertext trees.

Everything under each limb is linked in the same way, like the veins on a leaf, like the tributaries of a river, like neurons and axons. HTML is a software model of endless complexity, via simple branches.

The above routine converts a directory list to a series of URLs, or Universal Resource Locators. A URL connects a file on any attached server to the World Wide Web or to an Intranet Web. It's a message that never gets old: The Internet is a real network, with an infinite number of shared servers.

blast from the past

By clicking on a link, the user instantly retrieves the document. Compared to the traditional method of using the card catalog and then walking the aisles and searching the shelves of a physical library, the online catalog in a digital library can deliver the document directly to the user's desktop. Don't underestimate the fact that the library can actually be any spot in the world that is linked to the global Internet.

> **tip**
>
> **Since the Web Internet is a real network, many times the hard-wired lists we are describing here are actually generated "on the fly" when the results of a directory listing are served up to the user.**

All the provider has to do is create an attachment to the URL link by including the full path to the document from the Web. The Web server software takes care of all the technical details, such as the real IP address of the server as registered with the Inter-NIC and so on. Authors and publishers can build upon current network directory structures through this conversion of actual file names to Universal Resource Locators by connecting LAN and WAN systems to the Internet and Intranets.

Utilizing TOC, Index, Glossary, Appendices

The internal structure and built-in organization of many documents provide users with powerful, albeit manual, methods for the nimble handling of large quantities of information. Once again reaffirming the theme of this book, digital documents should work better than the traditional equivalents.

- Table of contents should offer elevator access → rapid level changes
- Index should offer escalator, level-by-level access → sequential changes
- Glossary, appendix should be value-added tools → universal access

Based on the principle that any hot link in a hypertext document can lead to anyplace else, whether it be a page or a library, HTML is built to offer author-published collections of files with a pre-defined series of links and logical paths through the documents.

Summary

There are a few principles of electronic document design that are just common sense:

- Make navigation tools always available; don't strand the reader in a sea of info.
- Make the reading as "thoughtless" as possible, as natural as possible, "just like a book."
- Deliver the desired information first, and presentation later.

html

documents:

creation,

editing,

management

PageMill: The Web Page Builder

Adobe PageMill was originally released for the Mac and later for Windows. It is designed to give even beginning Web authors simple and powerful tools for creating Web pages. The graphical user interface exposes all of the variables and formats of HTML, freeing the author from the need to learn the coding scheme.

The most important thing to understand about authoring HTML documents is that you are creating *content*, not *appearance*. This is not a vague philosophical statement; it is a fact of the HTML standards. The author can control such organizational (content-related) information as levels of headers, as well as such presentation elements as bold, italic, underline and so on. But unlike paper document production technology, the author can't control the actual appearance to the end user.

This is because in HTML and browser thinking, the end user is encouraged to choose his own presentation. As an HTML page downloads, it calls for only general behavior, and the user can configure his browser to utilize certain fonts and attributes. A general language is transmitted to the Web client, whether that client be Mac, Windows, UNIX or even character-based clients like LYNX. The local client displays your "universal" HTML Web documents in locally available fonts and graphics.

Text Enhancements

Text can be typed directly into the HTML editor, or HTML documents created elsewhere may be imported into PageMill for editing and enhancement. Plug-ins are available for importing other popular document types. Also, applications that support drag-and-drop copying allow quick pasting of files into PageMill.

To make information more easily accessible, or to achieve an attractive appearance, HTML text can be modified and enhanced. The two types of modifications are paragraph formats, to indicate headings, body text, lists and so on; and character formats, which enhance selected characters and words.

Paragraph Formats

- Paragraph format is the standard plain format for body text.
- Pre-formatted format is used for displaying fixed-width spacing to maintain all original spaces from a source document, such as a financial report or the output from a mainframe print file.
- Address format is used for email or postal addresses or phone numbers.

- Heading formats are available for the six levels available in HTML. Heading sizes are relative to one another, and their actual display is determined by the browser. Relative sizes ranging smallest, smaller, small, large, larger and largest are the six levels available, and in general the largest header is used for the main heading on a page.

- The List formats allow the user to create various types of lists, including Bullet, Directory, Menu and Numbered. Outline style lists containing multiple levels can be formed with the Indent command, and PageMill automatically assigns a different bullet or numbering style to each level. A feature that is very handy for glossary-type lists is Term and Definition List format, where the term appears flush left and the definition is indented beneath the term.

Paragraph alignment can be selected as left, center or right alignment, but not all browsers support the latter two displays.

Character Styles

There are two types of character styles, called physical and logical character styles. In Adobe PageMill, characters or words can be selected through the familiar method of using the mouse to select text by highlighting. When a style is selected by button or pull-down menu, it is applied to the highlighted text.

The physical character styles display the same across most browsers and allow the author to determine how specific text will appear. The four physical character styles are the familiar text attributes of plain, bold and italic, with the addition of a monospaced font called Teletype.

The logical character styles will appear in the flavor of the particular browser based on the way that browser interprets the label. The following logical styles are available:

- *Emphasis* calls attention to text, often represented as *italic*.

- *Strong* is a stronger form of Emphasis, often represented as *bold*.

- *Citation* is intended for titles of published documents and other media.

- *Sample* is used to depict computer status messages, usually monospaced.

- *Keyboard* is used to indicate where the user would enter text, monospaced.

- *Code* is used to represent computer code, monospaced.

- *Variable* is used to represent where text should be entered in an application.

Font sizes, like heading levels, are relative. Right now, only Netscape supports font size changes, so other browsers will not display this effect. For that reason, you should consider restricted use of this feature for special effects.

Relative font sizes allow the author to change font size in relation to surrounding text, even though HTML does not allow specifying the actual size for every browser. When absolute presentation control is required, Acrobat PDF is the Web format of choice.

Page Enhancements

Frames

Frames divide the browser window in separate sections, which can be edited separately, and the end user can sometimes scroll through a frame separately while other frames remain in place.

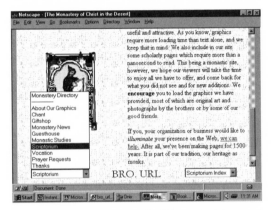

Frames are used on this page to allow user to point to the slider on the right to read a column of independently scrolling text while the graphic and JavaScript buttons at the bottom stay in their original places. Notice there are no borders on the frames. In this screen, the JavaScript pull-down on the left has opened a menu for quick navigation or other functions, such as making online purchases from the gift shop.

On many popular pages, such as the search engines and constantly updated vendor home pages like Adobe's, frames are used to constantly bring new articles to the user's attention. Pages such as these naturally draw mostly repeat visitors, so the Webmaster is challenged to keep the site interesting and attractive. Once again, this process is very much like a that of magazine or newspaper, where the basic format stays the same but the content is always changing.

Tables

Tables are the spreadsheet format of HTML, and they are likewise comprised of cells, columns, rows and a caption. But tables are not just for numerical information or lists; they can be used to organize many forms of information on a page.

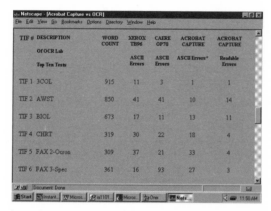

Tables can be used on simple charts to assure that columns of numbers will be aligned and easily readable on any browser.

Richer tables can contain graphics, columnar text, links, backgrounds and other elements in a clear presentation layout.

Tables can be imported Microsoft Excel tables, or they can be easily built with tools that will be familiar to anyone who has ever used a spreadsheet. PageMill offers simple visual tools for creating and modifying tables. A click on the Create Table icon allows the user to specify the number of rows and columns, along with such other basics as cell spacing, padding and border size. Cell spacing determines the amount of space between cells, which is the shaded line between cells. Cell padding specifies the distance between a cell's contents and the edge of the cell. Spacing and padding are measured in pixels.

A border can be added to a table to distinguish it from the rest of the page, and both the table width and the cell widths can be specified in pixels or percentages. Individual cells can be resized with the mouse by dragging the double-arrow pointer on the cell edge. Cells can also be joined to create larger cells that span multiple rows and/or columns in the original grid of same-size cells. These larger cells are typically used to include headings or images or other special elements. A caption can be added to either the top or bottom of the table to describe the contents.

The contents of a cell can be text, images, links or any other valid HTML element. Text can be entered directly, or objects may be simply dragged and dropped into a cell using the familiar cut-and-paste method. Each cell must be formatted separately, using the same techniques as those used to format text on a page, which means that character styles and paragraph formats can be applied to cells, as well as the alignment, color and relative font size of the cell's contents. In Adobe PageMill, the Inspector offers radio button convenience for specifying cell width, vertical and horizontal alignments and backgrounds, as well as check boxes to specify a header cell or no wrap within the cell.

Efficient Editing

Many elements can be used over and over in the Web site. Often-used specific objects such as navigation bars, logos and indexes can be easily referenced rather than copied to each page. The philosophy should be along the lines of, "Build it once, use it forever, as needed."

In PageMill, objects can be copied to the Pasteboard and used repetitively as needed throughout a page design and building session.

Backgrounds, Graphics, Multimedia

John Warnock, Chairman and CEO of Adobe, demonstrates easy animated GIF creation using Adobe Illustrator, Adobe Photoshop and GIFbuilder shareware at:

http://www.adobe.com/studio/tipstechniques/GIFanimation/main.html

A good practice is to limit images to 480 pixels, which is the default width of a Netscape window when displayed on a 13-inch monitor. This is the lowest common denominator of Web browsers and ensures that the images will be useful for the greatest possible number of people.

The Adobe PageMill 2.0 Guide lists the following link for a 216-color non-dithering palette that is completely compatible with both Mac and Windows browsers. This palette has been posted by Lynda Weinman, author of *Designing Web Graphics*:

http://www.lynda.com

An invaluable resource is available that compares various image treatments for online display of every type of image from photos to text. There is no substitute for seeing exactly how it looks on the Web. This set of pages will save you tons of time, and the sturdy conclusions are supported by a dozen samples of various treatments on the same image.

- **Continuous tone images: JPEG with medium or low quality**
- **Flat-color images (anti-aliased): GIF with a minimum of colors, no dither**
- **Black-and-white images: GIF with very few colors, six colors work well**
- **Gradations: JPEG medium is best for maximum number of colors**

http://www.adobe.com/studio/tipstechniques/GIFJPGchart/main.html

(Photography by Doug Menuez/Illustration by Woods & Woods Design/B&W image from Image Club.)

Embedding PDFs And Other Media Elements

Adobe PageMill uses the same plug-ins as Netscape Navigator to handle multimedia elements such as Acrobat PDF, Quick Time video, and various sound files such as AU, AIFF, AIFC and WAV, as well as other media elements. As long as the supporting applications are installed in the PageMill Plug-ins folder, the process for embedding such media objects is very straightforward.

The toolbar offers the Place Object button, or the user can pull down the File — > Place option to enter an object at the cursor point on the page. Images, movies or sounds can also be copied from the Pasteboard, which is handy for repetitive objects that are used on many pages.

When adding images to pages, users with character-based browsers, or those who choose to turn off graphics, should be accommodated by inserting an image label within the browser. This gives the reader of the page an idea of what appears in the missing image space. Parts of images may be made transparent to blend with the page, and the images may be resized to better fit the page. It must be noted that resizing does not affect the size of the image because it is not downsampling the image to a smaller file. Adobe Photoshop can be employed for such advanced manipulations. Images can also be used as page backgrounds to create a dramatic effect. This technique must be carefully employed so that text is not difficult to read.

Interlaced images are specifically designed to enhance the end user's experience by downloading the entire image in a form that gradually reveals the details of the image rather than painting it line by line over an empty white space. Adobe PageMill offers a clickable icon that creates interlaced images from standard GIF images.

tip

The Download Statistics tool under the Edit menu in PageMill shows approximately how long it will take to download a particular object at a range of connection speeds, from a slow 9.6 KB per second (9600 baud) to full ISDN speed of 128 KB per second.

T Working With JavaScripts

PageMill 2.0 does not test or preview JavaScripts but may alter HTML inside the scripts if Tags are included. To avoid this, the place holder feature of PageMill 2.0 should be used:

To add a place holder:

1. Open the page in a text editor before you open it in PageMill.

2. Immediately before the script, add the comment < !—NOEDIT— > to your file.

3. Immediately after the script, add a < !—/NOEDIT— > comment.

4. Save the page; then open it in PageMill.

The NOEDIT comments tell PageMill to leave the enclosed HTML alone so that your script can not be altered.

Management with SiteMill

Adobe SiteMill brings drag-and-drop functionality to the task of managing large and complex Web sites. The contents of most Web sites will follow the model of a magazine, where the collection changes constantly, rather than a model of books in a library, where the information remains static. Even Web sites that primarily serve the role of digital libraries will most likely have changing contents such as updates and new additions. And of course, just as with magazines, there is a need to provide access to archives of previously published articles. (Adobe SiteMill for Mac and Windows includes all of the page-authoring and editing functionality of PageMill.)

In a state of such dynamic flux, it becomes a challenge to maintain the links between growing collections of interrelated documents. In a traditional database management approach, all of the links within a collection of HTML documents comprise singular indexes of links between individual documents.

For example, a technical manual often contains many references to certain drawings, procedures or further reference materials. Adobe SiteMill provides a site view that examines all of the links within a collection and provides great help for managing changing Web collections, and repetitive links.

Whenever either end of a link is changed, SiteMill alerts the Webmaster and provides a simple drag-and-drop means of cleaning up any broken links.

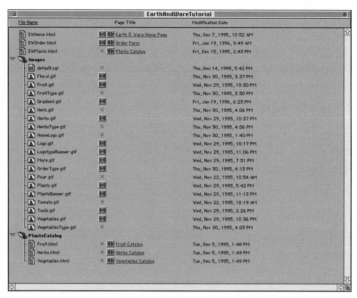

SiteMill provides vital information about links between pages in your site, all in one bird's eye view.

Links In Large HTML Collections

HTML links will be subject to dynamic change as new documents are added to the collection. The entire concept of "new" documents should be directed to all documents entering the collections, not necessarily just the latest "new" documents added to the collection.

Adobe SiteMill provides a visual layout of all of the connections between various links and pages, including error views that indicate broken links and stranded, unlinked documents.

Compared with simply adding files to the directory or file structure, this organizing software provides views into the relationships between files. This type of view of the entire site should be considered an absolute requirement for any successful, ongoing Web site.

As files change, and even as versions of files replace earlier versions, it is crucial to maintain links to the most valuable information on a site. As both source and reference sites evolve and change their contents and URL addresses, Adobe SiteMill tracks these changes programmatically and offers fixes in a graphical display.

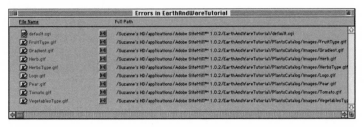

SiteMill summarizes error messages and shows file paths to facilitate site management.

Summary

The enhancements discussed in this book are primarily directed at making the information within a Web site more accessible to end users, rather than concentrating strictly on the presentation of the information. However, tools like Adobe PageMill serve both purposes by vastly simplifying the tasks of the Web page author.

Drag-and-drop functionality encourages experimentation, and the ability to easily copy and reuse elements throughout a Web site or HTML document not only saves time, but also adds an identity that allows the user to feel comfortable. For example, a navigation bar, like that seen on the Adobe Web site and others, offers a quick and convenient way of taking full advantage of all of the resources on a site.

Most Web authors will already be familiar with using the mouse to select text and graphics and using drag-and-drop techniques for copying. These simple techniques are extended to all of the functions necessary to create Web pages and manage Web sites with Adobe PageMill and SiteMill.

Dynamic change is the nature of the Web, and every Webmaster will face the responsibility of maintaining order and functionality in this environment. Adobe SiteMill provides a graphic depiction of all the documents and links on an entire Web site, making this a very manageable task.

part
5

advanced
resource
guide

advanced searching techniques

chapter twelve

Advanced text searching tries to mimic the way humans remember and find things. These techniques try to overcome the "yes/no" and "on/off" nature of computer information. Databases require the user to know exactly how a word or term appears in the data, and usually he also must know which field the data appears in. The nature of the information in document management systems will often not be bent to such narrow indexes.

For this reason, libraries of digital information are expected to offer this human-like accessibility. The user thinks: "If I'm going to a digital library, I expect to be able to search every single word in every book in the whole library. Otherwise, I could just go to the old library with the paper card catalog."

This is perhaps a primal reaction to computers: "Okay, if you're so smart, prove it." If the computer is hard to use, or if the user can't find what he is looking for, the computer is the dumb partner, not the user.

| example |

People expect to be able to search for ideas much the way they do in common conversation:

DAVE: I want to read about that inventor who made those great spy planes...

HAL: Did he build the Blackbird spy planes?

DAVE: Right, and he built the P-38 and the U-2.

HAL: Did he work for Lockheed?

DAVE: Right, Lockheed Skunkworks.

HAL: Kelly Johnson appears in most articles on the Skunkworks and Blackbird, so you must be looking for Kelly Johnson.

In the above example, we used celebrity stand-ins from the Stanley Kubrick film 2001: A Space Odyssey. The human star was Dave, and the famous movie star computer was HAL9000. Advanced text-searching systems provide the kind of access that was fantasized about in this 1969 sci-fi epic and Academy Award-winning movie.

Methods For Advanced Searching

In a recent interview, Phillippe Courtot, CEO of Verity, Inc., one of the world's leading text search vendors, explained the goals of text-searching systems: "When the user asks the question, 'Who is the president?,' they want the answer! They don't want documents. They want 'Bill Clinton.' "

Traditional text-search engines bring back a series of articles. The user then reads the articles and arrives at the answer, or the information he sought. Courtot is referring to the next step of automation, where the computer reads the articles and brings back the answer. Here again, we are asking the computer to perform a human function; we are trying to mimic or automate thinking. This is a fundamental key of true instant access. This section goes beyond the basic searching capabilities of the Acrobat family by introducing compatible search features by other developers: natural query language, concept searching, fuzzy logic, intelligent agents and more.

There's a great article on this subject called "Chatterbots, Tinymuds, and the Turing Test: Entering the Loebner Prize Competition," by Michael L. Mauldin of the Center for Machine Translation at Carnegie-Mellon University. The content areas include: natural language processing, believable interactive characters, the Turing test, and the philosophy of AI.

Find this article on the Web via the URL, or search for the author and title!

http://fuzine.mt.cs.cmu.edu/mlm/aaai94.html

tip

Two levels of query expansion:

Lexical: Word stemming, wildcards, fuzzy, pattern recognition

Logical: Word thesaurus, dictionary, concept relations

For example, if you were searching for the "inventor of copiers," a lexical expansion would modify the individual search terms by narrowing them down to root words and then adding pieces to that root. The term "inventor" would at least be reduced to "invent" and all versions such as invented, invention and so on. With right and left truncation, or word stemming, other terms such as vented, inventory, prevention and so on might be created from the core form of the word. These types of query expansions may or may not help you find the "inventor of copiers."

On the other hand, a lexical expansion might offer you additional meanings of the query term. Perhaps a thesaurus or dictionary would suggest the word "xerography" in place of "copier" and lead to Chester Carlson.

In a nutshell, lexical expands the specific query term or word, while logical expands the meaning of the original query.

235

Natural Language Query

A natural language query capability allows you to "speak" to the computer in the same language commonly used to speak to humans. This is usually accomplished by a program that "parses" the user input query by stripping out stopwords and inferring relationships between the words in the query.

Stopwords are words that are purposely ignored in many text search engines; they usually include prepositions (of, in, to) and articles (the, a, an). The reason they are ignored is that they are considered too common in most collections to be useful, and the index can be made smaller and faster by ignoring them.

As an alternative to the more formal language of Boolean queries, natural language queries are especially helpful for new and unfamiliar users. With the widespread adoption of text-searching applications on the Web and everywhere else, the ability to form Boolean queries may one day become as common as the ability to type on a keyboard, but in the meantime, natural language query capability will be highly desirable.

For efficiency, experienced users may always rely on the more structured Boolean query language because the results are highly predictable and the terms can be controlled and modified with great precision.

The Excite Web searcher is available at:

For a taste of how a natural language query text-searching system performs, the Excite for Web Servers software runs on many Web sites, including the Adobe site. The Excite Web search engine is also available to search the Web itself.

http://www.excite.com

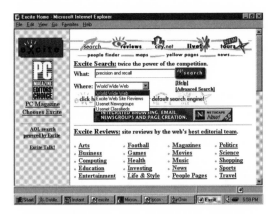

Excite is designed to help the user who may not know exact topics or keywords.

Concept Searching

If a computer is going to think like a human, then it should be able to handle many related ideas as if they are all part of one big concept. This is the quantum leap where advanced text searching loses the surly bonds of conventional computer databases.

On a very mechanical level, a form of concept searching can be handled by simple, brute force techniques. Wildcards are the original brute force technique. Searching with wildcards can extensively plumb the depths of text collections. Many text searchers use word stemming as a built-in wildcard function, and simple word or term entries are automatically expanded.

What wildcards and stemming do on an individual word level, concept searching does on the entire query level. In a concept search, the user can enter a number of words or terms of interest, and the software will expand these particular terms in a number of logical ways.

| example |

Building on the Dave and Hal interaction:

The term "spy planes" might expand via a thesaurus to include the most popular terms such as Blackbird, U-2, Stealth and so on. The advanced text-search software serves up Blackbird as a potential "expanded" search topic.

By having the computer continue the conversation, by sensitively mention-ing relevant topics, the text search proceeds in a way that intuitively blends the user's intentions with the computer's ability.

For a look at Vector Space Similarity Searching, try Fulcrum's Web site:

http://www.fultext.com

Automatic Summary

When talking to another person, large bodies of information can be assumed in just a few words.

───────────────────────| example |───────────────────────

DAVE: Do you know the fastest planes that were ever built?

HAL: Yes, I'm a big fan of all forms of supersonic flight. Which ones are you most interested in? The experimental planes, the military planes or other high-performance aircraft?

DAVE: I'd like to know about the fastest plane that takes off and lands like a regular plane and gets the fastest speed records.

HAL: Do you mean sustained speed, operational speed or some special post-to-post race speed ?

DAVE: I mean the plane that is the fastest overall. The fastest plane in my definition has the highest number of common, day-in and day-out missions that register the highest speeds and altitudes.

HAL: The SR-71 Blackbird appears in the majority of highest absolute speed records for conventional aircraft.

Automatic summary provides assistance in understanding the contents of the hit articles. In a way, this can be considered a form of advanced browsing rather than searching. Rather than just providing a ranked list of hit terms in response to a query, automatic summary will write a small report or abstract of each hit.

For some applications, these summaries may provide all of the information necessary from the hit articles and save you time retrieving and reading each article. In the example above, each of the iterations of the computer's response in the form of HAL's conversation reveals progressive summaries of the information available. Based on these summaries, Dave can quickly move to the articles that are of primary interest.

Fuzzy Logic

DAVE: I wonder what is the fastest plane that I could fly on?

HAL: Fly on as a regular passenger, or a custom flight on some special deal, or just what is physically possible ?

DAVE: What plane flies faster than anything else, that I personally, a non-pilot, could actually fly in?

HAL: Of a number of two-seater supersonic aircraft, the fastest is the SR-71B trainer. It can exceed Mach 3 in normal flight.

Fuzzy logic can be thought of as an "Expanded Or" search, where you want to find as many of your query terms as possible, but not necessarily all of them. Fuzzy logic attempts to perform the rough grouping that a human mind can.

In the example, the original query has to do with the fastest plane ride theoretically available. After one iteration, the query is narrowed down to a more focused search. This second search effectively finds the fastest planes and then narrows that down to planes with at least one passenger seat.

Another form of fuzzy logic that is relevant to text searching is the ability to recognize incomplete hits in the text. This can be very important where documents contain errors or variables in the words and terms. For example, documents that are converted through optical character recognition (OCR) may have many misrecognized characters within words.

These types of errors can not be completely compensated for by wildcards and word stemming because there is no way to predict where the errors may occur. If the error occurs in the stem word, these methods are ineffective.

Fuzzy logic in this case effectively does a wildcard-type search, where any of the letters in the words may be the wildcard. The fuzzy logic determines that if the hit term has at least some of the characters of the query term, it may be a valid hit.

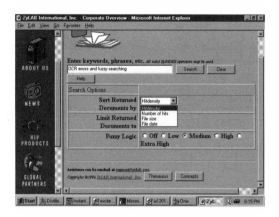

To take a tour of fuzzy logic text-searching capability with a specific adaptation to overcome OCR errors, try ZyLab's Web site:

http://www.zylab.com

ZyLab offers ZyIndex, one of the venerable and perhaps most popular of traditional text search engines. Since Jon Karlin added document-imaging capability and many other updated features, a new product ZyImage has emerged as a uniquely well-integrated solution for scanning, recognition and text retrieval.

Semantic Word Relationships

In the previous examples, we discussed using a thesaurus to perform a concept search. For example, rather than searching for a "shoe" we could search for many kinds of shoes simultaneously. The query for "shoe" would also search for "boot," "sandal," "sneaker" and so on because all of the terms might occur in a thesaurus listing of the term "shoe."

To get a feel for semantic searching that employs dictionaries as well as thesauri and gives you the opportunity to choose the expanded query terms, try the Dataware Technologies or Excalibur Technologies Web sites:

http://www.dataware.com
http://www.excalib.com

In semantic searching, the terms can be expanded to a whole class of objects of the original query. In this type of concept search, or expanded term searching, "shoe" could be any article of clothing, not just something worn on the feet. Now the query "shoe" may also search for "hat," "gloves," "coat" and so on.

This prosaic example of "shoe" is overly simple. Loftier examples might include searching for "passion" in Shakespeare's plays, where the query "passion" is expanded to include all the array of emotions between love and hate, fear and joy, and the words and concepts that portray passion.

Intelligent Agents

Intelligent agents are also known as persistent searches, which continuously or period-ically perform the same queries, which may employ any of the methods discussed previously.

For example, the intelligent agent could be constructed by a user to collect specific in-formation from any number of sources. This is particularly relevant in constantly up-dating pools of new information. A very simple example of this functionality is offered by the automated clipping services that will constantly watch any number of news feeds and immediately tag any article that matches the query, just as traditional clipping services have done on paper.

Web robots and spiders are specialized forms of intelligent agents that constantly roam the Web and bring back indexes of the information available at certain URLs. Many of the large Web search engines employ these Web robots and spiders to con-tinuously search and map the World Wide Web. In effect, the spider replaces a large number of humans doing manual searches and creating infinite bookmarks pointing to interesting information on the Web. Every user of the search engine enjoys the beneficial results of the labor of these tireless bots.

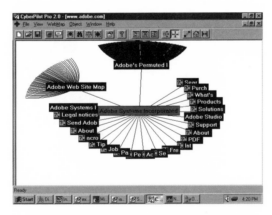

For the searcher who doesn't want to surf, a personal info-gathering bot like NetCarta's CyberPilot Pro maps
Web sites for enhanced insight into contents.

Relevance Ranking And
Term Weighting

Relevance ranking refers to the order in which the hit list is presented to the user. The feature is designed to save the user time by presenting the most "relevant" documents first. Some search engines offer relevance ranking on the fly, such as Acrobat Search's "Rank By" option.

Term weighting allows the user to assign more or less importance to each term in the query, thereby directly modifying the relevance of each term.

Relevance ranking refers to the way the results of a query are returned to the user. There are many ways to determine relevance, and each vendor tends to offer a variation on the theme.

In general, the purpose of relevance ranking is to present the user with the documents that are most likely to satisfy the intent of the query. Because there are many methods of determination, and several search engines actually use more than one method, the rank is often determined numerically.

There are other ways of determining relevancy, and each vendor's approach to the question is described in the vendor profiles at my Intelligent Imaging site:

Relevance rank may be determined by:

Total number of hits in the document;

Hit density which is determined by hits vs. total terms in the document;

Hit clustering which is determined by adjacency of the hits;

All of the query terms appear, rather than many instances of one or two terms.

http://www.onix.com/tonymck/ocrlab.htm

Term weighting is a way for the user to add emphasis to certain terms in the query, to add relative importance to particular terms or words. In effect, term weighting allows the user to influence or completely determine the relevance ranking of hit documents.

For example, if a user is searching for information on the SR-71 Blackbird reconnais-
sance plane, he might use term weighting to tailor the search to return only the most
likely relevant documents. If the following three query terms are used, each could
have separate weighting:

Query: SR-71 + + +, Blackbird +, Beatles---

In this case, three (+) or three (-) would be maximum positive and negative
weighting for relevance:

SR-71 + + +   Most important term; return every document with this term.

Blackbird +   Neutral importance term; may be relevant; return hits.

Beatles---   Least important term; not likely to be relevant to the query.

> **(t i p)**
>
> **Always take at least a quick look at the user guide whenever
> using a new search engine. They all perform similar functions,
> but they all have their idiosyncrasies. For adding emphasis to
> a term, they may agree to "+" as the identifying operator,
> but that doesn't mean they agree that the "+" appears at
> the beginning or end of the term. For example, +agree or
> agree+?**

Advanced Text Searching
In Action

In this section, we'll show advanced searching in action to achieve instant access. You
should concentrate on the contents of your electronic document system while considering the usefulness of the features discussed here.

At the heart of this discussion, consider simple and advanced text searching to have a
relationship comparable to that between arithmetic and advanced mathematics.
While the truth of arithmetic operations is never compromised by advanced calculus,
the formulae of calculus can arrive at solutions that would be extremely tedious or

even impossible to arrive at by extensive arithmetic operations. In a similar way, many of the advanced text-search features described here are often actually automated or combined operations of simple Boolean text-search operations.

Exploiting Verity Search: A Boolean Primer

In 1961, the late Gerard Salton received a grant funding his group's research into information retrieval (IR). His test bed, SMART, is the most widely used research tool in the field in the 35 years since its inception. Dr. Salton is one of the leaders, if not the leader, in the field of IR.

Boolean search can be complicated for the uninitiated but worth the effort for improving search results. The following techniques can be used alone or in combination with other search methods.

Expressions Within Fields

All of the Boolean functions described earlier in this book operate within Document Info fields the same way as they do in text searching. This of course means that the And, Or, Not operators can be used singly or in combination to retrieve a group of documents.

For example, for a system managing software documentation, the user might enter "Adobe **Or** Microsoft **Or** Oracle" in the Author field to retrieve all files produced by those three vendors.

For more information on the pioneering work in the field of pattern recognition in general, and specifically in text searching, visit Cornell on the Web. Start at this page, and then backspace to /Info and resume your browsing:

`http://www.cs.cornell.edu/Info/Faculty/Gerard_Salton.html`

 **Special Operators For Document Info Fields**

The following operators are designed to be used only with the Document Info fields:

Operator	Semantics
=	matches exactly (for text, numeric and date values)
~	contains (for text values)
!=	does not contain (for text, numeric and date values)
<	is less than (for date or numeric values)
<=	is less than or equal to (for date or numeric values)
>	is greater than (for date or numeric values)
>=	is greater than or equal to (for date and numeric values)

The comparison operators "<," "<=," ">" and ">=" function just like the mathematical relations that they symbolize, namely less than, less than or equal to, greater than and greater than or equal to. These operators can be used only with values of the same type because, as everyone knows, you can't compare apples and oranges. Therefore, these operators can be used only with date or numeric values.

In terms of text, the new operators just refine earlier Boolean operators. The = operator provides for an exact text match for the entire field, while the ~ (tilde) operator simply requires that the search term be contained somewhere within the field. The != for text is equivalent to the Not operator for exact matches.

Expressions Within Multiple Fields

A query can be designed to use Boolean operators and multiple Document Info fields. As mentioned earlier, the large size of the Find text box suggests the extended queries that can be built in Acrobat Exchange. The Find text box is also used to enter query arguments that can include multiple Document Info fields combined by multiple operators.

By using the name of each Document Info field as part of each query term, the Verity search engine will look for the term only in that field. If we extend the mathematical explanation of the process one more step, we can say that this capability adds a "value" to each query term. However, unlike the simple positive and negative values of numbers in arithmetic, this system offers many "values" for a term.

Instead of just plus or minus, a query term may have a "value" of Title, Subject, Author, Keywords, Date Created or Date Modified. This capability of assigning a value to each query term allows a skilled user to perform very powerful combined text and database searching.

---
example

The example given in the Acrobat Exchange Help file follows:

"You can build a Boolean expression that uses more than one field by combining the field expression with the search expression in the Find text box. For example, if you enter:

("Sixteen to one project" **Or** "16 to 1 project") **And** (Author ~ Raskin)
And (Keywords ~ "slide show" **Or** keywords ~ presentation **Or** keywords ~ spreadsheet)

in the Find text box, the search returns only documents that contain either the phrase "sixteen to one project" **or** "16 to 1 project" **and** have an Author field that contains "Raskin," **and** have a Keywords field that contains **either** the phrase "slide show" **or** the word "presentation" or "spreadsheet."

The first part of the query is the argument defined by parentheses

("Sixteen to one project" **Or** "16 to 1 project")

which demonstrates the use of double quotes to define a phrase rather than a word search. The reason that double quotes are required is that the stopword "to" is a part of the phrase, and without the quotations the "to" would be ignored during the search.

The use of the Boolean operator Or within the first set of parentheses makes this a query argument rather than a term because the contents within the parentheses are determined by the operation of the Or. That means that this "term" is actually one of a set of terms.

The first argument is then combined with the second argument via the And operator

(Author ~ Raskin)

which demonstrates the Document Info field search capability. Within this argument, which is once again the result of an operation rather than a single term, the ~ operator is used to select only those documents that contain "Raskin" in the Author field.

Both of these arguments are combined via the And operator with a selective search of the Keywords Document Info field. At this point in the math-like operation of the query, the user has defined two versions of a phrase that must have been published by one author, and the user has finely focused the search operation.

No matter how large this collection, the user will retrieve only one author's mention of the key phrases "sixteen to one project" or "16 to 1 project." The next argument will retrieve only such mentions as appear in slide shows, presentations or spreadsheets.

In this example, you would be excluding all other potential mentions of these query terms in the database that might have popped up in e-mail, proposals, training documentation, and other material that may not be useful for the purpose at hand.

Perhaps you are preparing a paper or presentation and need only the author's finished materials for reference. All other materials would be less meaningful because they may have just been part of the preparations for the documents represented by slide shows, presentations or spreadsheets.

The final argument

(Keywords ~ "slide show" **Or** keywords ~ presentation **Or** keywords ~ spreadsheet)

assigns the "value" of keywords to every term in this inclusive Or statement, which means that these terms must appear in the Keywords Document Info field.

Summary

As stated at the beginning of this section, the builder of an electronic document system should consider all of these approaches in terms of the content he intends to offer. In most cases, there are ways to adapt text-search engines to accomplish these functions once the desired functionality has been identified.

There is an entire education in this field freely available over the World Wide Web. The engines are all running out there, ready for test drives on the road to instant access.

The Boolean query translation project mentioned in Chapter 3 is one response to the opportunities and challenges of the new global library. It seems logical that one commonly accepted set of query grammar and syntax rules will become standardized, if only informally. Concept-search software will follow the same imperatives of market demand. Most users come to the Web hoping to find an easier way of accessing information. The concept-search software will interact with the user to refine expanded concept queries by suggesting options and techniques.

tapping the web:

a fountain of information

chapter

thirteen

"We're not in Kansas anymore, Toto." This is Oz; we're on the World Wide Web. We should be able to find anything we want just by typing in the words we want to find!

It's not quite that simple, but several big engines are running out there, indexing tens of millions of pages, just so the user can type in words associated with the topic. It is commonly taken for granted that the computers know everything, and that we should be able to ask them simple questions and they will tell us everything we need to know.

Well, the World Wide Web is not the whole Internet, and the Internet itself is a single-digit fraction of all the knowledge in the world. But the fact remains that more information is now literally at our fingertips than was ever even dreamed of. Vast information resources are now available in a globally accessible library that defies the imagination.

Search engines, the combined hardware/software systems that provide the indexes for the ever-changing content on the Web, allow users to perform global research on the Internet.

(t i p)

Read the Help files at each site!

Searching the WWW: Tools To Target Your Information Hunt

(http://www.altavista.com)

(t i p)

Searching for plain old "Java definition" and the more tightly defined "Java NEAR definition" on AltaVista yields a vastly different number of hit documents, but the same document appears at the top of each search.

Such documents are worthy of study of their construction and contents. Check out the "Java definition" example.

This is the summary of the top page on the hit list on both vague and precise searches for "Java definition" (about 100,000 hits) and "Java **Near** definition" (500 hits).

Java: Definition

Java: Definition. Java: Definition. Cool Object Oriented programming language designed from the ground up to be secure. Including garbage collection, http://search.netscape.com/misc/developer/conference/proceedings/j4/tsld003.html - size 737 bytes - 27 Mar 96

Considering the URL, it's not so surprising that the Netscape Developer Conference Proceedings might have a clue about getting documents to rank high.

In this example, the words "Java" and "definition" comprise 42 characters out of a total file size of 737 bytes (characters) much of the remaining material is comprised of stopwords, and therefore unindexed and unranked in the hit list. This is a simple but extremely effective example of using the keyword and concept at the level of the Web document.

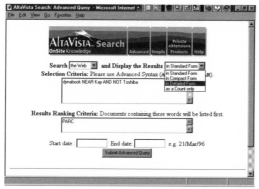

The AltaVista Advanced Search screen allows the user to specify where to search, the organization of the hit list and date ranges, and it has generous screens for complex Boolean queries and term weighting entries.

Excite

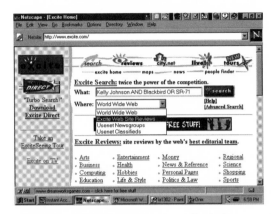

Excite and Magellan merged, and their home page offers both concept searching and the Magellan editor's reviews.

Search Philosophy

Excite is designed to help users find information when they don't exactly know what they seek. They characterize searching in three generations: first, keyword searching; second, thesaurus-aided keyword searching; third, a concept knowledge base.

Paraphrasing the corporate explanation, the Excite index maps information in N-space to construct relationships between terms based on a probabilistic technique. A smoothing technique is used internally to clean up the matrix.

The resulting knowledge index points to statistically significant sentences because the Excite engine is never working directly with just words. Architext's engine concentrates on concept search rather than keyword search.

In layman's terms, N-space means that individual terms are related by their co-occurrences in the database. For instance, if the name "Kelly Johnson" often appears within the same sentences, paragraphs or sections as the terms "SR-71" and "Skunkworks," these terms will be close in N-space. Therefore, a concept search for any one of these terms may retrieve items that mention the others. A search for "SR-71" might also find articles on "Kelly Johnson's" other planes, such as the WWII twin-fuselage P-38 Lightning.

Compared to semantic term expansion, which is based upon fixed associations between terms, such as those found in dictionaries, thesauri and other reference sources, N-space term expansion is built upon the relationships computed between terms within a particular collection. Specifically, the indexing process creates these relationships between terms, which is referred to as N-space because it has unlimited dimensions or relationships between terms.

Smoothing may refer to processes that control or prevent overly wide term expansions.

Functional Description Of The Search Engine

The user is presented with a field for natural language entries, with radio buttons to select either Concept or Keyword search.

The first 10 hits are served up, with automatically generated summaries of the hit documents. The Web Click-to-Go-To feature is used to view the documents. Users may change from Sort by Confidence to Sort by Site.

While Architext uses a natural language for queries and differentiates itself from the rest of the field through concept searching, suggested advance search techniques are built upon traditional information-retrieval techniques. All of the tips on the Boolean And, Or and Not search operators in Chapters 7 and 12 are valid in this concept engine.

HotBot

http://www.hotbot.com

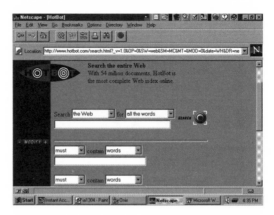

HotBot offers sophisticated features such as term weighting and phrase searching in this painlessly simple menu, which appears upon clicking the Modify button on the initial search page. HotBot is also the first Web search engine to allow you to specify a media type as a Smiley Face: "%-}" and so on.

> **At the SAP Sapphire User Group meeting in Philadelphia in September 1996, Bill Gates shared the happy news that Microsoft was finally "totally pure." Mr. Gates was referring to the fact that the last mainframe-style mini-computer applications within Microsoft Corp. were now running on networks of micro-computers. This step was, of course, largely helped along by Microsoft Windows NT.**

"Slurp the Web Hound" is the name of HotBot's robot that downloads 10 million Web pages per day. A joint production of HotWired magazine and Inktomi is interesting for both its simple user interface and the massively parallel architecture that it runs on. Inktomi is a company founded in February 1996 in Berkeley, California, to build massively parallel systems using large numbers of low-cost computers on high-speed networks.

In the case of HotBot, this NOW (network-of-workstations) architecture employs many PCs to perform both the indexing "Slurp the Web Hound" functions and the search functions required by Web users. The idea is that this architecture is vastly expandable with the simple addition of disk drives, cheap processors and network services, as needed.

Like Architext's Excite search engine, HotBot offers this excellent "free" service as its initial product. Of course, it generates revenues through advertising space on its pages, but Web users do enjoy an excellent free searcher.

e x a m p l e

Four Searches On HotBot For "Quark to PDF":

Searching for the phrase "Quark to PDF" with the **Must Contain** modifier terms "Quark" and "Acrobat" retrieves 12 documents, most from the PDF-L Listserv Archives and Newsletters.

Without the **Must Contain** term-weighting operator, the search retrieves 19 documents, which include less-relevant items, such as Seiko's printer driver Web page.

If the **All Of The Words** operator is used (which is an **And** search) instead of **Phrase,** the search retrieves 2,122 documents.

Searching for **Any Of The Words** (which is an **Or** search) retrieves 214,021 documents.

Even in the last example, several of the same documents appear in the top 10 hits for all searches. Closer study of the hit summary for each one of these consistent hits would give insights into HotBot's relevancy ranking.

> **From the HotBot FAQ: Overview at:**
>
> http://www.hotbot.com/FAQ/ faq-overview.html:
>
> **HotBot's cryptic operating instructions also add:**
>
> *HotBot is a search engine. HotBot does not care which realtor you use.*
>
> *HotBot works for a magazine. HotBot does not like long documents.*
>
> *Do not taunt HotBot.*

Infoseek

http://www.infoseek.com

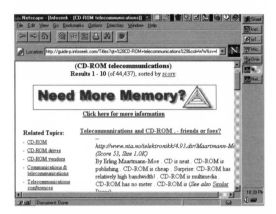

The Frames presentation offers a main results list on the right two-thirds of the page, with conventional related topics on the left third. As in photography, the Rule of Thirds often leads to pleasing page layouts.

---

example

Searching for the "definition of ActiveX" on Infoseek, consider the results of the simple proximity operator:

Search for "ActiveX definition" with no query operator: *21,108 hits*

Search for "[ActiveX definition]" with **Proximity** operator: *10 hits*

It is much more likely that you will *find the definition of ActiveX in the focused 10 hits* than in the impenetrable mass of hits of the simple search. Note that the brackets "[ ]" are the **Proximity** (or **Near)** operators here.

Big Iron On The Web

One of the most striking things about these engines is their impressive speed. While it is almost impossible to pinpoint the performance of any particular Web session, all of these search sites are noticeably quicker than the average site. And the indexes being searched must be very large. AltaVista claims to index 50 million pages and more than 3 million Usenet articles. Open Text states that it indexes every word on the WWW.

To accomplish such blazing performance, these search engines are running on high-end platforms. Understandably, DEC's AltaVista runs on the vaunted 64-bit Alpha processors. Since Sun Microsystems sponsors Excite, users enjoy the pleasures of the 8-CPU Sparc 1000E. Although the platform for Open Text is not disclosed, suffice it to say that its architecture is designed from the ground up to run in a multi-processing environment.

Steve Kirsch of Infoseek provided the big picture in the November 1995 issue of Boardwatch magazine: "We have a bunch of Sun machines, a T3 and a T1 coming in, a couple of routers, and about 350 GB of disk space. All together, there's 30 CPU's." So, if you want your Web site to be speedy, there's the blueprint.

(t i p)

This is how Infoseek explains the basics of searching:

"Five Quick Secrets To Better Searching"

1. **Capitalize names and titles, such as December and Star Wars.**

2. **Use double quotation marks or hyphens to group words that are part of a phrase. This offers multi-word string matching.**

3. **Use brackets to find words that appear within 100 words of each other, such as words you would expect to see in the same sentence or paragraph. This is the Proximity or Near operator.**

4. **Put a plus sign (+) in front of words that must be in documents found by the search. This is the weighting element that affects relevance in the hit list.**

5. **Put a minus sign (-) in front of words that should not appear in any documents found by the search. This is the Exclude function that allows a user to specifically list an entire set of erroneous "noise" hits for an otherwise effective query.**

If you're looking for information on OCR, you probably don't want to retrieve the OCR Orange County Registry, which is some sort of matchmaker
service. By using the **Exclude** operator on "Orange County," articles that include both your intended string "ocr" and the excluded term will be ignored
or ranked very low.

Open Text

(http://www.opentext.com)

The Open Text Web index is unique in the focus upon exact words. In addition,
queries can be directed to specific content:

Summary   URL   Title   Hyperlinks   First Heading   Anywhere

The focus capability of this search engine is available via pull-down menus and gives
users the tools to easily construct highly specific queries.

In addition to these field operators, the Open Text Web index also offers the standard
Boolean operators, which include:

Near - Proximity   **Or** - Loose Accrual   **Followed By** - Order of Terms

And - Specific Accrual   **Not** - Specific Exclusion

Here's the X Dimension view of complex collections, allowing users to "fly" through docs.

Lycos

http://www.lycos.com

The Lycos site shows its heritage in a very functional but still comfortable style.
Lycos offers filtering and organizing services, and everything is easily accessible through a smart,
simple interface.

Yahoo!

http://www.yahoo.com

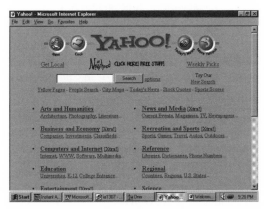

Yahoo! is a classic secondary publisher, like BIOSIS (since 1926) and Lycos,
and it provides the excellent service of reviewing and organizing raw info resources.

www.Search.com

http://www.search.com

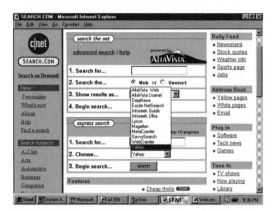

A place on the Web that stables the horses of all the Web searchers. This site is crammed with searching options. Its raison d'etre is to further the state of Web searching. "Choose your weapon," as the menu says.

Getting Noticed:Attracting Humans And Electronic Spiders

Everyone wants to take advantage of the "free advertising" by putting up billboards on the Information Superhighway, by posting pages on the World Wide Web. Just as with all advertising, it doesn't work if no one ever sees it. The Web search engines are being used every day by millions of people around the world, and well-designed pages should attract tons of interested readers. As in conventional advertising, the right product with the right packaging could be a gold mine on the Web.

The topic of how to attract spiders has become hot, and many articles and even books are being written on the subject. To show up at the top of the hit list on the big search engines is highly desirable. In effect, today's Web page designer must write for two audiences: the potential readers or customers (the humans), and the spiders (the robots), which determine the relevancy of the page, and determine whether a page is number 1 or number 100 on a results list.

Each of the search engines offers advice on how it performs its indexing and hints on how to catch the spider's attention. Unlike conventional advertising, sex doesn't necessarily sell. Repeating the word "sex" on your page may not attract exactly the clientele you are hoping for, unless you are hoping for perverts and the FBI. So, Rule Number 1 is to pick the subject of your page and concentrate on it.

Though the various spiders go about their business in different ways, they will all start at the top of the page. The top of an HTML page contains the Title and Heading fields. Some spiders are only going to dip into the page a little bit, like maybe only the first few hundred characters, so it is important to use those characters well. So, Rule Number 2 is to use a Title and Heading that describe the core offerings of the page.

In addition to the HTML fields that are displayed by browsers, there are an additional class of tags called Meta Tags. As the name implies, these fields are used for information about the page. Specifically, the Meta Tag can be used to enter up to 1,000 characters of keywords, which may then be used by the spiders. So, Rule Number 3 is to use Meta Tags.

Finally, as Web users become more sophisticated, the content of the page becomes of paramount importance. The Web surfer is spending time and effort seeking valuable or interesting information. So, *Rule Number 4 is to concentrate on content and offer some real and unique value to readers of your page.*

T How They Work: Spiders, Robots, Web Wanderers

The Web search engines depend upon a process of constantly indexing the ever-changing galaxy of information on a myriad of sites and pages. The World Wide Web is built on the HyperText Transfer Protocol, which provides instantaneous hypertext links between any two sites anywhere on the Internet, as long as they both support HTTP. This infinite interconnectedness spawned the image of a "web."

It's only natural that a web should have spiders walking on it. Spiders are also known as robots or wanderers that peripatetically follow hyperlinks around the Web and index the sites and pages they find.

Meta Tags

Meta Tags are elements in HTTP headers that can be included in HTML documents for search and management purposes. They do not display in normal view. Meta Tags provide custom index fields in the HTML environment, which can facilitate complex searching.

---
example

The following is the top of an HTML page, illustrating the use of Meta Tags. All comments are in italic.

<!DOCTYPE HTML PUBLIC "-//IETF//DTD HTML 2.0 plus SQ/ICADD Tables//EN" "html.dtd"> *Document type declaration, inserted by HTML editing program.*

<HTML> *This signifies the beginning of the document, and a corresponding* </HTML> *tag is found at the end of the document.*

<HEAD>

<TITLE>OCR Lab, Optical Character Recognition, Document Understanding, Text Searching</TITLE> *One of the elements that comprise a valid HTML document (head, title, body). This title is normally displayed in the browser title bar.*

<META NAME = "keywords"

CONTENT = "OCR Lab, Optical Character Recognition, OCR, Document Understanding, Text Searching, Information Retrieval, Web publishing, digital documents, PDF, Portable Document Format, text retrieval, search, Acrobat, Kofax, Cornerstone, Intrafed, Xerox, Caere, TextBridge, Omnipage document understanding, sgml, html, icr, forms">

<META NAME = "description"

CONTENT = "Where Paper Documents become Digital Documents, how to get There from Here!"> *These two Meta Tags, Keywords and Description, are designed to attract Spiders to index the page under these words in the search engine index, especially Keywords.*

</HEAD>

<BODY>

<H1> **From Books to the Web**
 The On-line OCR Lab </H1>

This is the first line visible in a browser in normal mode.

<HR> <UL> <LI> <P><EM> **Optical Character Recognition -_-_- Document Understanding -_-_- Text Searching _-_-_ Digital Libraries _-_-_-** </EM> </P> </LI> </UL>

These few items are designed to let a reader immediately understand the type of material found at this site, and also to attract those spiders that index the first few lines of a page. Many search engines also include the first several words in a quote or summary in the hit list. It's important to make them meaningful so they stand out on the hit list that the humans read, no matter where they are ranked by the robots.

> **tip**
>
> On a search engine that allows field searching, all Meta Tags are searchable. Any search for "Keyword Field CONTAINS OCR" or "Description Field CONTAINS paper AND digital documents" would retrieve the document in the above example.
>
> In this sense, a very sophisticated database can be constructed from simple HTML conventions, as long as all the users understand the particular conventions that have been added to a collection.

Smart HTML vs. Spamdexing

"Spamdex is a method used by a number of promotion companies in an attempt to push a site to the top of search results for certain keywords you specify," according to www.exploit.com. According to Lycos, spamdex is a "data manipulation trick ... we're happy to report no longer works in Lycos." Infoseek also advises against spamming your Meta Tag, saying that any tag containing a term repeated more than seven times will be ignored.

> **tip**
>
> Some spiders dip into the page by reading only Header 1, 2, or 3 information. Put your key words and concepts into your headers! They have to be readable by both humans and robots.

To understand the open nature of the Web, it's important to remember that HTML is a simplification of an earlier ideal representation of info called SGML, or Standard Generalized Markup Language. SGML was originally proposed decades ago as a universal format that would span all the end-user operating systems and all the communications media. Like UNIX and the Internet, HTML was designed to be "open" and easy to use, which opens the door to abuse.

For example, since Web browsers are designed to display both text and inline images, the user wouldn't be surprised to browse to a page that is mostly just a .GIF graphical image. It takes a little longer to download, but it just pops up in the browser. So, a "page" in Netscape Navigator or Microsoft Internet Explorer could display text and graphics but really only be showing a .GIF image displayed inline with no need for user intervention. The user, staring at the screen, is seeing words; it's a simple inline GIF image but it looks like text. When you View Source (in your browser) you will see that there is no information, only a clever inline Graphic Image Format file with tons of Hot Terms buried in invisible text. These spurious spider attractors garner a high ranking for the page, but the page is usually a dead end leading to some marketing deal, which almost always is a waste of time for the erstwhile information seeker on the Web.

The Excite engine serves as an excellent spam detector because it generates a "summary" of the page, and on these spamdex pages the search term is repeated ad infinitum. On the hit list, these spam pages stand out. The Excite summary exposes many excellent examples of how not to design Web pages.

(t i p)

Most Obvious Spamdex Move Number 1: Use "invisible text" to repeat search phrases.

Most Obvious Spamdex Move Number 2: Re-register and deliver the same info over and over.

In the long run, justice is done because the human Web searchers are seeking content, and when they are tricked into viewing an empty hole, they will not to go back to it.

!Register-It!

This great resource on the Web allows you to directly register your page to many search engines in one fell swoop! Suddenly everyone in the world can find your page on the Web.

```
http:www.register-it.com
```

T **The !Register-It! FAQ**

This is an excerpt from the FAQ (Frequently Asked Questions archive) that illuminates the far-reaching effect of the !Register-It! Service:

Exactly which sites will I be registered with?

We maintain a database of over 1,000 sites on the Internet where your potential customers may find you. Depending on your industry, geography and several other factors, we register you with over 300 of these sites.

How long does it take you to register my site once I sign up?

We send your site out for registration with all relevant sites on our list within 24 hours of receiving your registration. But please note that several search engines and popular sites may take several weeks before registering your site.

Summary

These Web search engines offer the fulfillment of technology prophecy. From Vannevar Bush in his epic "How We May Think" article from the *Atlantic Monthly* in 1945 to Bucky Fuller in the Education Automation sermons he delivered in the 1950s, today's World Wide Web offers the true embodiment of a technological vision. What used to be just an unusually compelling and popular sci-fi prediction is now an increasingly popular reality. Anyone with a computer and a phone connection, from anywhere in the world, can navigate a vibrant and expanding global library of information.

document management:

information as a corporate asset

Some of the earliest pioneers of document-management systems have been law firms, whose life blood is documents. In fact, law firms were coincidentally among the earliest adopters of word processing, which led to the need for document management.

In the earliest word processors, where documents were stored on magnetic cards, it was necessary to manage those cards. Even as simple a document as a greeting letter would be standardized if it met the needs of a large number of people. If an individual modified that widely reused standard letter, chaos would ensue. In the earliest days of word processing, only the most senior, responsible secretaries (hey, this was the '70s!) would be allowed to record anything because accuracy was everything.

This manual process of controlling the important magnetic documents worked well, and a trained operator could use the cards to produce "fill in the blanks" documents that were personalized for each letter. Eventually, there were machines that held two cards, and a card full of names and addresses could be shuffled into a standard letter, the original list/merge function.

When early standalone word processors evolved into "shared systems" in the late '70s, many people began sharing common collections of electronic documents. Law firms, for example, shared collections of contracts, agreements, letters and so on. Immediately, the need arose to distinguish original from modified documents, and then to pick out various versions of documents.

As surely as the big law firms evolved to Novell networks and WordPerfect, they adopted increasingly sophisticated document-management systems to answer this key requirement. In a profession where words count for everything and literally define the product, it is imperative to maintain the integrity of the documents.

This chapter provides an overview of the key issues of ownership, permissions, version control and audit tracking.

Document management as a specific discipline is dissolving into the larger world of increasing acceptance of digital documents. As discussed in earlier chapters, the rudiments of document management are included in the Document Info fields of Acrobat, Word and most other modern applications. As we move rapidly toward universal document sharing, this crucial concern will be blended into the general milieu. But the critical function of providing for the integrity and unique identity of individual documents will never diminish in importance.

Document Management Principles

Common sense applied to document management quickly arrives at a few basic rules:

1. Documents must be secure; access must be firmly controlled.

2. Given access permission, user changes must be tracked in an audit trail.

3. Any document/version must be traceable anywhere on the network.

4. Supervisory functions are usually available across the collection.

In order for globally dispersed users to confidently use the digital collection, very tight controls must be in place. A source document must be inviolable. The envelope of document-management information is the best first step to security.

We discussed in earlier chapters the elements of document management. Early, forward-looking applications like Adobe Acrobat, Microsoft Word and many earlier programs all built Doc Info fields into their file structures.

Those early Author, Subject, Title, Keywords, Date Created, Date Modified and other Meta-info fields included in the file structure offer the foundation for sophisticated document management.

For more information on document management, check out these sites.

Open Text Web site:
http://www.opentext.com

Documentum Web site:
http://www.documentum.com

PCDocs Web site:
http://www.pcdocs.com

Saros, a Division of FileNet, Web site:
http://www.saros.com

Classic Doc Management Fields

Assuming that anyone reading this chapter desires to share digital documents among large communities of users, I confess I've taken a shorthand view of the issues involved. All of the following fields are dynamically tracked in a true document-management system. Audit trails are available for each document, monitoring each access and action that has occurred in the life of that document. In any document-access system that involves changes to the documents themselves, tracking the overall processes that have occurred on the document is critical.

In Chapter 4 we discussed the Doc Info fields and their function as rudimentary document-management tools. There are similarities and differences between the fields for managing documents and the system of permissions and audit trails for actually controlling the documents, as shown here:

Document Management Field	Acrobat Field
Name	Title
Category	Subject
Owner	Author
Description	Keywords
Created	Created
Last Modified	Modified
Size	File Size

Document-management systems control documents through a series of permissions and audit trails. All levels of access to a document can be controlled either by an individual user or by groups. For example, the supervisor usually has over-riding capability to manipulate documents, whereas individual users may be limited to certain functions such as See Document Citation, See Document Contents, Modify Contents and so on. In addition to user permissions, the versions of the documents are often stored separately, along with an audit trail of all accesses and operations.

Status

This field describes the current status of a document, like a book in a library, or a movie at the video store. The field determines if the document is reserved to a particular user and, if so, the period of time it will be unavailable.

Version

As documents are checked out, modified and returned in new forms, various versions are tracked, with the number of versions kept determined by the administrator or individual users. In areas of collaborative use of pooled documents, it is crucial to identify individual versions to avoid misspent time and energy on out-of-date documents.

MIME Type

MIME type is crucial for Web applications because it allows a user to take advantage of his own installed software for optimum viewing of all retrieved files. MIME types are recognized by the browser by their file extensions. For example, if the user's browser is properly configured to recognize the MIME type, it will open Word to view a .DOC file, Acrobat to view a .PDF file, etc. Otherwise, unregistered MIME types will be simply stored on disk. While it is desirable to receive certain files directly to disk rather than display them, such as compressed files, it is best to configure the browser to handle all expected MIME types. In Intranet business applications this will be less of a problem because the universe of possible file types will be predictable, unlike the Web itself.

Doubling security, each PDF document can be password-protected with multi-level permissions.

One of the biggest bonuses any Webmaster or Intranet Sysop can give to their users is a simple list of pre-configured MIME types. That way, the browser will be fully configured for at least the anticipated business documents. No users will complain that they couldn't read a spreadsheet or word processor file or some other commonly accepted business document format. They may complain that they can't read the latest 3-D VR space or some other fun stuff, but that's on them.

Another enhancement offered in the new Intranet business suites of software is an included viewer. The viewers can display and usually print "views" of 40 or more common document formats, or MIME types. While these can not be edited, the information is available to users without the source application.

For example, a browser configured to recognize the MIME types .DOC and .RTF as Word files will launch Microsoft Word on the user's computer. If Word or another compatible word processor is not installed on that computer, a viewer could be used to display the file.

To round out the discussion, it should be noted that Acrobat offers three additional useful Doc Info fields, plus Document Password Security.

Creator: specifies the source application, such Word, Page-Maker, Illustrator, whichever.

Producer: lists the PDF source application, Distiller, PDFWriter or something else perhaps.

Optimized: is a simple yes/no on this efficiency enhancement introduced with Acrobat 3.

Security: offers two password options, one to open the document and another to change security options. The four controlled options are:

Printing

Changing the Document

Selecting Text and Graphics

Adding or Changing Notes and Form Fields

Assembling Virtual Docs On The Fly

The supreme advantage of high-tech document-management systems is the ability to assemble up-to-the-minute reports from all of the best sources of original information.

Rather than create a large, aggregated document where many files are copied into one megalithic mass, you can create an elegant set of references within your short summary. This function is comparable to the way a word processor can assemble many separate chapters and sections into one long document for printing.

The hyperlinks of HTML take this feature one step further, where each document is composed of a number of links, and each link refers to a dynamically changing document, which may in turn be updated separately or draw its contents from remote sources.

You can make your points in confident shorthand and refer all doubting Toms to the URLs from which you arrived at your conclusions.

This ability to create dynamic documents through included references will never diminish in value. This function of dynamically created documents through organized links is fundamental to the value of the Web and Intranets.

Workflow: Assembly Line Style

Workflow is the ultimate brute-force document-imaging application where the main benefit is moving images of documents over a network rather than moving paper documents between numbers of people and offices. Workflow, as originally realized in a couple of billion dollars' worth of business applications, concentrates on the organized movement of document images among the various business functions, treating documents as so much raw material in a fixed business process.

In this process, there are various nodes, corresponding to programming branch points. For example, if a flood of documents comes pouring in through a high-speed scanner, the various batches of images can be handily distributed to any number of human processors to enter all the data and resolve all the questions.

Document Workflow

In theory, workflow starts in the mailroom, where all documents are scanned and sorted into batches, after which all documents flow through an evenly distributed cycle of human decision procedures.

If the documents themselves can be organized into batches and carry their own unique index and status information, the complicated task of document handling may conceivably be automated. In fact, many very complex processes involving document handling have already been efficiently automated through workflow. But only well-thought-out and carefully analyzed high-volume, repetitive operations return a value on this investment.

The key is the transaction. If a set of documents is closely coupled to a business transaction, where real money changes hands, it makes sense to look into workflow. If it's just a once-in-a-while thing, where you are fishing for benefit/payoff, workflow is just a red herring and should be ignored.

Complex Doc Management Via RDBMS

To understand the desirability of managing documents in a database, you only have to ask a Webmaster what his job is like. Documents constantly change, with new documents replacing old documents, or usually just succeeding them in an ever-growing aggregate. It falls to the Webmaster to track all the links between the new and old and maintain order. In computer science, this task was cracked long ago in Relational Database Management Systems (RDBMS).

In very large collections of documents, you want to retrieve information rather than search for information. By their very size and volume, it becomes impractical to follow hypertext links to desired information. The oft-stated goal of "three clicks and you're in" is virtually impossible to achieve once the number of documents grows to the thousands and beyond. So large collections are untenable not only from the Web-master's system-management point of view, but also from the end user's convenience and efficiency point of view.

The solution to both of these bookend requirements is to incorporate RDBMS tech-niques and technology. These are the engines that drive the big business applications and routinely handle tens of thousands of users and millions of transactions. Think of the automated teller machines that sit out in the cold and rain and sleet and snow and reliably debit your account no matter which bank it may be in and within sec-onds hand you a short pile of cash. That complex transaction requires far-flung com-munications and transactional processes between very large financial databases, and it takes less than a minute. These transactions are performed, logged and verified by huge online systems. They are usually running under proprietary megalithic in-house programs or on commercial databases such as IBM DB2, Oracle, Informix, Sybase, SAP and others.

With increasingly sophisticated security software on the Internet, the big database vendors are bringing their power to Internet applications. For example, Informix offers a series of Datablades to allow new functionality that can be built within the robust architecture of its RDBMS. One announced Datablade allows the Excalibur information-retrieval capabilities to be applied to data and information residing within Informix databases.

This convergence represents several breakthroughs in efficiency. This is the economy of supporting one combined system for information retrieval rather than running par-allel systems with all of their recurring costs and burdens. For example, in the past all of the business applications would be run on the "Big Iron" and RDBMS software, while "soft functions" such as search, document management, workflow and collabo-ration would run on secondary, or parallel, systems. Combining these functions on the primary systems currently supported by IS budgets makes a very persuasive cost and procedural argument.

Another advantage is that free-form information collections can enjoy the benefits of transactional speed and verification, including automatic instantaneous updates, which are common in RDBMS applications.

The major benefit of this convergence is that all users may utilize all of the processing, communications and stability of the larger system, enjoying the synergy of conver-gent purposes. It makes common sense to have all the documents and all the data available to the users in one collection and through one interface.

Summary

Web-accessible document-management systems allow large and widely dispersed groups to refer to, modify, copy and otherwise employ remotely shared collections of documents. This ability to dynamically share the creative and editing processes is referred to as collaboration software on LANs, WANs, and the Internet and Intranets.

Workflow is a concept from the document-imaging industry, where complex, repetitive document-handling processes were automated through network-based transfers of electronic documents. The prototypical workflow applications were employed in insurance claims processing, manufacturing work orders and other document-based applications. As an evolutionary adjunct of document management, workflow is the programmed movement of documents through a specific process.

The entire process can be automated in a workflow system, and any participant in the process can be notified when his participation is required, and he can also view the current status of the process. In repetitive processes, workflow offers enormous improvements in efficiency through automation.

The ideal document-management application is the repetitive query that generates a constantly updated report. A number of "views" of extremely complex operations can be constantly updated and instantly available. All key reports from R&D, Marketing, Accounting, Personnel and so on can be generated from a single dynamic document-management process that always reports up-to-the-minute views of the entire process.

publishing on cd

chapter

fifteen

For conveying large amounts of information, CD can be much less expensive than on-line distribution, and it can sometimes even be quicker!

For example, CDs can be distributed by overnight mail to 1,000 locations for about $12,000, including production of the CDs and automated shipping and handling.

> **(tip)**
>
> **A 650-MB CD can store about 13,000 TIFF images, along with a simple index and a viewer to handle the documents. Compared to the simple cost of copying and shipping 13,000 paper pages, CD distribution offers tremendous financial and environmental advantages.**

If it costs two cents per page to duplicate a 13,000-page rich text or image document, that means production cost for each document is $260. Even if it cost one cent/page on a web press to print the copies, that's still $130 per 13,000-page document. Getting paper and toner costs that low is virtually impossible, not to mention the cost of hardware and labor.

And printed on 20-pound bond paper, those 13,000 pages weigh 130 pounds, so shipping will not be cheap. And if the cheapest methods are used, it will not be fast. Obviously, it's financially impractical to ship 130-pound documents to 1,000 different locations very often.

At the famously advertised price of 10 cents per minute, it would cost $378 to transmit over a 28.8 modem the contents of one CD-ROM full of information.

On a straight cost basis, mass-produced CD-ROM titles, in quantities as small as a few hundred copies, are very inexpensive. If the CD printing costs 50 cents per copy in quantity, that's a rate of 260 nominal image pages for one cent.

The cost comparison is overwhelming, and the communications time comparison also favors CD-ROM distribution for large quantities of information. To move 650 MB to each of these 1,000 locations through a 28.8 modem running at 3K/second would take 63 hours. So it would require a minimum of three modems at each location just to match the speed of CD distribution via overnight shipping. Considering the connect charges, whether they be simple long distance or some sort of leased line, it is easy to conclude that communications charges will far exceed the cost of $12 per location offered by CD.

To move 650 MB to each location through a 56-KB line running at 56 KB/second would take 3.3 hours. Obviously, telecommunications options are available that can and do easily move this volume on a constant basis. In fact, 56-KB lines are among the slowest of the advanced communications available, compared to ISDN, T1 and T3 lines. But the cost of communications follows the simple market rule of "you get what you pay for," and high speed comes at high cost. If a dedicated 56-KB line is $650 per month, at each of the 1,000 locations in this example, the communications cost can rise astronomically. No one can happily justify a $650,000/month phone bill to move this amount of information.

---

tip

A different problem arises when very large volumes of digital files must be accessed by many people in dispersed locations. At a point that can be easily measured in dollars and number of users, the original cheap data dissemination technology still makes sense: a dial-up bulletin board system, or BBS.

To distribute hundreds of thousands of images daily among many hundreds of data entry operators working at home, a dial-up BBS and a 28.8 modem is the proven winner. It's cheaper and faster than all the alternatives.

Electronic distribution of this magnitude will be more practical when ISDN is universally available. After all, at 128 KB, 650 MB can be moved in just about 87 minutes. At two cents a minute, transmission costs would be only $1.74. Even at a rate of 10 cents per minute, a dual-channel ISDN could move the CD's worth of data for less than $12. And the information would get there at least 20 hours quicker than overnight shipping.

And technically, 87,000 minutes of total transmission time would be required to move these 13,000 pages to 1,000 locations. But that happens in a "lights-out" mode, so it does not figure into the equation. However, that's a lot of bandwidth, and bandwidth is like water, a shared resource.

And, of course, on the receiving end a spare 650 MB of storage would be necessary. A pittance on a network, perhaps, but a fairly demanding load for a laptop. Information shipped on a CD comes with its own portable storage media, a considerable advantage.

Type of communication	Megs per minute	Estimated Total Cost	Comments
CD - Shipped Overnight - 18 Hrs.	0.6 Mb/Minute	$25.00	Cost includes CD, duplication, shipping
Paper - Shipped Overnight - 18 Hrs. for 13,000 pages*	0.6 Mb/Minute	$560.00 ($300 ship, $260 print & paper)	Cost includes duplication (and paper), shipping
28.8 modem - 63 Hrs.	0.17 Mb/Minute	$378 @ .10/min.	Slow & expensive for large volume
ISDN - 15.75 Hrs. (112 Kbps)	0.69 Mb/Minute	$18.90 @ .02/min.	Cost includes .02 per minute charges
56 Kb - 31.5 Hrs.	0.34 Mb/Minute	$56.87 @ .015/min.	$650 / Mo. Flat Rate
T1 - 1.544 Mbps - 70 Min.	9.26 Mb/Minute	$1.96 @ 0.28/min.	$1200 / Mo. Flat Rate

Estimated costs to ship 650 Mb coast to coast.

*Note: assumes 13,000 pages of images at 50K/page. At 2K per page for text, 650 Mb of data is 343,455 pages.

[T] Sony Explains The Technology In 8X CD Drives

"Sony designed the CSD-880E CD-ROM drive to overcome problems inherent with high-speed performance. The new, more robust spindle motor minimizes vibration, spins the disks more smoothly and lasts longer. Sony also expanded the frequency bandwidth of the optical pickup, improved the RF (radio frequency) amplification circuitry, and developed a new digital signal processor for better control over functions such as error correction and speed. All of these improvements combine to lessen vibration and maximize readability for superior performance and faster data access.

"Besides including components for 8X performance, the CSD-880E CD-ROM drive is also designed to utilize very little CPU processing power to increase net system performance. In addition, a large 256-KB buffer enhances system throughput.

"Whether viewing a full-motion video clip, looking up information in a multimedia encyclopedia or playing the latest action-packed game, the CSD-880E CD-ROM drive retrieves information fast and opens files smoothly. Not only does the drive feature a quick average access time of 160 milliseconds, but its high data transfer rate of 1.2 MB per second enables support for MPEG-2 video."[1]

From The Foreword To CD ROM: The New Papyrus

"Microsoft is extremely excited about the vast potential of this emerging CD ROM technology for a number of reasons. For one thing, CD ROM is quite different from any other medium in existence, whether it be television, movies, video, slides, audio, books or personal computers. In fact, one might look at CD ROM as the summation or combination of almost all of these. But what is it that makes CD ROM so special? On the technical side, because all the information is stored in digital form, the medium is similar to floppy disks, hard disks and other magnetic media. However, the transportable nature of the compact disk and the cost per bit put CD ROM in a class all by itself."

William H. Gates, Microsoft Press, © 1986

Archiving to CD

CD offers an excellent means of relatively short-term archival storage, for example, for the next several years. Compared to physical or even microfilm archives, documents may need to be stored for 100 years or more. Some of the manufacturers have introduced CD media that is projected to have a 100-year shelf life, but no one expects CD media to last that long. So even though the media is perfectly fine, it may be difficult to maintain the drives themselves for such periods.

Therefore, if we embrace the rate of change, we see the digitization of the information as the ultimate archive technique. Digital documents can be easily migrated to each new generation of storage media as they are developed and attain widespread acceptance.

Write It Once

If possible, the entire collection should be organized and written once to the CD to take optimal advantage of storage space and file structure.

The content manager, whether called a digital librarian, Webmaster or collection director, must always put the needs of the user foremost in determining the optimum file characteristics of a particular collection. There are also industry standards to be considered, for easier access for the reader:

"One thing described in these standards is the physical format of the information recorded on the compact disc. The physical format refers to not only the dimensions of the disk, but specifies how the information is laid out on it.

"Think of it like a book. Suppose that all books were made in one standard size, perhaps the size of a paper-back novel, and contained the same number of pages. These are the physical dimensions of the book. Now if a book standard describes the size of the type, spacing between lines and page margins in the book, it specifies how the information is formatted. This is the same way these standards document the format of information on a compact disc."

— "A Brief History of CD Development," which notes the various Color Book conventions developed primarily by Sony and Philips

This site offers a concise, in-depth history of the development of CD technology:

http://www.octave.com/ricoh/why.html#stand

> **tip**
>
> In a mass production of hundreds or thousands of CDs, the collection must be tested in the folder and directory structure on hard disk before being mastered for CD publication. It's the only way to ensure that all links will remain intact and that indexing will function.

T **CD Speeds: 1X, 2X, 4X, 8X ...**

In the ISO 9660 standard, upon which the original music CDs were designed, the data-transfer rate was 150 KB per second, and this became the basis for "1X." By this measure, a 4X drive has a speed of 600 KB per second, an 8X drive has a speed of 1.2 MB per second (1 MB per second is 10 times faster than 1 KB per second) and so on. The original music CDs, at 1X speed, had a maximum playing time of 74 minutes, so it would have taken 74 minutes to read the entire contents of one CD. At the task of pure data transfer, an 8X CD drive could read all of the data from a full CD in a little over 9 minutes. Of course, these peak speeds are not useful for all applications, such as audio and video, where the presentation speed of the CD contents is of primary importance.

The content manager must also decide on PDF creation options in Distiller and PDF Writer and indexing options in Catalog. Such features as Word Stemming and Thesaurus add to the overhead of the database, increasing the size of the files required for the index.

If the collection of documents is relatively small, and let's face it, the 650-MB capacity of a single CD-ROM makes most requirements relatively small, every single Search Expansion option should probably be included.

But in voluminous applications, every variable should be explored and the value of each should be weighed. Of course, it is nice to include Bookmarks, Thumbnails and every possible Search option in the database, but the value of such luxuries must be judged for each application.

You should publish a few sample collections to judge the effectiveness of search tools and options on a specific set of documents. You can experiment by doing Web searches on

> In the PDF format files created by Distiller or PDF Writer, there are many options that affect the size of the files. And in HTML, many options affect the files' size of a page, including graphics, backgrounds, Java applets, animated GIF, frames and so on. The author and publisher and Webmaster must look carefully at both the benefits and costs of rich content.
>
> In many cases, CD-ROM publications can go all out with the relatively luxurious capacity of 650 MB and the extremely high-speed access of 8X CD reader drives.

The High Sierra Standard

Philips and Sony did not define the file structure or the logical file format for CD-ROMs. They left that up to other manufacturers concerned with digital computer data. This could have resulted in utter chaos because each operating system had a different format.

Two people working at Silver Platter, Bela Havatny and Parke Lightbown, called a meeting in 1985 of all companies working with CD-ROMs. Individuals from such companies as Digital Equipment Corp. (DEC), Microsoft, Hitachi, Sony, Apple Computers, Philips and 3M attended the meeting.

The meeting took place at the High Sierra Casino and Hotel in Lake Tahoe, Nevada, so when they formed a committee they called themselves the High Sierra Group. They defined a standard that was based on the Yellow Book, a standard owned by Philips and Sony. The standard addressed the requirements of reading CDs on various platforms: Macintosh, MS-DOS, UNIX and VMS. It also was set up as an international standard so foreign characters such as Kanji could be used. It was even designed to later accept WORM (Write Once, Read-Many) drives and rewritable media.

The Birth Of ISO 9660

"The High Sierra standard was accepted by the majority of CD-ROM manufacturers at the time. Within a year it was adopted by the International Standards Organization (ISO) with minor changes. They gave it the cryptic name ISO 9660. It is, however, an important name to remember."[2]

Now that most CD drives come bundled with the computer, standardization is virtually complete. However, when deciding upon CD-recording hardware and software, it is very important to be sure that the equipment meets the predominant industry standards to assure the future usefulness of your published CD.

services such as InfoSeek or Open Text. The more you practice, the more you'll understand what tools and options will deliver the results your audience will appreciate. See Chapter 7 for details on Acrobat Search and Chapter 12 for details on advanced searching techniques.

For the latest information on CD-ROM developments and standards, go to:

http://www.uscchi.com/cdrom/

http://www.nta.no/telktronikk/4.93.dir/Maartmann_Moe_E.html

Acrobat Catalog And Search on CD

On CD-ROM, user software is usually included on the CD. The fact that ISO 9660-compliant CDs can run on many platforms, from DOS to UNIX, makes CD an ideal medium for physical distribution of digital documents.

An example of this is the Adobe Acrobat search engine, which can be used to publish a CD-ROM. A content manager can use Acrobat Catalog to index the collection, to create a database of documents that will be fully searchable on the CD-ROM.

By including the Acrobat Reader for all platforms, users on DOS, Mac, UNIX and Windows can enjoy the benefits of this CD-ROM. The storage requirement for all four readers is about 6 MB.

Production Via CD-Recordable

CD-R drives now cost less than $1,000 and come complete with software for writing files to so-called CD-ROM disks. Since the original acronym of CD-ROM meant Compact Disk-Read Only Memory, it's a bit of an oxymoron to say "CD-recordable." Of course, the technology itself is a great combination of widely readable media, a modern-day floppy disk, with the new CD-recordable drives that allow writing files on CDs.

These CD-Rs can be expanded beyond individual usage by simple "ganging" on a network to produce multiple copies of a collection simultaneously. Ganging refers to the practice of connecting tens or hundreds of low-cost disk drives to the network. The alternative for offering network access to large numbers of CD-ROM disks is to connect a jukebox to the net. However, even if the jukebox has multiple picker arms and multiple drives, the ganged array of many CD drives containing many CDs is inherently faster. Since CD drives cost less than $100, they can be arrayed in stacks. The advantage to the user and the network is that there is no latent or waiting time while a jukebox robots seeks, grabs and loads a CD. All CDs are online, as opposed to the near-line storage of jukeboxes on networks.

Of course, absent intense usage and faced with large volumes of CDs, jukeboxes offer excellent performance and great value.

CD-R is also very useful in producing copies of voluminous collections on an ad hoc or demand basis. In either case, it is essential to have a single-source database complete with all files and indexes to write in one shot to the CD.

Mass Production

Mass production is the next step for volume more than you realistically produce one at a time on an individual CD-recordable.

When considering the potential of mass CD-ROM publication, you must weigh costs vs. potential enjoyment by thousands of users. The same 40 or 50 cents per page will produce a high-performance CD-ROM collection or a massive collection of boring accounting data. Let's face it; even the most interesting CD encyclopedia is boring compared to best-selling game of Myst.

The reason for the excitement of Myst is that it embodied all of the smartest technologies that could possibly be put on CD. When you installed Myst, you got a Windows version of Apple's Quick Time movie viewer. And you got a database that tracked your progress through an extremely complex series of situations and choices. The CD offered movies, sound, interactive programming ... Myst first verified the richness of CD publication.

Now every user has cheap access to the tools that were used to create this groundbreaking CD adventure. All of the tools that were used to enhance this fantasy can be used to make all forms of information accessible:

- A tech manual can be enhanced through Quick Time movies that demonstrate a procedure in a way that a series of drawings could never convey.

- A drawing or graph can be mapped at high resolution to provide mouse-click access to information specifically related to that spot in the image.

- A verbal explanation can be heard through PC speakers with a click on a Hints box.

Web Links

Entering a Web link into an Acrobat file is simple.

Acrobat Web links connect the rich and sturdy format of CD-ROM diskettes to the ever-changing and updated World Wide Web.

The function of Web links depends upon a smooth integration of the user environment. For example, ideally a user could be navigating a CD-ROM publication and have access to some form of network connection to the Internet. This connection can provide access to constantly updated information referenced on the central source of the CD.

With so many Internet service providers offering "unlimited Internet access" for less than $20 per month, more and more people are going to have their remote PCs connected to the Web full time, 24 hours a day, seven days a week.

Home PCs this year are designed to cost about $2,500 and they offer an absolute treasure chest of power. Former luxuries are now included for the small office/home office market, such as 17-inch monitors, stereo sound and 3-D graphics. A PC with 32 MB of RAM, a couple of gigabytes of fast hard drive storage, running a 32-bit multi-tasking system like Win95 or NT can easily stay online constantly, performing complex tasks.

The Internet is just another network, so why not stay online?

Of course, you may need another phone line, or perhaps in the near future the phone company will offer ISDN, or the cable TV networks will offer two-way service, or perhaps even cel phone or satellite connection to the Internet will be affordably available.

Your configuration will determine the success of the linkage, depending on your Internet access and software setup. For example, if Acrobat is properly installed as the Helper App with Netscape Navigator, this linkage will be virtually seamless. If you're on a network with a direct Internet connection, you'll barely notice the leap from the CD to the Web.

T Naming PDF Files

The safest bet is to name files according to the least common denominator, which is the DOS convention for names. This means that eight characters can form the filename and three characters can form the extension. For example, FILENAME.EXT, where FILENAME equals the eight-character file name, and EXT equals the three-character extension.

To be fully compliant with the ISO 9660 Interchange Level 1 conventions, use only the letters A to Z, the numbers 0 to 9, and only the underscore and period characters in an eight-by-three file name.

Summary

Virtually every new PC now includes a CD-ROM reader drive, usually at 4X or 8X speed. A lot of new software is now distributed on CD, along with all user documentation. As a user, you'll print your own documents as needed—at your cost for toner and paper.

Distribution on CD-ROM can be very timely and very cost-effective compared to all other alternatives when a large volume of information must be conveyed. Documents with Acrobat Web links and other hyperlinks can be distributed on CD-ROM and have access to dynamic updates via the World Wide Web.

Looking into the future, with both the past of discarded technology and the present of new technology constantly being announced, it is logical to question the future viability of the currently ubiquitous CD-ROM media.

But even as we ask the question, the basis of the question is changing. One hundred years ago it was vitally important to print books in inks that would not destroy the paper pages. At the time, there was no new media on the foreseeable horizon that could replace paper and books.

Today, when it is obvious, given the history of 9-track tape and 8-track cartridges, that physical media comes and goes, the requirement to preserve information has a new solution. In the past, to move information from an outdated media to a new media, such as from paper to word processing or database format, required physical effort and labor.

Now that information is in digital form, it will be almost instantaneous to transfer the information onto whatever new media may evolve. The information itself, once embodied in digital form, is liberated from the physical media upon which it temporarily resides.

Given all the above, the current dominant, robust physical medium is compact disk. Of course, like all things, their time too shall pass. But because the information is digital, it will naturally migrate to the next hardware and software world.

footnotes

1 http://www.sel.sony.com/SEL/ccpg/text/ccpg/flash.html#pr3, Press Release, Multimedia Products Div. Of Sony Information Technologies of America, makers of Trinitron monitors, 6/3/96.

2 http://www.octave.com/ricoh/why.html#stand

index